"Eye-opening and groundbreaking. Kimberly Kay Hoang's tour-de-force ethnography inhabits and crosses multiple domains of desire-making to showcase the mutual construction of masculinities, financial dealmaking, and transnational political-economic identities. Through the innovative frame of desire as a force of production, this work dismantles the problematic analytic binaries of 'culture' and 'economy.' Specifically, by viscerally analyzing the role of confidence, the production of hierarchical status, and the buttressing of failure—all premised on particular performances of feminine submission— in creating the conditions of possibility for investment (and individual) potentials, Hoang delivers what many works have only promised: an example of how embodiment, inequality, and intimacy construct social economies. Differential masculinities and women's roles in brokering these differences while making space for their own life projects are the currencies of market development and action. Rarely ever has the relationship between desire, work, capital, and national identity been so clearly articulated. Truly an intrepid, captivating ethnography."

—Karen Ho, author of *Liquidated: An Ethnography of Wall Street*

"*Dealing in Desire* is obviously an exceptionally courageous book given the challenging fieldwork that Hoang engaged in. But equally importantly, it is a very astute book that connects different modes of presentation of the body by Vietnamese karaoke girls to specific organizational contexts and to macro structural transformations in East Asia. The book stands out as a signal contribution to the new sociology of transnationalism."

—Michele Lamont, Director, Weatherhead Center for International Affairs, Harvard University, and author of *The Dignity of Working Men*

"Boldly linking global political and economic transformations to intimate transactions, Hoang's *Dealing in Desire* offers a transformative account and novel analysis of sex work. A welcome contribution to gender studies and the economy of intimacy, this book will interest a wide audience."

—Viviana A. Zelizer, Lloyd Cotsen '50 Professor of Sociology at Princeton University, and author of *The Purchase of Intimacy and Economic Lives*

"The most extraordinary ethnography I have read in years. At a time when ethnographers in sociology seem inclined to write sensationalist accounts designed for mass appeal, Hoang represents the relationship between sexual and economic relations in Vietnam with exceptional thoughtfulness, methodological self-reflection, and theoretical sophistication. The book beautifully examines the relationships among masculinity, femininity, power, sexuality, and financial transactions among Vietnamese women and Western and Vietnamese men, making clear the many ways that sex workers and their clients or patrons manipulate their relations to meet complex personal and economic needs. Hoang's approach is masterful. She respects her subjects enough to avoid feeding two of the most common tropes in common representations of Asian sex workers, the exotic doll and the helpless victim. And she respects her readers enough to challenge us with a complex yet consistently engaging narrative. *Dealing in Desire* is a triumph."

—Mario Luis Small, Grafstein Family Professor, Harvard University, and author of *Unanticipated Gains: Origins of Network Inequality in Everyday Life*

"In *Dealing in Desire,* Hoang shows us how to look at the micro to learn about the macro. Her rich ethnographic account of the sexual industries in Vietnam situates our understanding of sex work in a larger political economy as it illustrates how race, nation, and class produce multiple masculinities and femininities."

—Rhacel Salazar Parreñas, author of *Servants of Globalization: Women, Migration, and Domestic Work*

"*Dealing in Desire* is easily the most deeply researched and rigorously argued book ever written about the Vietnamese sex industry, and it is surely one of the most authoritative studies currently available on the sociological dynamics of sex work in the current era of accelerated globalization. For a piece of serious academic scholarship, it is also a remarkably gripping read."

—Peter Zinoman, Professor of History and Southeast Asian Studies, University of California, Berkeley

Dealing in Desire

Dealing in Desire

Asian Ascendancy, Western Decline,
and the Hidden Currencies
of Global Sex Work

Kimberly Kay Hoang

UNIVERSITY OF CALIFORNIA PRESS

University of California Press, one of the most distinguished university presses in the United States, enriches
lives around the world by advancing scholarship in the
humanities, social sciences, and natural sciences. Its
activities are supported by the UC Press Foundation and
by philanthropic contributions from individuals and
institutions. For more information, visit www.ucpress.edu.

University of California Press
Oakland, California

Library of Congress Cataloging-in-Publication Data

Hoang, Kimberly Kay, author.
    Dealing in desire : Asian ascendancy, Western decline,
and the hidden currencies of global sex work / Kimberly
Kay Hoang.
        p.   cm.
    Includes bibliographical references and index.
    ISBN 978-0-520-27555-3 (cloth)
    ISBN 978-0-520-27557-7 (pbk. : alk. paper)
    ISBN 978-0-520-96068-8 (ebook)
    1. Sex-oriented businesses—Vietnam.   I. Title.
HQ242.5.A5H635   2015
338.4'7306709597—dc23   2014032692

Manufactured in the United States of America

24 23 22 21 20 19 18 17 16 15
10 9 8 7 6 5 4 3 2 1

In keeping with a commitment to support environmen-
tally responsible and sustainable printing practices, UC
Press has printed this book on Natures Natural, a fiber
that contains 30% post-consumer waste and meets the
minimum requirements of ANSI/NISO Z39.48–1992
(R 1997) (Permanence of Paper).

Cover art by Dinh Thien Tran.

In loving memory of Lois Mumm

*For Richard (Men), Nancy (Ha), Jamie (Che),
Andrew (Quoc-Viet), and Lillyan (Thuy-Tien)
Hoang for the material sacrifices you made in
your lives that enabled me to find the creative
space to write*

Contents

Acknowledgments

This book has taken me on an incredible journey filled with high highs, low lows, some tears, and a lot of laughter. When I embarked on this journey, I never imagined how many people it would take to guide and inspire me through the myriad twists and turns of this project, from the initial proposals to fieldwork and theorizing to writing and rewriting. Although I bear responsibility for whatever faults you may find with this book, I owe my work to so many people who generously provided me with their assistance along the way.

My greatest debt is to the men and women who let me into the most private and intimate spaces of their lives and who taught me how to manage a broad range of relationships in the field. The social debt that I owe these individuals is enormous. There are many whom I cannot name here without unnecessarily complicating their lives, but I would like to thank a few people using their chosen pseudonyms. First and foremost, I am deeply indebted to CQ, TTV, TinTin, Nguyen Nguyen, and Anh Cua Ti, who risked their reputations, businesses, and social connections to help me gain access to the most elite bar in Ho Chi Minh City, which catered to some of the most powerful local elites. These informants taught me how to manage a range of relationships with bar owners, local officials, the police, clients, mommies, and women working in the bars. To high-level officials, elite businessmen, and various others, they introduced me as a trusted researcher. Without their support, collecting this research would not have been possible. I also thank

Anh Nguyen, Lilly, and Tina, all of whom welcomed me into their bars, teaching me the ropes and allowing me to make several mistakes at their expense. I am enormously grateful to the women who "adopted" me into their bars, sharing their clothing, makeup tips, and other insights into managing clients. All the individuals described in my book had a huge impact on my life, forever transforming the way I see the world.

At the University of California, Berkeley, my faculty advisors provided me with a great deal of intellectual support. I thank, first, Raka Ray, my dissertation chair, for providing me with more intellectual and emotional support than I could ever have ever imagined. In this postmodern era, Raka met with me several times over Skype to guide me through my fieldwork and help me think through many of the emergent themes that eventually became the chapters of this book. She believed in me and trusted me to find my own way in moments of uncertainty. She also taught me the importance of learning how to find balance both in the field and throughout the writing process, so that I would bend rather than break when moving across rough terrain.

Barrie Thorne provided me with a great deal of mentorship and guidance along the way and pushed me to pay attention to subtle details, slippages, and contradictions in my data. She also taught me how to engage with larger theoretical debates while addressing the ethnographic detail that emerged in my field research. Irene Bloemraad read several drafts of my papers and pushed me to think about the empirical puzzle and how each piece fits with the others. She provided numerous insights and suggestions that challenged me to think not only about microprocesses in everyday life but also about how macroprocesses linked to the global political-economic structure shape relations on the ground. Peter Zinoman has been enormously supportive with his time, reading every draft that has come across his desk and providing me with valuable insights about Vietnam and historical works that describe colonial relations. I am grateful to Michael Buroway, Claude Fischer, Neil Fligstein, Marion Fourcade, and Anne Swidler at the University of California, Berkeley, for sharing their ideas and expertise with me and for critically engaging with my work.

At Stanford University, I had the privilege to be mentored by several great people, including Paula England, Monica McDermott, and Michael Rosenfield. I also benefited tremendously from the informal mentorship I received from Catherine Kay Valentine and Ann Morning. I thank Rhacel Parreñas for providing me with invaluable advice and intellectual support over the years. Paul Spickard, my undergraduate advisor, took me under his wing and equipped me with the tools to chase after my dreams.

At Rice University, where I was a postdoctoral fellow in Poverty Justice and Human Capabilities at the Center for Women, Gender, and Sexuality Studies and the Kinder Institute for Urban Research, my research found a home in several places. I am grateful to Michael Emerson and Diana Strassmann for their support and mentorship. Elizabeth Long and Sergio Chavez in the Department of Sociology helped me think through many of the ideas in this book. Tani Barlow and Anne Chao at the Chao Center for Asian Studies provided me with an academic home by supplying me with an office there, where I grappled with many of the puzzles in this book. Serendipitously, I arrived right when the Humanities Research Center brought in a group of scholars conducting research and writing on issues of slavery and antitrafficking—namely, Kerry Ward, James Sidbury, Sheryl McCurdy, Deliana Popova, and Jennifer Musto, among many others. I was told that being a postdoctoral fellow can be extremely isolating; however, I never experienced that isolation, thanks to the company of Jennifer Tyburczy, Ratheesh Radhakrishnan, Jared Piefer, Patricia Snell-Herzog, Jennifer Augustine, and Aynne Kokas, who were brilliant and collegial and made being at Rice University a lot of fun.

I feel so lucky to have found an academic home in the Sociology Department at Boston College, where I am in the company of wonderful colleagues who supported me as I wrote and rewrote the chapters in this book. I especially thank Sarah Babb, my department chair, who despite her busy schedule, found the time to read the entire manuscript for this book and provide insightful comments that pushed me to deepen my analysis and broaden my audience. Sarah also hosted a book workshop and allowed me to invite Michele Lamont and Karen Ho, who together helped me fall in love with the process of revising and rewriting. I also thank Eve Spangler, Zine Magubane, and Stephen Pfohl for reading various chapters of this book. The many conversations I had in McGuinn Hall with Charlie Derber, Brian Gareau, Paul Gray, Sharlene Hesse-Biber, Michael Malec, Shawn McGuffey, Sara Moorman, Gustavo Morello, Natasha Sarkisian, Julie Schor, and John Williamson helped to bake many of my uncooked ideas for this book.

Many of my friends and colleagues closely read different parts of my book and motivated me along the way. First, I thank Jessica Cobb for reading nearly every draft of this book and working with me as I assembled and reassembled the empirical puzzle over the course of nine years.

She pored over every last word and made laser-sharp comments and critiques that always pushed my writing to new heights. Jennifer Carlson's theoretical brilliance encouraged me to think critically about my data and reframe my analysis as I rewrote and revised over the years. Hana Brown and Jennifer Jones provided me with constructive criticism that fundamentally shaped many of the ideas in this book. Alan Chin, Barbara Brents, Ashley Mears, Kristen Schilt, and Robert Vargas read this entire manuscript and provided me with precious insights. I also benefited deeply from several writing groups, with Oluwakemi Balogun, Stanley Thangaraj, Suowei Xiao, Julia Chuang, Leslie Wang, Katherine Mason, Heidi Sarabia, and Tey Meadow, who provided valuable criticism and suggestions for improving the text. In the Boston area, Bart Bonaikowski, Larissa Buchholz, Margaret Frye, Laurence Ralph, Mario Small, and Ya-Wen Lei provided invaluable suggestions for dealing with issues of positionality. Sherine Hamdy spent days listening to me outline my book project and helped come up with the title for this book. I am also grateful to Abigail Andrews, Ryan Calder, Rafael Colona, Dawn Dow, Katie Hasson, Jordanna Matlon, Anthony Ocampo, Freeden Oeur, Nazanin Shahrokni, and Lilly Yu for their comments and penetrating questions throughout this process.

The research for this book was costly, and I would like to acknowledge several institutions and organizations that awarded me with generous grants and fellowships supporting my research. Stanford University provided full support so I could complete my master's degree and begin conceptualizing this research project. The University of California, Berkeley, provided me with generous support and funding over multiple years through both the chancellor's university multiyear fellowship—the UC Berkeley Dean's Normative Time Fellowship—and the UC Berkeley Institute for East Asian Studies Fellowship. I also received several grants while at UC Berkeley that together covered the costs of traveling to Vietnam to conduct my research. These were awarded by the Department of Sociology; the Women, Gender, and Sexuality Studies Program; the Center for the Study of Sexual Cultures; the Center for Race and Gender; and the Center for Southeast Asian Studies. The Ford Foundation provided me with funds that permitted me to spend a year writing my dissertation while among a community of scholars, who continue to inspire me. The Soroptimist Founder Region Fellowship enabled me to file my dissertation on time.

In the field, I was fortunate to have the support of many institutions and people. I thank all of those at Vietnam National University, especially Tran Thi Bich Lien and Dang Thi Tu, and those at the Southern Institute of Social Sciences—namely, Dang Thuy Duong and Bui Thi Cuong—for their support and guidance in Vietnam. In addition, several friends provided me with company and support along the way. Thank you to Danny Phan, Duc Le, Duy-Anh Nguyen, Linh Do, Laura Phan, Linh-Vi Le, Benny Tran, Chi Ha, Anh-Thu Ngo, Dong Ngo, and Micheal Ngo.

I had the privilege to present this book to numerous audiences, who provided me with an opportunity to try out my ideas and challenged me to reject or reformulate my arguments. These include audiences at Northwestern University's Department of Sociology Colloquium, Harvard University (History, Culture, and Society Workshop, Transnational Studies Initiative, Asia Center), University of Chicago's Department of Sociology Colloquium, Brown University's Pembroke Center, University of Connecticut's Department of Sociology Colloquium, Williams College's Department of Anthropology and Sociology Seminar, Yale University's Southeast Asian Studies Council Seminar, and the Women, Gender, Sexuality Studies Seminar at University of Massachusetts, Amherst. Portions of this book also appear in the journals *Social Problems* and *Gender & Society*.

I am grateful to Reed Malcolm, my editor at the University of California Press, for his support and expert editorial advice and for reading multiple drafts of this book. I am also indebted to Stacy Eisenstark and the entire production team at UC Press for the time and care with which they prepared this manuscript for production.

Several friends sustained me and nourished my soul along the way. Without them I would not have had the motivation to complete this book. Special thanks to Kristel Accacio, Lauren Beresford, Jessica Chen, Timothy Downing, Mimi Lam, Ellis Monk, Tianna Paschel, Saher Selod, and Jamie Tong. In Houston, Chi Thuy and Edward Rhee; Kathy and Richard Ong; Chi Thanh and Anh Diem Nguyen; Adam and Yumi Nguyen; Minh Dang; Katie Suh; and Elena, Kenny, and Jilly Marks graciously welcomed me into their homes with unforgettable southern hospitality. Robert Vargas helped to keep my spirits up by bringing warmth to the icy winters in Boston, planning wonderful escapes around the world, celebrating every triumph, and radiating a passionate energy that always seems to replenish my soul.

Lastly, I thank my family. My extended family is indeed large, and while I cannot thank everyone here by name, I thank in particular the people who made deep sacrifices that enabled me to write this book. My siblings, Jamie Jo Hoang, Andrew Quoc-Viet Hoang, and Lillyan Thuy-Tien Hoang, are the best siblings anyone could ask for. I missed out on many years of Andrew's and Lillyan's childhoods, but they have grown up to be incredible young adults. My sister Jamie stepped in and took care of my parents' business affairs when I could not fulfill my duties as an immigrant daughter; without her, I would not have survived graduate school or the first years on the tenure track. Finally, and most important, I thank my parents, Richard Men Hoang and Nancy Ha Hoang, for their courage, dedication, grace, support, and sacrifice. For as long as I can remember, they have worked eighteen hours a day, 365 days a year. They first ran a billiard hall that catered mainly to single immigrant men, and later a motel that provided a temporary home to migrant farmers, homeless families, sex workers, and men in transition out of prison. This was not just a family-run business; it was the home that anchored and humbled me. People often ask what my parents think of my research; and the truth is, they were far more concerned with how academia would affect my social well-being than with the underground economy of sex work. The motel was a universe of inequality and a home that grounded me and always compelled me to think about "bigger" issues. I owe my family everything, and for that reason I dedicate this book to them.

Introduction

Dealing in Desire

On a hot summer evening in 2006, I found myself sitting on the back of a stranger's motorbike as he gave me a tour of the local sex industry. How I got there was a combination of luck, naïveté, and a lack of options. I went to Vietnam with the intention of studying the commercial sex industry, but I had no idea how I would gain access to it or what I would find. Unsure of how to get started or where to go in Ho Chi Minh City (HCMC), I did not venture far. I walked into a bar located right outside my hotel that catered primarily to Western tourists.

My approach was simple: enter the bar, explain my research interests to the bar owner, and hope that the sex workers would speak to me about their experiences. Unsurprisingly, a foreign woman venturing into a bar alone does not inspire much in the way of trust. Dejected, I spent the night talking to a bartender, Duy, who convinced me that I needed to broaden the scope of my research project by first touring the different sites within Ho Chi Minh City's richly diverse sexscape.[1] He told me, "This is just one bar. There are many more bars out there that cater to different kinds of men." Though Duy did not personally know anyone who worked in other bars, because he could not afford to patronize them, he advised me to ask one of the motorbike-taxi drivers outside the Caravelle Hotel (a local five-star hotel in the heart of HCMC's business district) to show me the sex industry through his lens.

With no other leads, I followed Duy's suggestion, and at around midnight the next night I made my way to the Caravelle. There I met Anh

Bao, a thirty-two-year-old motorbike driver dressed in blue jeans and a black satin button-up shirt, with a cigarette firmly tucked into the left side of his mouth. I negotiated a price of twenty U.S. dollars (VND 400,000) for the night and asked him to show me the sex-work industry as he saw it.[2] Intrigued by my request and curious as to what a Vietnamese American woman was doing out late at night on the streets alone, he enthusiastically obliged. And on the back of Anh Bao's motorbike, I crisscrossed the city with him as he mapped out the different sectors of Ho Chi Minh City's sex industry.

For a long stretch of time we drove past parks and streets, before Anh Bao began pointing out the touristy areas most often frequented by Western men. These streets were lined with travel agencies, restaurants, and street-food vendors catering to Western tastes, children selling flowers and candy after midnight, and women on the patios of bars aggressively calling out to men passing by. Constant cries of "Come here! Come in, please!" ceased for only a moment when female tourists or couples walking together passed one of the dozens of bars.

Next, we drove past a series of high-end clubs with bouncers, strobe lights, booming music, and bars lit by LED lights that beamed through the windows. Droves of taxicabs dropped off overseas Vietnamese (Viet Kieu) who entered the club in groups. As I sat on the back of his bike, Anh Bao pointed out local sex workers he recognized as they walked out of a bar with their arms wrapped around Viet Kieu men. He had gotten to know these women when he parked his bike outside the bar around closing time to offer cheap rides home to the women who had been unable to secure a client for the evening. Over the course of nearly three hours spent circling the city, I took everything in—making mental notes of things I would later enter into my research. Anh Bao was a storyteller; and as we stopped outside each place, I sat propped on his bike laughing as he made up dramatic scenarios about the kinds of love affairs that occurred in each segment of the sex industry.

Contrasting the tourist bars—with their patios and women workers who called out to Western budget travelers—to the lavish clubs where Viet Kieus arrived in taxis and left with attractive sex workers wrapped around their necks, I began to cultivate an empirical puzzle. That first motorbike tour with Anh Bao opened my eyes to the heterogeneity within Vietnam's sex industry. To my knowledge, the literature on global sex work at that time did little to compare multiple markets that cater to different clientele from diverse socioeconomic and racial/ethnic backgrounds. I wanted to learn more about how sex workers made their way into the different bars, about the intimate relationships between men and women, and about the organizational structure and management inside those spaces. Why did some women go to bars catering to Westerners, while others chose bars catering to overseas Vietnamese men? How did the intimate relationships vary across the different bars?

And so I began my journey into the richly diverse social and cultural geography of Vietnam's sex industry. I set out to expand the sociology of sex work by incorporating a serious analysis of male clients into my study and to compare the different niche markets that catered to racially and economically diverse groups of men. My interest in the variation among segments of HCMC's sex-work industry led me deep within the bars and clubs that Anh Bao showed me on that first night, and also well beyond them. In addition to segments of the sex industry catering to Western budget travelers and Viet Kieus, I discovered two more niche markets, which catered to wealthy local Vietnamese businessmen and Western businessmen. Each niche market presented its own purposes, logics, and practices for ethnographic exploration.

Following seven months of preliminary research between 2006 and 2007, I returned to Vietnam in June of 2009, where I spent the next fifteen months conducting research for my dissertation. My goal was not to simply skim the surface and do a few interviews with sex workers and clients—I wanted the deepest possible understanding of the industry from both the worker's perspective and the client's. To attain this level of understanding, I had to immerse myself in each niche market by working as a hostess or bartender and developing relations of trust with workers and clients alike.

What I did not realize at the time was that I was conducting research in an area that was about to take a major turn. The 2008 global financial crisis that rocked the United States and Europe had the opposite effect on Vietnam. As the second-fastest-developing economy after China, Vietnam was a new international goldmine. Investors from around the world made their way to Ho Chi Minh City to capitalize on what they saw as a booming economy and a promising market for foreign investments. Talk about Vietnam's astonishing economic growth was rampant among everyone from street vendors to international businessmen. In the span of fifteen months, between May 2009 and August 2010, I watched as the state bulldozed several old colonial buildings and replaced them with steel-and-glass high-rises. Construction crews, machinery, materials, and jobs appeared on every block as new structures rose to be marveled at by global elites and poor locals alike.

These economic transformations, I discovered, were tightly woven into the social and cultural fabric that structured many of the relationships inside the bars I studied. In the most elite bars, men brokering capital deals spent exorbitant amounts of money on alcohol and women, and they made a point to pay with cash to display the vibrancy of Vietnam's economy to foreign investors. It was through these grounded interactions that I came to understand how the intimate relationships formed within different segments of the sex industry were embedded in the dramatic political and economic transformations occurring not only in Vietnam but also around the world.

This book draws on ethnographic and interview-based data that I gathered while working in four different bars of Ho Chi Minh City's global sex industry catering to local Vietnamese elites and other Asian businessmen, overseas Vietnamese men living abroad, Western businessmen, and Western budget travelers (backpackers). These multiple niche markets served a diverse group of men all tied to different kinds of global capital. For example, the market catering to local elites and their Asian business partners relied on the labor of hostess-workers to project confidence in Vietnam's booming market economy, a confidence that facilitated foreign direct investment through speculative capital deals. The market catering to Western budget travelers attracted a different kind of global capital, overseas remittance money that the male clients called "charity capital,"[3] through the labor of sex workers who portrayed Vietnam's Third World poverty. Thus, as I worked in each bar, I found myself enmeshed in a distinct social world of economic capital. Drawing on Viviana Zelizer's description of "market money," I watched as economic capital took on different social and cultural meanings within each bar, which became a site of interaction between global and local economies. "Not all dollars [we]re equal" in these four sites, and their meanings were expressed through interactions of race, class, and especially gender in each bar, a space charged with desire.[4]

Dealing in Desire explores how high finance and overseas economic remittances are inextricably intertwined with relationships of intimacy. For Vietnam's domestic superelite who use the levers of political power to channel foreign capital into real estate and manufacturing projects, conspicuous consumption provided both a lexicon of distinction and a means of communicating hospitality to potential investors. With the opening of Vietnam's economy to foreign investment, a new ultra-high-end tier of sex workers emerged who deployed vocabularies of consumption and sexuality in an elaborate symbolic dance tailored to the needs of individual capital deals. In a slightly lower-tiered niche market catering to overseas Vietnamese men, sex workers were valued not only for their beauty but also for their ability to project deference around their clients while highlighting Asia's rapid economic rise. Sex workers who catered to Western men in the two lowest-paying markets worked to project poverty and dependence to help men negotiate their personal sense of failed masculinity in the context of Western economic decline. As such, different configurations of racialized desires, social status, business success, and hope for upward mobility all play out differently in the four niche markets in which I conducted fieldwork. Through ethnographic fieldwork conducted over the course of five years in Vietnam, between 2006 and 2010, *Dealing in Desire* illuminates Ho Chi Minh City's sex industry not simply as a microcosm of the global economy but as a critical space where dreams and deals are traded.

CAPITALIST ASCENDANCY IN EAST AND SOUTHEAST ASIA

Most scholars who examine the coproduction of gender and global capital situate their studies within common frameworks that divide the world into two economic categories: "more developed" regions of the world, such as Europe, North America, Australia, New Zealand, and Japan; and "less developed regions," which encompass the rest of the world. As a result, maps of global economic flows tend to show the movement of money from First World Western nations like the United States and Europe to less developed countries through lending institutions like the World Bank and the International Monetary Fund, or in the form of private commercial lending through foreign direct investments (FDI).[5] In this context, those who look at the coproduction of gender and global capital tend to highlight the dominance of Western nations—and the *men* in charge of directing global capital flows from those nations—in transforming the social, cultural, and gendered relations of "less developed" economies.

This framework for organizing and understanding nation-based hierarchies that places the West at the top of the global order has been so powerful that even critical scholars like Aiwha Ong, Lisa Rofel, Julie Chu, Karen Kelsky, and others who work to deconstruct East/West or global/local binaries through theories of multiple or alternative modernities situate their frameworks in relation to the "originally" modern West.[6] Regarding East Asia, for example, Koichi Iwabuchi and Karen Kelsky describe how Japan—a country that is economically part of the

Global North—remained subject to multiple forms of Western cultural domination that racialized, emasculated, and rendered Japan as inferior to the modern West.[7] As a result, as Aiwha Ong and many others have noted, nations like Japan and China alone cannot contest Western cultural dominance; rather it is the collective rise of multiple countries within pan-Asia that has destabilized Western hegemony.[8]

The last ten years (2005–2014) have witnessed dramatic changes in global financial flows that have shifted the economic center of gravity more toward East Asia, raising important questions about the waning dominance of the West. Two major, simultaneous events in particular push us to rethink the World Bank's previous division of the world: the 2008 global financial crisis that rocked the United States and Europe and the concurrent rise of East Asia. According to the 2011 *World Wealth Report* by Merrill Lynch and Capgemini, for the first time in history there are now more millionaires in Asia than in Europe.[9] Moreover, in 2012, the World Bank reported that East Asia accounted for 32 percent of global market capitalization, ahead of the United States, at 30 percent, and Europe, at 25 percent.[10] The 2008 global financial crisis reversed the fortunes of leading global cities like New York, London, and Tokyo, which struggled to retain their lead in relation to Singapore, Dubai, Hong Kong, and Shanghai.[11] David Harvey dubs these transformations "the rise of rebel cities," where the rising skylines of Asian cities represent the new horizons of global markets.[12] Concomitant with the economic rise of countries in East and Southeast Asia, formerly dominant countries have felt the effects of Western decline. In her book *Citizen Protectors,* for example, Jennifer Carlson narrates a context of American decline in the United States, where the men in her study describe the loss of well-paying jobs, safe communities, and cheap goods that support breadwinner masculinity.[13] These shifts in global capital tell a revealing story: that the developing world is becoming a driver of the global economy. As this book highlights, these global economic transformations have produced new tensions as the fortunes of local Southeast Asian elites shift from depending on Western-based capital to depending on Asian-based capital flows.

WHY STUDY VIETNAM?

One way to understand the effects of this new pan–East Asian rise is to examine how people in less developed regions within Southeast Asia articulate their national ideals in comparison to people in more developed

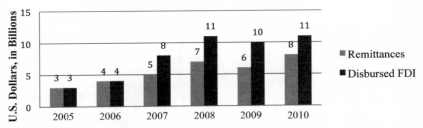

FIGURE 1. Overseas remittances and disbursed foreign direct investments (FDI). Source: General Statistics Office of Vietnam, 2011 data.

countries within Asia and to the West. With the rise of East and Southeast Asia, Vietnam, like other smaller countries in the region, gained a platform to articulate new national ideals that challenge common representations of poverty in the Global South and the latter's oppressed relation to the West; Vietnam did so by making itself an attractive site for East and Southeast Asian investment capital. At the same time, Western and diasporic men traveling to this region for business or leisure must contend with these transformations.

Vietnam provides a compelling site to investigate these complex processes of rise and decline. Largely unaffected by the 2008 global economic slowdown, Vietnam's economy grew nearly 8 percent each year between the point when it joined the World Trade Organization (WTO, hereafter) in 2006 and the time of this research. This growth attracted foreign direct investment. By 2010, annual FDI was nearly three times the amount brought into the country in 2006. Figure 1 shows two forms of capital: overseas remittances (money sent from foreign workers in the Vietnamese diaspora) and disbursed FDI (investment capital that has been registered and accounted through state banks). The General Statistics Office of Vietnam reported that FDI skyrocketed from U.S.$4 billion in 2006 to $11 billion in 2010.[14] By 2010, FDI disbursed capital was nearly four times as much as the foreign capital brought into the country in 2005 prior to WTO membership.

Figure 2 adds a third dimension to the flow of foreign capital: committed FDI. The difference between disbursed capital and committed capital is the difference between actualized money and promised money. For example, on a land development project with a projected investment of U.S.$50 million, a foreign investor might disburse $20 million in the first phase of construction and commit to bringing in anther $30 million in later phases of construction.

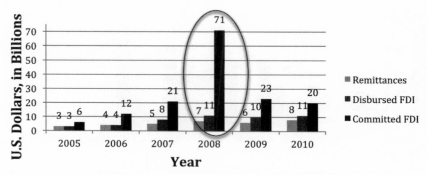

FIGURE 2. Overseas remittances, disbursed foreign direct investments (FDI), and committed foreign direct investments. Source: General Statistics Office of Vietnam, 2011 data.

Importantly, looking strictly at committed or promised capital, there was a major spike, to U.S.$71 billion, in 2008, which occurred at the height of the global financial crisis. Regardless of whether the committed capital actually made its way through state banks, the spike in 2008 hints at a rapid increase in the brokering of deals.[15] This is indicative of the highly speculative markets and the volatility emerging in the Vietnamese economy, as well as the rapid increase in the number of deals being brokered during that time.

But if the United States and Europe experienced a financial crisis in 2008, where was all this capital coming from? Before 2006, the United States was one of the largest foreign investors in Vietnam. Between 1995 and 2005, Australia, Canada, and the United States were the largest providers of FDI in Vietnam. However, by 2009, Western nations played a much smaller role in Vietnam's market economy as countries within the Asia-Pacific region began to take over. And by 2010, the six leading contributors were Taiwan, South Korea, Malaysia, Japan, Singapore, and Hong Kong (figure 3).[16] Capital from these sources overtook both Western investments and overseas remittances, giving an Asian face to wealth in Vietnam for the first time.[17]

The shifting sources of capital led to a rapid altering of the social and urban landscape as bulldozers tore down old colonial buildings, like the one in figure 4, to make room for new high-rises, as depicted in figure 5. During the fifteen months that I conducted research in HCMC, between 2009 and 2010, a new high-rise steel tower appeared each month; for this reason, foreigners and locals alike dubbed Vietnam the new "international goldmine." Investors engaged in major land speculation as they

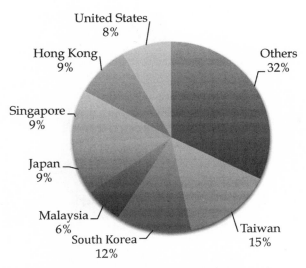

FIGURE 3. Sources of foreign direct investments in 2010.
Source: General Statistics Office of Vietnam, 2011 data.

FIGURE 4. An old colonial building that will be torn down and replaced with a new commercial development. Photo by Johanna Hoelzl, 2013.

FIGURE 5. A 2010 high-rise development project in the shape of a lotus, by Bitexco, a Vietnamese state-owned enterprise with a South Korean CEO. Photo by Danny Phan, 2014.

sought out development projects that were expected to yield rapid, high returns on their investments. By 2010, the manufacturing, real estate, construction, and hotel development and tourism sectors dominated Vietnam's economy, rapidly replacing the previous, agriculture-based economy that had dominated through the mid-1980s. These changes marked the beginning of a transition toward an industry- and service-based economy.[18] This economic shift created a new opportunity for Vietnam to reposition itself and decide how to imagine its pathway toward modern nationhood with respect to Asia and the West.

How do shifting global capital configurations destabilize the terms in which diverse men and women negotiate their perceptions of the rise of East and Southeast Asia and the simultaneous waning of the dominance of the West? The multiple niche markets in Vietnam's global sex industry offer insight into some of the larger macroeconomic shifts that reframe our understanding of the coproduction of gender and global capital.

THE HIDDEN CURRENCIES IN VIETNAM'S SEX INDUSTRY

Foreign direct investments are not disembodied flows of global economic capital. People broker capital deals. In an ethnography of Wall Street, Karen Ho engages with the works of Karl Polanyi, who reminds us that "economic practices take place in a complicated web of social relationships, which change in degree and form over time."[19] Ho argues that when we assume that financial capital is abstract, separated, or decontextualized from concrete lived realities, we run the risk of allowing elite players in the global economy to define and decipher our economic lives.[20] In Vietnam, FDI is embodied in entrepreneurial relations that are largely male dominated and heavily influenced by existing practices established in China, Japan, and South Korea, where men rely heavily on the sex industry to facilitate informal social relations of trust as foreign investors embed themselves in the local economy.[21]

Vietnam's transition from a socialist to a capitalist economy beginning in 1986 created a domestic superelite that was connected to powerful political figures. However, in a country like Vietnam, where the majority of investors do not have faith in *legal* contracts enforced by the Vietnamese state, or when they seek to bypass many of the bureaucratic hoops to obtain land and permits through informal social networks, the sex industry plays a vital role in establishing *social* contracts for state entrepreneurs with political capital to strike deals with private entrepreneurs and foreign investors.[22] In order to attract investments from foreign companies and negotiate contracts in the region, men rely on the labor of hostess-workers to ease the tensions between factions, facilitate personal relations of trust, and broker business deals.[23] As political scientist Thu Huong Nguyen-Vo writes, "During marketization, the state, which includes the Communist Party and government, endowed a class of men with certain state-owned capital and freed them to make entrepreneurial choices in an economy that now included private entrepreneurs and foreign capital. Entrepreneurial men used sex buying to establish personal ties facilitating their access to the means of production and exchange in an economy that was moving from central command to one that depended on" the brokering of relations between state officials, foreign investors, and private entrepreneurs.[24]

For local Vietnamese and other Asian businessmen, hostess bars are masculine spaces of leisure and consumption, where they can engage in deal-making practices crucial for organizing business ventures. Inside the bars, hostess-workers act as informal brokers of social capital, setting the stage for local elite men to dramatize Vietnam's potential as a lucrative place for foreign investment. In a highly speculative market driven by emotional calculations of risk and potential rewards, businessmen must establish informal relations of social trust to secure investment in speculative real estate markets and urban renewal land-development projects.

Hostess bars in Vietnam's sex industry have enabled local Vietnamese clients to secure business deals in an informal, nonbureaucratic, and culturally Asian setting, where they can build personal ties to mitigate financial risks through private and off-the-record knowledge of the economy.[25] As a result, a new high-end niche market of sex workers has emerged in tandem with the new Vietnamese political and economic superelite. These sex workers are valued not only for their beauty but also for their ability to deploy vocabularies of consumption that ease tensions between men in an elaborate symbolic dance tailored to the requirements of individual capital deals.

A look at local Vietnamese elites and their Asian business partners brokering capital deals tells only one part of the story: that of Asian ascendancy. By strategically looking at multiple segments of the sex industry, this book also examines how overseas Vietnamese men and Westerners simultaneously negotiate perceptions of Asia's rise and Western decline while recuperating their failed masculinity and marriages through personal relationships with local sex workers.

SEGMENTED NICHE MARKETS IN VIETNAM'S SEX INDUSTRY

This book brings sociological theories of globalization, markets, and gender into conversation to create a framework for analyzing segmented markets in the context of Vietnam's economic rise. Building on Zelizer's idea that markets and social life are inextricably intertwined, Rene Almeling argues that we should examine variation in how markets are configured.[26] I examine multiple niche markets of Vietnam's segmented sex industry to better explain how male clients and female sex workers negotiate their perceptions of Vietnam's repositioning in the global economy.

Dealing in Desire advances research on global sex work, research that has tended to focus overwhelmingly on female sex workers and either overlooks the experiences of their male counterparts or focuses primarily on Western men.[27] Interestingly, while most research assumes that wealthy Western men brokering capital deals command the high-end sexual markets, in this Asian-centered economy the local elites and other Asian businessmen command the highest-paid niche markets. I illustrate how the men in these different niche markets participate in different projects that involve divergent understandings of Vietnam's place and future in the global economy.

For businessmen tied to Asian financial capital, the sex industry allows men to broker deals by projecting confidence in the Vietnamese market. For Western men and overseas Viet Kieus, who are largely excluded from the segment of the sex industry linked to business trans-actions and FDI flows—since the vast majority of FDI into Vietnam comes primarily from Asia—the sex industry serves a different purpose, allowing men to displace their status anxieties onto women's bodies. The three other niche markets inflate the diminishing egos of Viet Kieus, Western businessmen, and Western budget travelers as sex workers help attract overseas remittance money into the local economy.

Taken together, the niche markets that cater to local Vietnamese businessmen, Viet Kieus, Western businessmen, and Western budget travelers highlight how the commodification of sexual labor can have multiple and varied effects as male clients and female sex workers nego-tiate their changing status—either by embracing the shifts in global capital flows that bolstered Asia's ascendancy or by reproducing old regimes of global power that hinge on Western dominance. Local elite Vietnamese men and their Asian business partners fall on one end of the spectrum, in a niche market where relations of intimacy are tied to the trappings of East and Southeast Asian foreign direct investments. At the other end, intimate relations are tied to the trappings of paternalistic charitable giving from Western nations. By comparing multiple markets and weaving distinct relational configurations into one transnational story, this research questions several assumptions found in existing the-ories of global sex work.

ECONOMIES OF DESIRE: SEX WORK IN THE NEW GLOBAL ECONOMY

Dealing in Desire looks at clients and sex workers in multiple markets to show that the worlds of high finance and benevolent giving are never divorced from the personal and intimate gendered spheres of the infor-mal economy. I examine interactions among men, and between men

nen, as they make emotionally calculated risks to fulfill individual desires that are intimately tied to their aspirations for the nation
during a time of rapid economic expansion coupled with a great deal of
economic volatility.

This book brings together three key theoretical insights crucial for
understanding desire. First, we must situate desires as they converge
and diverge across local, national, regional, and global social spaces.[28]
I highlight new forms of desire linked to the broader political economy.
The trappings of capitalist success and failure emerge in a context where
global economic market insecurities lead to the rise of new translocal
and transnational flows of money embedded in different race, class, and
gender relations.

Second, I augment current works on postcolonial and global theories
of intersectionality by stressing the material and cultural relations of
desire. More specifically, I examine how men's performances of masculinity and women's embodied and performed femininities hinge on their
structural locations within categories of race, nation, class, gender, and
sexuality.[29] As Anne McClintock points out, these categories "are not
distinct realms of experiences, existing in splendid isolation from each
other; [rather], they come into existence in and through *relations* to
each other."[30]

Third, by comparing multiple niche markets, I show how men's performances of masculinity and women's corresponding performances of
femininity are mobilized hierarchically in their desire to *affirm* Western
superiority in the markets that cater to Western men and to *contest*
Western dominance in the markets that cater to non-Western men.
Through these interactions in everyday life, men and women actively
work to construct competing hierarchies of race and nation in the global imaginary. A relational approach allows us to see how racialized,
nation-based, and classed relations are mobilized through different
intersecting relations. Men and women draw upon different consumption and production strategies in distinct spaces of leisure and entertainment in their desires to reimagine the developing world's place in relation to the West.

In other words, this book theorizes desire relationally as it moves
from the macro level of the national political economy, to the meso
level of the moral economies that structure different niche markets of
the sex industry, to the micro level of individual hopes, dreams, and
desires for upward mobility that connect particular men and women in
intimate relations. In using this scalar approach to trace new economies

of desire in Vietnam, I build on the work of Julie Chu by situating individual desires for mobility in a particular cultural-historical moment where desire meets potentiality.[31] In doing so, I focus on the productive frictions that shape men's and women's desires as they reflect the polarized tension between imaginaries of Vietnam as a nation on the move and as a former colony untouched by globalization.[32] Therefore, while changes in the global economy structure relations of intimacy between clients and sex workers, intimacy also serves as a vital form of currency that shapes economic and political relations.

MASCULINE DISTINCTION AND WOMEN'S AGENCY

By connecting the three levels of analysis, I show how competing masculinities are expressed, negotiated, and reproduced through the enactment of male *desires* that double as status within the broader political economy and in relation with women. At the micro level, this book pays close attention to what Doreen Massey calls "differentiated mobility"—the uneven and unequal positioning of different groups in relation to different flows of capital and movements of people[33]—to examine men's and women's hopes and aspirations to reimagine hierarchies of race, nation, and class differently in each niche market.

Men's desire for dominance over other men is enacted through the consumption of distinct types of sex workers in different spaces. For male clients, sex workers are products to be consumed in ways that enable them to enact distinction.[34] Chapter 3 brings together two key theoretical insights crucial for understanding multiple hierarchies of masculinities. First, I discuss how performances of masculinity depend on men's positions within global markets. That is, multiple masculinities intersect across local, national, regional, and global social spaces.[35] Second, I highlight new forms of privilege linked to the trappings of capitalist success and failure in a context where global economic market insecurities have led to the rise of new financescapes in Asia.

In the niche markets of HCMC that cater to Western men, masculinities are indeed mobilized to privilege an international hegemonic masculinity that *affirms* Western superiority.[36] However, I take this analysis one step further by illuminating a simultaneous process wherein local Vietnamese elites and Viet Kieus articulate their desire to imagine a new global order that no longer privileges a white, First World masculinity. These men construct competing notions of an international hegemonic masculinity that *contests* Western superiority in the Asia-Pacific region using personal wealth and Vietnam's access to Asian FDI as an indicator of national dominance. In other words, two simultaneous processes are at work in HCMC's niche markets—a recuperation of Western power and a contestation of that very power by those with aspirations for Asian ascendancy.

Masculine distinction in the bars depends heavily on the labor of female sex workers. As I illustrate throughout the book, workers perform *femininity* to enhance men's performances of particular *masculinities*.[37] I introduce the term *competing technologies of embodiment* with greater theoretical and empirical depth in chapter 6 to explain how sex workers construct desirable bodies in different ways to cater to male clients' competing aspirations. In order to entice clients, sex workers who cater to wealthy local Vietnamese men and other Asian businessmen construct themselves as distinctly *pan-Asian* modern subjects, while workers who cater to Viet Kieus construct themselves as *nostalgic cosmopolitan* subjects, and women who cater to Western men construct themselves as *Third World* subjects dependent on Western support, to satisfy their clients' racialized desires. These differing embodiments and performances of femininity have symbolized Vietnam's changing economy as it has pushed to emerge as a rising dragon in a new era that embraces capitalism and an open market economy. Through these performances, sex workers effectively work together with clients to *contest* and actively reshape global race-, nation-, and class-based hierarchies.

By detailing the complexities of HCMC's global sex industry, I examine how desire shaped by technologies of embodiment shape and reshape various relations of intimacy, client self-conceptions, and workers' patterns of embodiment, including their performances of femininity. These masculinities and productive femininities that hinge on male desire are precarious precisely because of the rapid economic transformations occurring in the broader political economy. Consequently, I show that racialized desires, social status, business success, and hope for upward mobility are both realized and shattered in the bars of Ho Chi Minh City.

TRAFFICKED VICTIMS OR SHREWD ENTREPRENEURS

It is difficult to write a book on the global sex industry without addressing the issue of sex trafficking. A burgeoning literature examines the plight of women as victims of human trafficking or as forced participants in the global sex industry owing to dire economic conditions.

When I began my research in 2006, I also wanted, as a feminist researcher and scholar, to study "trafficked women," or "victims" of the sex trade. However, I found that few of the women in my study were forced, duped, or coerced into the sex trade.

As far as I could tell, none of the workers I spoke with had been pressured by pimps or bar owners to have sex for money against their will. In fact, as I describe in more detail in chapter 5, the madams (locally referred to as mommies) in my study follow a strict moral code that prohibits them from taking a cut of their workers' earnings from paid sex. Mommies earned their money through a combination of business profits from the bars, alcohol sales, and tips from the clients. As a result, workers' autonomy and consent in the labor process were crucial to sustaining business across all four of the niche markets in this study.

While several scholars critically examine the issue of forced labor and human trafficking, I examine the broader structural conditions that shape the range of choices available to women as they enter the sex industry.[38] This book departs from the premise that all women in the sex industry are victims *forced* into the trade, or that they experience severe forms of labor exploitation, and instead follows the work of Denise Brennan, Rhacel Parreñas, and others by looking at women who *choose* to enter into sex work as a strategy to advance their economic and social positions in the local economy.[39] Many scholars of gender have shown that Third World women are frequently misrepresented as victims rather than as agents with motivations and desires that guide their actions.[40] Taking this work a step further, I illustrate how sex workers in HCMC act as astute entrepreneurs within existing structures of patriarchy.

For the women I studied who catered to wealthy local and other Asian businessmen, the sex industry allowed them to escape rural life and move into some of the most lavish spaces in Vietnam. These women earned more than white-collar professionals with master's degrees who worked in local businesses. Workers who catered to Viet Kieu men and Western men were women who either originated from HCMC or had migrated to HCMC several years earlier. They had all worked in the service economy and in factories, earning less than a hundred U.S. dollars a month with no possibility of upward mobility. Sex work provided these women with opportunities to advance economically and to escape exploitative working conditions. Critically, these women were not victims of trafficking. They were free agents who could quit working at any time. But while women were able to capitalize on Vietnam's rapid development, it is important to situate their mobility as constrained within structures of patriarchy. That is to say, the women's mobility hinged on their ability to appeal to their male clients' desires. Nonetheless, the contemporary sex industry provides sex workers with differing pathways of upward mobility.

Finally, people often ask whether the sex workers and clients in my study practiced safe sex. This book is not about their sexual-health practices. However, I will say that the vast majority of men and women in my study indeed used protection. In fact, safe sex was part of the workers' negotiations with their clients because it enabled them to stay in the business longer. Male clients, moreover, often encouraged safe sexual practices in order to protect their wives and their other girlfriends and lovers in their complex social circles.

THE SETTING AND APPROACH

To study HCMC's sex industry, I conducted twenty-four months of ethnographic research in two main phases—2006–2007 and 2009–2010—along with monthlong follow-up visits in 2008 and 2012. In the first phase, I conducted seven months of field research on three niche markets that catered to Viet Kieu men, Western tourists in the backpackers' area, and poor local Vietnamese men.[41] In the second phase, I returned to Vietnam to conduct another fifteen months of ethnography beginning in June 2009. In this phase, I built on the methodological approaches of Anne Allison, Tiantian Zheng, and Rhacel Parreñas by working as a hostess and bartender to better observe relationships among owners, mommies, police, clients, and sex workers in the bars and clubs.[42] I also added two new types of clients to my study: wealthy Vietnamese men and their Asian business partners, and Western expatriates.[43] While conducting this new research, I revisited spaces that catered to Viet Kieu and Western budget travelers to examine how the sex industry had changed in the three years since Vietnam's accession to the World Trade Organization.

I chose to work in four different bars to capture the diversity of the male clients involved in HCMC's sex industry. These bars include Khong Sao Bar, which caters to wealthy local Vietnamese elites and their Asian business partners; Lavender, which caters to overseas Vietnamese men living in the Vietnamese diaspora; Secrets, which caters to Western transnational businessmen and expatriates; and Naughty Girls, which caters to Western budget travelers. Chapter 2 provides a much more detailed description of the four bars where I conducted research, and I reflect on my research methods in depth in the methodological appendix.

Between 2006 and 2007, I interviewed 56 sex workers and 27 clients. Later, in 2009–2010, I interviewed 90 clients, 90 sex workers, 8 mommies, and 5 bar owners evenly distributed across four niche markets of HCMC's sex industry. In total, this book is based on participant observation and in-depth and semistructured interviews with 276 individuals in Vietnam between 2006 and 2010. In the methodological appendix, I provide a detailed explanation of how I obtained access to each bar.

Before soliciting interviews that would delve into some of the most intimate details of their personal lives, I had to become familiar with my subjects. At Khong Sao, Lavender, and Secrets, I worked as a hostess and a bartender, serving drinks, sitting with clients, singing karaoke, and standing in the lineup as men chose the women to invite to their tables.[44] In all three bars, I typically worked a twelve-to-fourteen-hour shift seven days a week for roughly three months. I diligently wrote field notes each morning before returning to the bar. After nine months of this work, which required me to drink alcohol nightly with customers, I decided to scale back. In Naughty Girls, the lowest-status bar, I conducted three to four days of fieldwork each week as an observer rather than as a worker.

In all four bars, the first two weeks were dedicated to learning the culture and unspoken rules of each space, the names of my coworkers and regular clients, and recording copious field notes every night. Once I became a fixture in each bar, I began to systematically conduct informal interviews with my research participants. Interviews with the women usually took place "backstage" during downtime as we waited for clients to arrive or to be seated at a table.[45] I interviewed the men in a variety of settings—bars, coffee shops, their offices, and on car rides to project sites.

I prepared and memorized two interview guides, one for clients and one for sex workers, which allowed me to conduct two to three interviews per night. Each interview flowed as an informal conversation that lasted anywhere from two hours to seven hours. I began the interviews with basic background questions about where the participants were from, their occupations, their experiences prior to bar work or arrival in Vietnam, and their recent activities, such as traveling or working in Vietnam. I then began to ask intimate questions about their private lives, which included marriage and family life, extramarital affairs, and details about their relationships, emotional experiences, expectations, and anxieties about topics such as love, care, and deception.

MY DEALINGS WITH DESIRE

As a young graduate student looking to study globalization and gender, I was told by several senior sociologists not to study Vietnam. White men and good-hearted women of color alike warned me that a study of Vietnam would marginalize me either as an "area-studies scholar" or as someone who does "me-search." As an Asian American woman in the academy, I have often felt like a triple minority: first as a woman, then as a Vietnamese American, and lastly as someone who has chosen to study men and women in Vietnam's sex industry.

My beloved advisor Raka Ray once told me that every time I presented my work, I needed to make sure to desexualize my own body with suits or dresses that covered most of my skin. She told me that as an Asian American woman, I could not afford to give a presentation that was undertheorized, because a presentation that lacked theoretical and empirical rigor would allow audience members to ask questions about my positionality, sexualize my body, and ultimately delegitimize my project. She was right.

I have presented various pieces from this book numerous times in a variety of academic and public contexts. I have almost always received a question from someone in the audience asking, "So how far did you go for the sake of gathering data?" I understood this politely phrased question as a subtle way of asking whether I engaged in sex work. Each time someone asked this thinly coded question, I always wondered if male urban ethnographers were regularly asked if they partook in acts of violence, engaged in drug activity, or participated in sex work with and around their research participants.

Indeed, some of the classic ethnographies of our time have depended on ethnographers developing close and highly intimate relationships with their research subjects. While many of these ethnographers have been explicit about the fact that they did not sell drugs or engage in sex work during their fieldwork, it is often unclear whether the formation of their relationships in the field involved having sex with or doing drugs with their research subjects. Certain close relationships developed in the field are subject to greater scrutiny than others, depending on the gender, race, and class background of the research subjects and the researcher herself. The types of relationships that I had to develop in the field receive far more scrutiny than the types of relationships that other ethnographers develop, because of my gender and racial-ethnic background as well as those of my research subjects.

As I wrestled with these issues, I had what Randol Contreras refers to as a "standpoint crisis," where I had to grapple with the contradictions of feminist standpoint work that calls on researchers to be reflexive of their own subject position in relation to their research subjects, as well as confront my own hesitancy in addressing the type of questions those audience members asked. I often felt as if those subtle remarks were a testament to the unspoken differential rewards and consequences for those racialized as "outsiders" and "insiders" in relation to their sites of study.[46]

In his book *Stickup Kids,* an ethnography of drug robberies in the South Bronx, Contreras turns the feminist epistemology on its head by asking: who really benefits from a reflexive turn to address their positionality? Earlier feminists like Sandra Harding, Dorothy Smith, and Patricia Hill Collins called on researchers to reflexively contextualize their unique race, class, and gender standpoints in situating their research. Yet twenty years later, I find myself asking why reflexivity benefits "objective outsiders" who dive into poor neighborhoods with people of color while simultaneously delegitimizing the very scholars of color studying poor communities who are really at the heart of feminist epistemological inquiry.

As I pondered these questions, I began to deconstruct my own impulse to answer "no" to the question Did you engage in sex work? By saying that I did not engage in sex work, I would delegitimize the work of many feminist scholars who came before me, like Wendy Chapkis, who did engage in sex work to advance research agendas on women and labor. Distancing myself from sex work would also inhibit feminist scholars emerging after me who might *choose* to engage in sex work to advance their own research agendas. Moreover, the question of whether I did or did not engage in sex work completely misses women's experiences and overlooks the different kinds of emotional and bodily labors that sex workers performed outside of "sex-for-pay." I strongly believe that it would be disrespectful to my research participants if I made some kind of claim about whether or not I engaged in a sex act for pay, because of the implied moral implications that accompany this statement. I do not believe that having sex for pay is shameful.

But what if I answered "yes"? While I have never been included in the club of "cowboy" ethnographers who study drugs, gangs, or violence, reviews of my work have always been lumped into that category of research. *Cowboy ethnography* is a term used informally among sociologists to loosely describe researchers who study dangerous or hard-to-reach poor populations, and who enable readers to go on voyeuristic journeys with them as they detail their heroic efforts to break into dangerous field sites.[47] The phrase not only captures the informal gendered divides among male and female researchers "studying down," but it also alludes to the ways that the academy valorizes male ethnographers while simultaneously delegitimizing female ethnographers studying illicit economies. Men are heroic researchers while women are sexualized objects both in the field and in the academy.[48] By answering "yes," I would risk playing into these same exoticizing dynamics while simultaneously marginalizing myself and my research subjects.

In the end, I decided not to disclose whether I engaged in sex work. I have chosen to answer this question with another set of questions of my own: Why is it that when sex moves into the realm of pay that this intimate question suddenly becomes appropriate to ask? And why is this question, and others like it, used to scrutinize particular scholars, often scholars of color?

As a participant-observer in Vietnam's global sex industry, I performed a deeply embodied ethnography in which I had to learn how to manage a broad array of relationships with the local police; the mafia members behind some of the bars; and the bar owners, madams, male clients, and female sex workers in these bars. For twelve to fourteen hours a day nearly seven days a week, I became engulfed in the Vietnamese sex industry, subjecting myself to submissive performances of femininity and an incredibly powerful male gaze that constructs notions of female desirability.

In order to make myself useful in my field sites, I had to do what most ethnographers are afraid to speak of—I had to engage in my own dealings with desire. Letting go of all the markers of respectability that I had acquired in the United States as a highly educated woman from prestigious universities, I engaged in a deeply embodied ethnography that transformed who I was. This external shift humbled me, brought me both great pain and great joy, and ultimately became the catalyst for an internal shift that altered the narrative of my research. The stories of the men and women I interviewed cast a new light on the sex industry and provided me with a deep sense of respect for the men and women whose honesty and friendship led to my greater understanding of the coconstitutive relationship between gender and global capital flows.

So many of the rich stories that fill these pages came with what I call an embodied cost. Some ethnographies are so deeply embodied that they forever transform the researcher conducting them. They color the way we see the world, manage our personal relationships, cope with pain, and experience the joy that comes with the deep connections we build in the field. Over the course of several years, I learned how to theorize and ask big questions crucial to the formation of this book. However, I truly found my place in the world through my experiences in the field.

As an ethnographer, I entered into a space where I could experiment with different aspects of myself. Each bar required a different kind of embodied engagement, and it was in those spaces where I learned the tremendous power of humility and empathy that enabled me to dig deep within myself and others to pull out the stories that make up the empirical puzzle of this book. It was only by experiencing firsthand the subjective power of male desire—including feelings of utter invisibility and undesirability—that I could begin to understand why nearly all the women I worked with were willing to undergo surgical procedures to permanently alter their bodies.

And it was only by spending hours listening to men's aspirations and feelings of loss, failure, and loneliness that I could turn away from writing about these men solely in terms of sexual desire. In fact, this is not a book about sex or sexual relations; rather, men's and women's participation in HCMC's sex industry involves much more than the purchase of sex. Men purchase status and dignity as they work to protect their precarious—whether ascendant or declining—positions in the global order. As male clients and female sex workers interact, they reproduce hierarchies of desire and desirability in the mundane discourses and practices that construct new hierarchies in everyday life.

As I moved through the field site, I always knew that I could hit the eject button at any moment and put an end to my research. In this way, I was a temporary insider and forever an outsider, because my life and livelihood did not depend on my ability to be a successful hostess-worker. In a deliberate attempt to move away from voyeuristic ethnography, I have specifically chosen to focus this book on the experiences of my research subjects rather than write about my ethnographic journey. Aside from in this section of the book, I do not appear much throughout the text; this is a deliberate effort to place the stories of the men and women of my project at the heart of my analysis. In taking this turn, I hope that a new generation of male and female ethnographers will engage in a reflexive dialogue about the racialized, gendered, and classed relations that differentially reward and discipline white scholars, as opposed to scholars of color and male and female scholars from diverse class backgrounds. I also hope that more scholars of color will feel inspired and compelled to study, with theoretical depth and empirical rigor, the very poor and marginalized communities that we were once told to stay away from because we bring a whole different set of sensitivities and insights worthy of academic scholarship.

OVERVIEW OF THE BOOK

This book forges a new direction in studies of the relationship between sex work and the political economy in three ways. First, I show that sex work is not economically isolated from other industries but is coconstituted with local and global economic processes. Second, I illustrate how crucial HCMC's sex industry is to the development of the nation and the construction of new non-Western masculinities and femininities. Lastly, I show how sex workers activate the local market and contribute to Vietnam's dynamism by directly and indirectly facilitating the flow of foreign capital and overseas remittances into the country.

Chapter 1 demonstrates how HCMC's sex industry has transformed as Vietnam moved from French colonialism and U.S. interventionism culminating in the Vietnam War and a period of isolation to eventually opening its doors and becoming a player in the global economy. Chapter 2 describes the contemporary setting with an in-depth portrait of each of the four bars where I conducted my ethnography. Setting the stage, this chapter describes the organization of each workspace and the analytical puzzle that drives the remaining chapters of the book.

Chapter 3 delves into the coconstitution of gender and global capital to demonstrate how new capital flows create possibilities for men to renegotiate race-, class-, and gender-based hierarchies. By employing a relational analysis of four different niche markets of HCMC's sex industry, and contrasting the present arrangements to those in 2006, chapter 3 shows how male clients engage in a variety of practices to establish a sense of status within global hierarchies that were rendered unstable by the movement of both men and money between the First and Third Worlds. Local Vietnamese elites and Viet Kieus rely on female sex workers to contest Western superiority, while Westerners in this cityscape turn to a different set of hostess bars to affirm Western superiority.

Chapter 4 examines the social and economic trajectories of the mommies, who embody entrepreneurial success, defying common assumptions about sex workers as victims of human trafficking or economic exploitation. Chapter 5 highlights the importance of autonomy and consent in sex work by examining the moral codes in the labor process that influence sex workers' decisions to engage in sex work after leaving factory work, domestic work, or other forms of service work. This chapter also illustrates the distinct relations of intimacy that emerge between men and women in different niche markets.

Chapter 6 introduces the concept of competing technologies of embodiment to show how sex workers' surgical and cosmetic bodily projects represent different perceptions of an emerging nation's divergent trajectories in the global economy. Sex workers construct desirable bodies that appeal to male clients' different projections of Vietnam's place in the global economy through three competing technologies of embodiment: pan-Asian modernity, nostalgic cosmopolitanism, and Third World dependency.

Finally, chapter 7 examines the varied trajectories of economic and social mobility that sex workers trace as they migrate from villages or move from factories or service-sector work into the sex industry. Sex work, I show, provides many poor urban and rural women with hope and pathways for mobility that would be unimaginable in factories, where women work twelve to thirteen hour days for less than a hundred U.S. dollars a month, which pales in comparison to the two hundred to seven hundred U.S. dollars a month they earn in paid sex work. Sex workers actively destigmatize their work by converting their urban income into social status and respectability in rural villages. Workers I interviewed sent remittances home and built new houses that fundamentally altered the physical landscape of their hometowns and local perceptions of their work.

Dealing in Desire takes seriously the labor of the women I studied. This book views women as, in the words of Caitrin Lynch, "creative agents in their own lives, not simply as pieces in some global monopoly played by capitalists and state representatives."[49] The bars of HCMC tell a story that extends far beyond intimate relations between men and women; these quotidian interactions provide a window into the racialized sexual desires, competing status claims, capitalist greed, and hope for economic mobility that drive sex workers and their clients into these bars, where shrewd deals are made to fulfill global fantasies.

1

Sex Work in HCMC, 1867–Present

The urban geography of Ho Chi Minh City (called Saigon until the end of the Vietnam War) is shaped by a multilayered history that structures the spaces occupied by Westerners, Viet Kieus (overseas Vietnamese men), and local Vietnamese men as clients of the contemporary sex industry.[1] Economic and geopolitical shifts transformed the structure of the sex industry under French colonialism, under American imperialism during the Vietnam War, and in the aftermath of Vietnam's reunification and eventual accession to the WTO. Men's differentiated participation in the contemporary sex industry is part of a long history of imperial domination coupled with recent economic transformations occurring in Vietnam. As men participate in the multiple niche markets of HCMC's sex industry, they may draw upon contemporary imaginaries of Asian ascendancy in a globalizing economy or of First World benevolence toward developing countries, but both of these tropes are drawn from the shadows of Vietnam's colonial and imperial past.[2]

The stratified structure of Vietnam's contemporary sex industry in HCMC is embedded in three major shifts in Vietnam's political economy. In the first shift, Western men embedded themselves in the highest-paying markets of prostitution under French colonialism and U.S. occupation until the fall of Saigon. In the second, Vietnam's economic liberalization under the 1986 Doi Moi (economic renovation) program attracted Viet Kieu to Vietnam in droves. These men established themselves in the highest-paying niche market of HCMC's global sex industry through the first decade of the twenty-first century.[3] Under the Doi Moi program, Vietnam effectively transitioned to a market economy as the Communist Party maintained its political monopoly, opening the country to foreign trade, investment, and large-scale tourism and marking the beginning of Vietnam's prolonged and continuing period of growth and development.

Doi Moi set the stage for the third political and economic shift that transformed the HCMC's stratified sex industry: Vietnam's accession as the 150th member of the World Trade Organization, on January 11, 2007, which led to the subsequent boom in foreign direct investments (FDI). In the wake of the 2008 global financial crisis that rocked the United States and Europe, Vietnam began to rely less on the West as a source of foreign investment and more heavily on capital investments from the more developed economies in Asia.[4] These new economic arrangements allowed local Vietnamese and other Asian businessmen, responsible for directing foreign investments from Asia to Vietnam, to replace Viet Kieus as key players in the highest-paying niche market of Vietnam's global sex industry.

In short, the historical tensions between Westerners, Viet Kieus, and local Vietnamese elites matter because their relationships are fraught with histories of sexual domination, not merely of sex workers, but also of other men and other nations. The historical context provides a backdrop for the contemporary stratification of HCMC's sex industry through an exploration of geopolitical and economic power relations. Specifically, it examines the frictions produced by the long, gnarled transition from French and U.S. dominance (from the late 1800s to the mid-1900s) to Asian ascendancy in a neoliberal, globalized marketplace. Historical and contemporary hierarchies of men and nations clashed as Vietnam began to imagine its pathway toward modernity and set the stage for competing hierarchies in Vietnam's contemporary sex industry.[5]

FRENCH COLONIALISM, 1867–1954: THE PRESTIGE OF WHITENESS

French involvement in Vietnam began after Britain acquired Hong Kong in 1842, when France worked to establish a trading base in Southeast Asia.[6] In 1867, France invaded southern Vietnam (known as Cochinchina) and developed a French colony. Then in 1883, France invaded and seized northern Vietnam (Tonkin) and central Vietnam (Annam), establishing these regions as French protectorates. In 1887, France created the Union Indochinoise, which consolidated the territory by bringing together Cochinchina, Annam, Tonkin, Cambodia, and later Laos. Under French colonialism, a culture of large urban centers—with new concentrations of administrative power, trade, and financial services—replaced a predominately rural peasant culture. Saigon's population rapidly increased from 13,000 in 1883 to 250,000 by 1932.[7]

This urban growth fueled new forms of prostitution that catered to French men.[8] Saigon-Cholon (renamed Ho Chi Minh City after the Vietnam War) became known as the "pearl of the Far East," a place where Westerners could partake of exotic cuisine, trinkets, and women while enjoying the comfort of French influence.[9] In the early years of French colonialism, the influx of unmarried French soldiers created an unbalanced ratio of seven men for every woman in the European community. This imbalance, alongside the permanent establishment of French troops in Saigon, fueled the growth of local prostitution.[10]

In cities like Saigon, colonial men and colonized women interacted intimately with one another, often in commercial relationships. To protect colonial men from sexually transmitted diseases, the Hanoi Municipal Council officially passed legislation in 1888 to regulate prostitution.[11] This legislation required prostitutes to register in local municipalities and created several dispensaries in which to examine the women's bodies for venereal disease.[12] However, underground prostitution rings dominated the sex trade, and the burgeoning sex industry was difficult to regulate.[13] By 1936, Saigon-Cholon had an estimated five thousand women working as prostitutes. Of these, only six hundred were registered at local dispensaries, while the rest were involved in clandestine prostitution rings operating out of "singing houses," where men went to listen to women sing; opium dens; cafes; and dance halls.[14]

In Saigon and Hanoi, a variety of establishments ranging from cheap brothels to expensive hotels catered to men of different classes, including minor civil servants, French businessmen, army administrators, and servicemen.[15] Prostitutes who operated in a low-end local Vietnamese niche market provided low-cost services to local men in thatched huts, while wealthier French male clients could afford to have relations with prostitutes in upscale hotels.[16] It has been documented that French colonial military men were generally the highest-paying clients, especially in relation to local Vietnamese men.[17] Although there is little documentary evidence on relations between prostitutes and local Vietnamese men in the French or Vietnamese national archives, the writings that do exist indicate that the French allocation of military funding created a racial hierarchy that privileged whites.[18] The prestige of whiteness transformed local brothels from the exclusive domain of literate Vietnamese elites to spaces for male European office workers engaged in commerce.[19]

After almost a hundred years of colonialism, the French were defeated in 1954 at the battle of Dien Bien Phu, marking the end of French involvement in Indochina. This defeat culminated in the country's division along the seventeenth parallel between North Vietnam, led by the Viet Minh, and South Vietnam, led by Ngo Dinh Diem. Following the withdrawal of the French military and French economic aid, the United States increased its involvement in South Vietnam by providing political advisors and hundreds of thousands of troops to the South to fight the Viet Cong (the North Vietnamese military). The replacement of French colonialism by United States political and military interventionism fundamentally altered the structure of the commercial sex industry in Southeast Asia.

U.S. INTERVENTION, 1962–1975: R&R FOR AMERICAN GIS

U.S. involvement in South Vietnam dramatically transformed the local political economy, which triggered major transformations in the sex industry. During the Vietnam War, the U.S. military fought alongside the South Vietnamese republican forces against northern Vietnamese communist fighters. Between 1962 and 1975, the United States spent more than U.S.$168 billion on the Vietnam War. This was more than the total amount of economic aid given to all other developing countries during those years.[20] This massive injection of U.S. capital into Vietnam triggered the large-scale growth of prostitution, not only in South Vietnam, but also in other parts of Southeast Asia, as outlets for rest and recreation (R&R) were established to entertain foreign soldiers. In addition, forced urbanization, bombings, and defoliation caused an estimated 10 million Vietnamese to flee their villages between 1965 and 1973, eventually swelling Saigon's population from half a million to 4 million people.[21] As a result, the traditional economic marketplace was drastically altered by war and overpopulation, substantially altering the commercial sex industry as new niches rapidly took shape in the urban centers of Saigon.

During the Vietnam War, the official policy of the U.S. Department of Defense was to suppress prostitution wherever possible.[22] However, unofficially, the U.S. military relied on prostitution to ease American soldiers into the country and help them cope with battlefield trauma.[23] After soldiers spent several months fighting in the war, the military sent them off for R&R in Tokyo, Seoul, Hong Kong, Taipei, Manila, Bangkok, Kuala Lumpur, Singapore, and Hawaii.[24] In each of these locales, hundreds of nightclubs, massage parlors, and bathhouses lined the streets, featuring local female entertainers awaiting the arrival of American GIs.[25] Visits to Southeast Asian brothels and bars became so prevalent that the U.S. military produced films to brief soldiers about local customs, attractions, and dangers.[26] Officials warned GIs of getting robbed when drunk and highlighted safe sex practices that would prevent the spread of venereal disease.

Although most men left Vietnam for their R&R, by 1966 the city of Saigon contained over one thousand bars, one hundred nightclubs, and thirty cabarets.[27] At the height of the war in 1968, there were over two hundred agencies that recruited women into prostitution and thousands of bars, hotels, and brothels offering sex for sale in a national sex industry involving five hundred thousand women.[28] The streets of downtown Saigon and those near U.S. housing compounds and military bases were thick with bars that catered almost exclusively to American men.[29] At the time, Senator J. William Fulbright said that U.S. forces in South Vietnam had turned the city of Saigon into a "brothel."[30] Unlike the class-segmented sex industry of the French colonial era, this "brothel" was structured by access to U.S. dollars, with American GIs commanding the vast majority of the sex trade. There were, however, subtle status markers that differentiated sex workers catering to American GIs on the streets and in inexpensive bars from the higher class of sex workers that catered to U.S. civil servants in hotels or discotheques.[31]

Two narratives exist of women's experience of prostitution during the Vietnam War. The first, advanced by feminists like Susan Brownmiller and Kathleen Barry, asserts that women refugees had little choice but to engage in prostitution to sustain a livelihood for themselves and their families.[32] Women brought into military compounds as the "local national guests" of the United States lived and worked in curtained cubicles, where they provided "quick, straight, and routine" sexual services for which they were paid as little as two dollars per sexual transaction.[33] In addition, rape and sexual violence were prevalent in Vietnam's sex industry during the war.[34]

A second narrative of sex work during the Vietnam War emphasizes pleasure, desire, and mobility as a part of women's stories. In one of the first oral histories conducted of bar girls working during the Vietnam War, Mai Lan Gustafsson captures the stories of women who described their work in the bars in positive terms, as full of good times, camara-

derie, and exhilaration.[35] All thirty-two of the women whom Gustafsson interviewed reminisced that the war represented one of the best
times of their lives, mentioning that prostitution allowed them to break
free from gendered "traditions" and expectations that were imposed on
women by local society. These two narratives—both reflexive of real
aspects of women's experiences—highlight the complexity that characterized relationships of intimacy between local sex workers and Western clients during the Vietnam War.

As prostitution burgeoned in the South, the Viet Minh in the North
worked to abolish all forms of prostitution as part of their efforts to
equalize men and women and to incorporate women into the military.
Women from Hanoi and the countryside fought alongside their male
counterparts in the Viet Cong against the South Vietnamese government and its French and American allies between 1945 and 1975.[36] The
national liberation movement held a strict code of ethics that prohibited
the rape and prostitution of local women. As such, according to official
records, prostitution was virtually nonexistent in Hanoi.

COMMUNIST PARTY RULE, 1975–1986: RECOVERING
THE "FALLEN SISTERS" OF IMPERIALISM

On April 30, 1975, the war between communist North Vietnam and the
government of South Vietnam culminated in the fall of Saigon. South
Vietnam crumbled as Americans evacuated and thousands of Vietnamese fled the country. The capture of Saigon by the Viet Cong in 1975
marked the reunification of North and South Vietnam and the expansion of the Soviet-style closed command economy. During the period
between 1975 and 1986, the state defined prostitution as a vestige of the
imperialist American presence and the southern puppet regime.[37] The
protection of women from sexual exploitation thus allowed Vietnam to
assert a new sense of nationhood defined against Western imperialism.

The revolutionary society sought to conquer the social evils of prostitution that were left behind by the American military with a campaign
to "lead the fallen sisters back to a happy future life."[38] Under the
"Recovery of Human Dignity" campaign, the state sent former prostitutes to schools organized by the Vietnam Women's Union. There,
women were treated for sexually transmitted diseases and provided
with vocational, cultural, and academic training to become productive
laborers.[39] Northern leaders cited the absence of prostitution as evidence of a successful new regime.

In this era, prostitution emerged as a pawn in the political economy as the Communist Party used its eradication as a symbolic weapon against Vietnam's imperial past. It was not until Vietnam reopened its doors to the global economy that signs of a commercial sex industry began to reemerge.

DOI MOI, 1986–2006: VIET KIEUS' NOSTALGIA AND CONSPICUOUS CONSUMPTION

The fall of Saigon in 1975 marked the end of over one hundred years of foreign colonial domination and military occupation in Vietnam. While this political triumph created independence, it did not deliver economic prosperity. The nation remained poor and underdeveloped in comparison to Western countries and other industrializing Asian economies. In 1986, after a decade of lagging productivity and rapid inflation in the context of communist reform and other worldwide transformations (glasnost and perestroika in the Soviet Union and the Deng Xiaoping reforms in China), Vietnam introduced the Doi Moi program of economic liberalization, which effectively transitioned Vietnam into a socialist-oriented market economy in which the Communist Party maintained a political monopoly. These reforms opened Vietnam to foreign trade, investment, and large-scale tourism, setting off a prolonged and continuing period of economic growth and development.

Between the late 1980s and the middle of the first decade of the twenty-first century, the local economy was bifurcated between those with access to U.S. dollars and those who could access only the local currency.[40] The normalization of ties with the United States in 1995 provided Vietnam with access to American markets and a sizable Vietnamese-American community, dramatically reorienting the local economy. Viet Kieus and Western tourists began to return to Vietnam in large numbers, increasing the flow of overseas remittances to the country from U.S.$35 million in 1995 to nearly $3 billion by 2005.[41] The United States and Europe were the two main sources of overseas remittance money brought into Vietnam.[42] The new flows of foreign tourists into Vietnam helped to fuel the local economy in such a dramatic way that Viet Kieus with access to U.S. dollars commanded the highest-paying niche markets of Vietnam's sex industry.

In 2006, the highest-paying clients in the sex trade were overwhelmingly Viet Kieu men who engaged in transnational forms of conspicuous consumption.[43] Their lavish recreation in Vietnam was made possible by the differences between their earnings abroad and very low Vietnamese wages. Their impact on the local economy was profound. Overseas remittance money flooded the country, transforming the local landscape with new modern houses funded by Viet Kieu remittances, which stood next to shacks. In contrast, most Western tourists frequented a renowned local bar called Apocalypse Now. Founded in 1991, Apocalypse Now was a place where vestiges of Vietnam's history of foreign occupation were mobilized anew in the local culture of leisure as Westerners reminisced about the war over a bottle of cheap beer in the company of sex workers. In short, while Western tourists sought out spaces that allowed them to reimagine the "good old days" of U.S. intervention, Viet Kieus carved out new niche markets in more luxurious spaces where they could order bottles of cognac or whiskey and receive an entirely different kind of VIP treatment.

Under Vietnam's market liberalization, land was controlled by the state along with several other state-enterprise monopolies in banking, mining, communications, and so on, which meant that key information about the market was not available without strong political connections.[44] While Western investors hesitated to move into this new market, Taiwanese investors began to find ways to embed themselves in the local economy.[45] In this political and economic context, a burgeoning number of private entrepreneurs and Taiwanese investors relied heavily on state entrepreneurs to provide them with access to contracts tied to state-owned assets and enterprises.[46]

Under these arrangements, male private entrepreneurs and foreign investors used hostess bars and the purchase of sex as avenues through which to establish the personal ties necessary to facilitate access to land and the means of production controlled by the state.[47] As a result, during marketization the government also had to grapple with conflicting state agendas that involved cracking down on low-end sex workers working the streets and simultaneously turn a blind eye to segments of the sex industry that catered to a burgeoning group of foreign and local entrepreneurs, as well as Western and Viet Kieu tourists, all of whom were fundamental to building Vietnam's economy.

Echoing China's campaign on "evils," "pollution," and "poison," Prime Minister Vo Van Kiet established the first campaign against "social evils" (*te nan xo hoi*) in 1995.[48] The government issued a series of decrees and directives to control "pollution" arising from Vietnam's increased inclusion in the world economy because of the Doi Moi policy.[49] Under these new mandates, the Vietnamese government targeted places that housed sex workers: karaoke bars, video shops, massage parlors, and so on.[50] However, in a study of Vietnamese karaoke bars, David Koh argues that there were two forces shaping state policies designed to eliminate social evils in Vietnam: the Vietnamese Communist Party, which led the state in making top-down decisions, and local administrators who were paid a paltry salary to enforce these policies.[51] In this bifurcated state, business elites at the top, who depended on the commercial sex industry to broker business deals, often evaded the laws addressing social evils by bribing lower-level officials charged with enforcing such laws.[52] And foreigners continued to participate in the local sex trade because their foreign-citizenship status granted them a degree of impunity not accorded to locals. Consequently, because the increase in private and public business linked to foreign investments hinged on men's ability to establish informal relationships of social trust in local karaoke bars,[53] these mandates were unequally enforced and the crackdowns mostly affected lower-end street workers, who operated in the public eye without any political ties.

VIETNAM'S ENTRY INTO THE WORLD TRADE ORGANIZATION AND THE RISE OF ASIAN FDI: 2006–PRESENT

In November of 2006, President George W. Bush visited Vietnam to attend the Asia-Pacific Economic Cooperation summit in an effort to normalize trade relations and prepare for Vietnam's entry into the World Trade Organization. Before his visit, President Bush had also committed the U.S. government to leading the world in combating human trafficking, and the U.S. State Department's *Trafficking in Persons Report* designated Vietnam as a Tier 2 country on the agency's watch list. The Tier 2 ranking marked Vietnam as a country whose government does not meet the minimum standards of the Trafficking Victims Protection Act.[54] To demonstrate compliance with the act and appeal to potential investors from Western nations, the Vietnamese state responded by criminalizing prostitution. However, no one could have anticipated that the 2008 global financial crisis would put pressure on Vietnamese state officials to adopt contradictory approaches to enforcing these laws. Just two years after Vietnam's entry into the WTO, Western capital was no longer the main source of foreign capital in Vietnam. As FDI capital from East and Southeast Asian nations began to pour into Vietnam, the Vietnamese state also had to accommodate the mounting interest of these new investors, who preferred operating through informal deal brokering. As a result, the government adopted a contradictory approach, simultaneously enacting repressive measures to crack down on low-end street prostitution and, among wealthy elite businessmen, permitting consumption tied to commercial sex work.[55]

At around the same time as President Bush's visit, the Vietnamese government launched a five-year, $30.5-million program to crack down on prostitution.[56] Phan Van Khai, then prime minister, advanced its early campaigns to get rid of social evils by directing the Ministry of Labor, Invalids, and Social Affairs to formulate and implement the National Plan of Action to Combat Trafficking in Persons. The Social Evils Department of this ministry and the Criminal Police Department worked in cooperation with Vietnam's Ministry of Justice, the Vietnam Women's Union, and the United Nations Office of Drugs and Crime.

This campaign was part of the prime minister's larger effort to respond to the outcry of U.S. government agencies and international religious and secular nongovernmental organizations devoted to rescuing poor "Third World" women deemed at risk of sex trafficking. Even though no research had been conducted to verify whether trafficking was a problem in Vietnam, the government nonetheless responded to sensationalized, unfounded media reports on the plight of "trafficked" women in Southeast Asia. As a result, the police shut down hundreds of bars and karaoke lounges and took to the streets to arrest sex workers.

Street prostitution became an easy target for state officials because those involved did not have ties to men with any kind of political power. Women who worked as freelance entrepreneurs in the sex industry were often *misidentified* by local police, NGOs, and the state as victims of human trafficking in need of "rescue and rehabilitation" and sent to confinement rehabilitation centers for sex workers and drug users.[57] The campaign to clean up the streets of HCMC was also part of a larger public effort to transform Vietnam's international image from that of a corrupt socialist country to that of a potentially attractive destination for Western investment. The strong arm of the state in charge of cracking down on social evils, however, rarely arrested sex workers in higher-tiered markets catering to foreign investors from Asia.

Following the 2008 financial crisis, the stratification of Vietnam's sex industry shifted once again as local Vietnamese elites in charge of brokering foreign investment deals from Asia gained the upper hand, replacing the overseas Vietnamese men as the clients who commanded the highest tier of sex work. The upsurge in Asian-based FDI in Vietnam's financial markets (described in greater detail in the introduction), coupled with global economic insecurity in the West, profoundly transformed the contemporary sex industry. The rapid shift in sources of capital via FDI from Asia, along with the upsurge in the number of deals being brokered, meant that local Vietnamese elites depended heavily on the commercial sex trade to secure capital from Asian investors. Today, the stratification of Vietnam's sex market mirrors stratification in the country's economic field. Despite the relative prestige of Western transnational businessmen elsewhere in the world, they no longer represent the most elite segment of the market for commercial sex in Vietnam. Rather, by 2009, the highest-paying sector of the sex industry was composed of wealthy local Vietnamese elites with access to Asian-based FDI capital.[58]

Despite state efforts to implement harsh punishments for sex work, the illicit trade thrived in the underground world of nightclubs, bars, cafes, and massage parlors because sex work was integral to economic practices in Vietnam. As the police took to the streets, sex workers moved to indoor venues, where they could disguise their work and operate outside the purview of local enforcers and often with the *protection* of higher-level state officials. Following early practices of deal broking through hostess bars under Doi Moi, Vietnamese elites continued to rely on the sex industry to play a critical role in brokering trilateral business deals among state officials, private entrepreneurs, and foreign investors from Asia.

These entrepreneurial activities are largely male dominated and heavily influenced by existing practices established in China, Japan, Taiwan, and South Korea.[59] In her book *The Ironies of Freedom: Sex, Culture, and Neoliberal Governance in Vietnam,* Nguyen-Vo examines contradictions in how the state deploys freedom in the economic sphere, where neoliberal leaders promote free-market forces and free economic agents while simultaneously governing sex workers' bodies. She argues that the Vietnamese socialist state is the biggest stakeholder in the sexual market, actively promoting entrepreneurial and consumerist freedoms as sex has become integral to entrepreneurs' way of doing business in Vietnam's marketized economy.[60] The rise of a permissive culture around sex work in high-end niche markets is due, in large part, to the importance of personal and business relations facilitated in hostess bars and gendered spaces of commercial sex work.

Because of the Vietnamese government's promotion of entrepreneurial and consumerist freedoms—as early as the establishment of the Doi Moi and more vigorously after the WTO accession and the upsurge in

Asian-based FDI—commercial sex has become a fixture in Vietnamese society. It provides local elite men with a space to build social ties, make status claims, and contest social hierarchies within Vietnam that once privileged Western and Viet Kieu men in the nation's sex industry. In fact, by 2012, NGOs, governmental agencies, and religious organizations began to realize that they had misidentified many "sex workers" as "victims of trafficking" and started referring to them more generally as "workers" to avoid conflating sex work with sex trafficking. This linguistic, legal, and symbolic shift highlights the importance of women's labor in spaces of leisure and entertainment. Moreover, despite protests from the Vietnam Women's Union and other antiprostitution campaigns concerned with women's rights and the spread of venereal disease, the Vietnamese government moved to decriminalize prostitution.[61] On June 20, 2012, the party enacted the new Civil Violations Punishment Law to eliminate the rehabilitation centers and release sex workers from their confinement. While sex work continues to be an illegal/illicit trade, the government has taken formal steps away from criminalizing the women who work in this trade. Thus, the structure of the contemporary sex industry reflects tensions between socialist values and capitalist desires within Vietnam's wider gender order.

The current (re)stratification of HCMC's global sex industry is embedded in a context rife with tensions between the city's place in the contemporary political economy and the residues left from its history of French and American occupation. As nation-states reposition themselves in the context of the 2008 global economic slowdown, diverse groups of men in Vietnam use the sex industry in different ways to assert masculine superiority in markets that exude the vibrancy associated with the rise of Asia or to recuperate relations tied to the Western hegemony that was prevalent in the region for so long. The imperial past casts different shadows onto each of the four niche markets as clients come to terms with remnants of the past that are being restructured by the shifting geopolitical arrangements of the present.

In the late 1800s through the late 1900s—the era of French colonialism and the Vietnam War—the dominance of the West in the region prevailed as white men commanded the highest-paying segments of Vietnam's sexual economy. Military funds that were directed into this region during times of war fundamentally altered the social landscape of these spaces. The racialization of Vietnamese women in sex work conferred prestige on whiteness during times of war and conflict, in places where Western men, through their sexual relationships with Vietnamese women, sought refuge from killing Vietnamese men.[62]

After defeating its foreign occupiers, Vietnam used the rejection of prostitution as a symbolic weapon against Western imperialism. However, with the opening of the economy to foreign investment, the regulation of prostitution was formally used to appeal to Western and Viet Kieu visitors from Europe and the United States looking to enact feelings of superiority through nostalgia and conspicuous consumption. Finally, in the modern era, prostitution is used once again by local Vietnamese political and economic elites as a symbolic tool to oppose Western dominance—not through the abolition of prostitution but by using spaces of sex work to facilitate ties among investors in charge of directing Asian-based capital. The configurations of capital sources shifting from the West to Asia brought on new tensions as new groups of local elites in HCMC worked to reimagine a global hierarchy in which Asians reign over their own region and local elites have risen to the top of the local order.

2

The Contemporary Sex Industry

Contemporary Ho Chi Minh City is marked by a distinctive *sexscape* where multiple niche markets in different areas of the city cater to global and local men who travel in and out of HCMC for business and leisure.[1] Each market presents a unique configuration of gender and global capital that influences men's perceptions of self and nation. Taken together, these markets challenge simplistic notions of Western dominance as men assert their places in a shifting global economy in the company of hostesses.

Thick descriptions of four types of bars illuminate the fact that gendered relations are also inflected with race and class in the clients' competing desires to affirm Western superiority or assert Asian capitalist ascendancy.[2] I focus on four specific bars that represent niche markets in which sex workers perform intimate labor for (a) local Vietnamese business elites working to attract foreign direct investments from their Asian business partners, (b) Viet Kieu men tied to nostalgic remittances, (c) Western men investing in small-scale businesses through benevolent remittances, and (d) Western budget travelers who still view Vietnam as a poor Third World country in need of aid or charity through benevolent remittances. In the space of each niche market, the formation of social contracts—among men and between men and women—depends on women's embodied labors designed to access distinct sources of foreign capital.

A comparison of these four markets—through an analysis of how race, class, sexuality, and nationality intersect in constructing multiple masculinities and embodied femininities—complicates our understanding of the sex industry in "Third World" nations by challenging ideas of Western dominance. This approach has material implications for how we think about global capitalism and new differences in wealth between nations. Sex work provides a unique perspective through which to examine not only how transformations in the global economy reshape intimate life but also how the emotional intimacy (and not merely sex) provided by sex workers serves as an important currency in attracting transnational capital.

KHONG SAO BAR: WEALTHY LOCAL VIETNAMESE AND OTHER ASIAN BUSINESSMEN

Khong Sao Bar was hidden deep in the heart of District 1—HCMC's vibrant business district, where wealthy local elites and tourists have easy access to some of the country's finest restaurants, hotels, and shops.[3] With no signage or street number on the outside of the building, this exclusive bar was available only to clients who had an existing relationship with the head mommy or who were introduced by a top-paying regular client. The bar catered to local elite Vietnamese businessmen who operate some of the country's top finance, real estate, and trade companies. All the men who had access to Khong Sao were part of a privileged class embedded in a small, tight-knit network of political elites who had access to the resources and bureaucratic power crucial to brokering deals. These men typically arrived in the afternoon or late in the evening after dining with their partners at another location. Because the bar was so difficult to locate and enter, local elites escorted Asian investors to the bar as part of their entourages.

Upon the arrival of a group of clients, three to five male service workers greeted them and escorted them to a concealed door that opened into an elevator. The guests rode up several floors to a very plain reception area. There, they greeted a woman in her midfifties who always dressed as if she were hosting guests in her own home. Her primary job was to monitor the cash register for the mommies and bar owner. Behind her cash drawer, a bright neon sign with the words *karaoke luxury,* in English, hung against a wall covered by chipped white paint. Nothing about this outer space conveyed luxury; instead it was designed to disguise the scene in case unwanted guests ventured into it.

After greeting the men, the older woman summoned one of the mommies to greet them. One of the bar's three mommies stepped out of a private room, bowed her head to greet the men, and proceeded to guide them down a stained dark-red carpet and into one of five private VIP rooms. Each room was decorated with nonmatching wallpaper patterns and disco lights that created a dizzying effect. Sofas lined three of the walls, creating a U shape, and two coffee tables for food and drinks stood in the center; a small dance floor and a television and karaoke set were situated across from the couches.

This setting symbolized a shift from an old bureaucratic culture to a newly entrepreneurial culture where men used relationships to broker deals. This was a comfortable space where rituals related to drinking had much to do with understanding and establishing social relationships among the men and little to do with Western conceptions of etiquette related to drinking and dining. In these simple physical surroundings, men displayed their membership in an affluent social class through their choice of expensive alcohol, the branded keys to high-end luxury cars on their key rings, their Vertu cellular phones, and expensive accessories.

Once the men were inside the private room, the mommy directed the barbacks (male service staff in the bar) to bring out the finest whiskey so she could pour a toast of welcome. Then she summoned the hostesses into the room and took a seat next to the most senior local Vietnamese man at the table while the hostesses lined up in two rows on the dance floor. It was implicitly understood that every man had to select a woman to sit with for the evening. In the event that an individual requested to sit alone, his male business partners often ridiculed him for being "gay" or unmasculine. Women in the bar also pressured men to sit with someone so they could help their friends earn tips. Each man typically sat with one or two workers, whose job was to ensure that the client enjoyed his time in the bar. The hostesses' services for clients included pouring drinks, feeding them, serenading them, dancing with them, and initiating drinking games.

The bar was also staffed by mommies and male service workers in addition to the hostesses. Hanh, the head mommy, a woman in her late twenties, ran the bar along with Quynh and Lan-Vy, two junior mommies who helped manage the workers. These three women always wore perfectly tailored black suits accentuated with designer tops, belts, and accessories, or long gowns of the type one might see at a red carpet event. In addition, ten male service workers provided the bar with private security, ran errands for clients and sex workers, and worked backstage delivering supplies and fixing broken equipment when necessary.

About twenty clients regularly brought their friends and business partners to Khong Sao. They visited the bar three or four nights a week, spending an average of U.S.$1,000–$2,000 per night and $15,000–$20,000 per month. Incredibly, the bar usually generated around U.S.$150,000 a month in revenue from alcohol sales alone. This space of leisure was crucial to local Vietnamese elite men, allowing them to establish social and personal relations of trust that enabled them to broker deals worth millions of U.S. dollars involving a broad array of projects, including land development; exports of steel, rubber, wood, textiles, and agricultural products; and commodity trading. In these spaces of leisure, men claimed their active role in a particular version of Vietnam with a vibrant economy.

Despite its high receipts, the bar did not pay any of the women or the mommies a wage for their work. Instead, their income depended on tips. At least one of the three mommies accompanied the hostesses to each table. The mommies earned U.S.$3,000–$4,000 per month in tips (in comparison, women with master's degrees in managerial positions made roughly U.S.$2,000 per month in HCMC) and received a small percentage of all alcohol sales in the bar.[4] As I discuss in greater detail in chapter 5, the mommies did not take a cut of the hostesses' earnings, did not force any of the women to have sex with clients against their will, and did not receive kickbacks from the women who engaged in paid sex. There was an unspoken rule in the bar that the women were to arrange all sexual transactions on their own. The mommies trained hostesses in how to sit, drink, sing, dance, and negotiate relations of paid sex.

During my fieldwork, roughly twenty-five women worked in the bar, along with fifteen others who cycled in and out as they accompanied men on business trips throughout Vietnam or overseas. They ranged in age from sixteen to twenty-two years old.[5] Two-thirds of the women were recruited from poor rural villages by the mommies. The remaining third came from poor urban families. None of the women in the bar were college educated.[6] This allowed powerful elites to maintain a degree of anonymity inside the bars, because hostesses did not move in their social circles. Workers earned roughly U.S.$2,000 per month in tips for joining men at their tables and U.S.$150–$200 for each sexual encounter.[7] They were permitted to keep all the money they earned from both tips and sex work.

Although the women's primary source of income was their hostess work in the bar, they often served as escorts, accompanying the clients to lunch, dinner, shows, clubs, and on vacations. The women earned tips for their company and for sexual services, as well as gifts of perfume, expensive cell phones, jewelry, clothing, and accessories. The most common exchanges of sex and companionship for money were limited in duration, but a few women were provided a monthly income to service clients in longer-term relationships as *gai bao* (hired girl-friends). In the time I spent at the bar, three of the women were even able to get their clients to buy them small houses or provide them with capital to start their own businesses.

LAVENDER BAR: VIET KIEU MEN

Situated on the third floor of a modern-style building, Lavender was an upscale bar located within five minutes' walking distance from the three five-star hotels in the heart of District 1. Unlike Khong Sao Bar, Lavender was out in the open for everyone to see. The owner had worked with an architect to construct an exterior design that would convey high-end luxury. They settled on an innovative double-glazed glass wall that allowed passers-by to hear the booming music that roared from the inside and see the flashing lights on the dance floor while providing exceptional privacy by obscuring the darkened interior.

The clientele of Lavender, primarily Viet Kieu, most commonly arrived in cabs. Every night, seven to ten male service workers dressed in all-black suits stood outside waiting to greet them. As the cabs pulled up to the curb, three service workers approached the vehicle, opened the doors for the guests to step out, and proceeded to escort the guests up to the bar. Men who had reserved table service and whose names were on the guest list were admitted directly to the bar, but a velvet rope cordoned off a queue for guests without reservations and guests whose membership in a party with a reservation had to be verified. Though the length of the queue primarily depended on capacity, it was an unspoken rule that Western men generally had to wait in the queue unless they were accompanied by a group of overseas Vietnamese or local Vietnamese men. The symbolic and systematic denial of Western men from these bars made Lavender one of the most attractive sites for Viet Kieu men, who operated in a more expensive niche market than Westerners.

After entering the bar, men were greeted by a mommy, who, along with her entourage of male barbacks, created a walkway using their bodies and flashlights to enable clients and their guests to make their way through the crowded room to VIP tables. There was a circular bar in the middle of the room, where bartenders and hostesses mixed drinks.

A large, handcrafted chandelier in the shape of a phallus hung from the ceiling above the bar and provided the room with dim white and yellow lighting. To the right of the bar was a stage where professional singers performed live or a DJ played mixes of American, Vietnamese, and Korean pop music. The circular design of the bar allowed the bar owner to maximize the number of semiprivate VIP rooms lining its perimeter.

The rooms were separated by long, thick, purple-and-white drapes that were pulled halfway open so that customers in the bar or on the dance floor could easily view the VIP customers. Each space contained plush white sofas and its own chandelier. In between the private rooms and the main bar were several round tables where non-VIP customers could stand or sit on stools. Each table had its own group of male service workers, hostess-workers, and mommies who attended to the clients. It was the service workers' job to help the mommies remember each client's name, the type of alcohol he preferred, and the hostess-workers who had previously accompanied his table.

Although the bar served a variety of mixed drinks, most men ordered "bottle service"—where a bottle of vodka, cognac, or whiskey costing between one hundred and two hundred U.S. dollars was shared among the men at the table. The vast majority of clients were Viet Kieu men visiting Vietnam to see family or their ancestral home. Roughly a third of the Viet Kieu men that I studied in these bars had set up permanent lives in Vietnam, working for foreign companies or owning small businesses such as restaurants, bars, or small IT companies. Bottle service enabled these men to differentiate themselves from Western expatriates and tourists in HCMC, who typically ordered beers or mixed drinks to avoid the markups on bottles. Lavender offered a deal—buy two bottles, get one free—so most tables ordered three bottles for the night (at two hundred to four hundred U.S. dollars).

After the clients ordered their drinks, the service workers brought a fruit platter, some dried jerky, and salted nuts to the table; and shortly after that, a mommy returned to greet the men again. She poured their glasses of alcohol and then raised her glass to salute them. Then she would ask them to invite hostesses to accompany them for the night. Although the bar did not require clients to sit with a hostess, most men chose to have company.

If it was early in the night and the bar was not full, the men would scan the room to look at the hostess-workers who stood around the perimeter of the bar and tell the mommy which woman they would like to invite to their table. However, if the bar was full, the mommy would instruct a group of women to line up in front of the table so that the men could select their company for the night. Hostesses attended to each client's needs by making sure his glass was always full and he was well fed, and by dancing and flirting with him throughout the night. They carefully crafted ways of ensuring that their clients always felt taken care of and desired—not to support business deals, as in Khong Sao Bar, but to support their clients' feelings of having returned to a Vietnam that had triumphed over the West.

The two mommies who ran the bar—Tho and Huyen—were in their late twenties and midthirties, respectively, and worked to set the stage for Viet Kieu men looking to experience the new Vietnam with vestiges of a nostalgic past. Tho and Huyen generally earned an average of three thousand U.S. dollars per month from alcohol sales and tips. They always dressed in tight suits or long gowns that made them appear older and more distinguished than the hostesses. The mommies recruited hostess-workers for this bar through their networks of promotion girls, who promoted various alcohol brands; or women got jobs in the bar after an introduction through a worker in the bar. Hostesses earned roughly one thousand U.S. dollars a month from tips for accompanying clients in the bar, plus about one thousand U.S. dollars for sex. Most women charged one hundred U.S. dollars for sex, and they left with a client once every few nights.

As at Khong Sao Bar, the women in Lavender could choose whether they wanted to sleep with a particular man. The mommies served as facilitators, introducing their workers to clients, but never took a cut of the pay women earned from having sex with clients. On several occasions, the mommies protected women who refused to leave with clients. Most often, however, women left the bar upon the requests of clients, because it meant they would make extra money; it also made them feel desirable.

Among the twenty-five women I studied, all were from either poor rural villages or poor urban families. The women who came from villages had previously been employed as maids, hotel receptionists, or restaurant servers, chasing fantasies of global-economic upward mobility. They ranged from eighteen to twenty-seven years of age. Like the women at Khong Sao, workers supplemented their incomes by working as escorts, accompanying men to restaurants and on vacations. Most of these exchanges were limited to the evening or to the duration of a trip, except in the cases of four women who developed short-lived remittance relationships with clients. Though some women hoped that hostess work would help them meet Viet Kieu men to marry and, thus, permit them to migrate, this was a rare occurrence, because most Viet Kieu men who married in Vietnam found wives through friends or family members who served as matchmakers.[8]

SECRETS: WESTERN EXPATRIATE BAR

From the outside, Secrets was indistinguishable from a typical "girly bar." The windows were heavily tinted to reveal only dim pink and yellow lighting. When the front door swung open, outsiders caught a view of women dressed in short, skintight Chinese-style dresses or leather dresses. There was no exclusivity to the bar; any man could recognize the bar from the street and enter.

But Secrets was clearly a male-dominated space; as I witnessed on multiple occasions, when white foreign women opened the front door, they immediately turned away as if they had witnessed something private and quickly left the bar. Men generally went there to drink with the expectation that they would receive the exclusive company of an attractive Vietnamese hostess.

The clients who spent time in this bar were mostly Western white men from the United States, Western Europe, or Australia who either lived in Vietnam or flew there frequently on business. Clients visited the bar Monday through Saturday; Sundays were family days in Vietnam. Most clients came in between 4 P.M. and 7 P.M., which was the bar's happy hour and a time when men were getting off from work. Many men also came in around 8 P.M., after they had had dinner with friends or family, and often stayed until midnight or 1 A.M.

The inside of the bar was roughly nine hundred square feet and rectangular shaped. To the left of the entrance was a long bar that ran the perimeter of the room. Behind the bar were mirrors that opened up the space and two flat-screen TVs on which men sometimes watched sports. To the right of the entrance was a dark-gray wall with several posters of the workers posing as models in bikinis. The women generally sat on one side of the bar and opposite their clients, or right next to them. The bar, which was roughly twenty feet long, was set up so that every male customer could sit at a stool where one hostess-worker would give him her undivided attention. Unlike Khong Sao Bar or Lavender, the men in Secrets always ordered beers or individual mixed drinks. The average bill was about fifteen U.S. dollars for three to four drinks. During the time that I worked in the bar, only two clients ordered bottle service.[9]

Lilly, the owner of Secrets, opened the very first bar of this kind, in 2008, in order to capitalize on the growing number of Western transnational businessmen who had suffered during the 2008 financial crisis and traveled to Vietnam to rebuild their professional lives. Lilly's mother, a prostitute during the war who worked mainly for American GIs, had encouraged her daughter to develop relations with Western men that would enable her to either marry and migrate or find the capital to start her own business. Lilly's mother had consulted with her on the drink menu, which included several mixed drinks whose names invoked wartime nostalgia, including "B-52," "Me Love You Long Time," and even "Cu Chi Blow Job," named after an infamous group of underground tunnels dug out by the North Vietnamese forces during the war. When men ordered this shot for a hostess, the woman would put her mouth around the glass as it sat on the bar and throw her head back to drink the shot in an erotic performance. In this particular niche market catering to Western businessmen, the erotic comingled with the military to invoke nostalgia for Western might.

When Lilly first opened Secrets, she hired twenty women from her HCMC neighborhood and the village where she grew up, paying each woman roughly one hundred U.S. dollars per month in wages. While this figure may seem low, other bar owners in the area did not pay any wages but instead expected hostesses to rely on client tips and sex work for their income. To encourage drink sales, Lilly also paid the hostesses 50 percent of the price of any drink men purchased on the women's behalf. In addition to these wages, the women also received tips from clients, which were generally one to two U.S. dollars per bill (the same as restaurant tips). These tips were placed in a jar to be divided among the women at the end of the night.

When the workers drank with the clients, the men typically stayed longer and bought more drinks. However, unlike in Khong Sao Bar or Lavender, the workers could choose not to drink. When I asked Lilly why she paid the women to drink, she responded, "I don't force the girls in here to drink. I don't want them to drink and get drunk and hurt themselves. Your body changes a lot when you drink. You get old really fast, and it is hard to stay in this business. So I pay them for drinks." Between their salary, tips, and earnings from drinking with clients, the women earned an average of U.S.$250–$300 per month. They rotated shifts to take one night off per week to relax and run errands, though many women came to work on their evenings off because they were bored at home and enjoyed their work. Roughly eighteen women worked in this bar at any given time.

Although the women earned a monthly income that enabled them to turn down many of the clients' requests for sexual services, they found other creative means to make money. Sometimes the workers charged their clients to run small errands during the day, accompanied clients to dinner after hours, and traveled with them on vacations to nearby beach towns in Bali, Phuket (Thailand), or Hong Kong. After a few months of building a relationship with a client, many of the women asked for gifts of gold jewelry or expensive perfumes bought in duty-free shops that they could easily sell on the black market. Women also asked for money to expedite a passport or to find deals on airfare, which allowed them to pocket U.S.$300 when planning a vacation.

While none of these women referred to themselves as sex workers, they talked very openly with one another about how to use the "boyfriend-girlfriend" framing as a strategy to get more money from their clients (referred to as *khach* in Vietnamese). Women in this establishment rarely engaged in direct sex-for-money exchanges but nonetheless expected to be compensated for their services. Secrets hostesses also created fictitious stories of crises, such as a dying parent or a debt they owed to the mafia, to access gifts of large sums from their "boyfriends." Hostess-workers earned between U.S.$300 and $700 per month from these boyfriend-girlfriend relationships.

NAUGHTY GIRLS: TOURISTS AND BUDGET TRAVELERS IN THE BACKPACKERS' AREA

Naughty Girls was located in the heart of the backpackers' district of HCMC, a part of town that catered to budget travelers looking to explore Vietnam as a Third World country. The area was home to travel agencies, budget hotels and hostels, tour and bus companies, and restaurants catering to foreigners. The district was known for its thriving nightlife, as one of the few areas without curfew restrictions on bars. As an area of the city that never slept, the backpackers' district had a Las Vegas–like ambiance, which made it easy to lose track of time there.

Located on the street, Naughty Girls had a large, warehouse-style open entrance exposed to all the street traffic and pedestrians, so that those passing by could see the entire bar from the outside. There was a front patio that bordered the sidewalk, where clients and hostesses sat and drank together or lounged in the sun. Inside, Naughty Girls was a small space, roughly thirty feet long and fifteen feet wide, with a bar taking up about a quarter of the room. The bar was painted dark brown, and, above it, multicolored neon lights hung from the ceiling. There was a black chalkboard wall, where clients and workers sometimes played drinking games or exchanged English and Vietnamese language lessons. On the front porch of the bar were four outdoor lawn tables and bamboo chair sets, where clients could sit and watch the activity on the street.

Tina, the twenty-seven-year-old owner of the bar, did not do anything to disguise this space. She wanted to make it clear that this was a "girly bar," where female tourists were not welcome. Workers in this bar were all very dark skinned and wore heavy makeup and simple clothing to cater to their Western backpacker clients' racialized desires (described in greater detail chapter 6). Most of the women wore tank tops, jean shorts, and Lucite high heels. They often sat outside and invited male passers-by into the establishment, crying in unison, "Come in! Come in please!" Women who walked by the bar with their husbands usually turned their heads in a different direction.

Whenever the police drove by, the women scrambled to bring the lawn furniture into the bar and close the doors. This activity was a formality of local governance, because Tina paid off the local police to leave her bar and its workers alone. But in addition to navigating relationships with the police, Tina had to contend with the local mafia, whose drug activity was visible in this area. However, Tina was able to use the mafia to her advantage by paying its members to inform the women when police were making rounds and to manage bar fights or unruly clients. At first I was intimidated by the presence of the mafia, but over time I realized that although they were affiliated with criminal activity, these men did not act as pimps who forced women to have sex with clients, did not try to get money from women, and did not even procure clients for the bar. While there are pimps in Vietnam who manage street workers in Vietnam, the men linked to Naughty Girls acted both like brothers to the women and as contract employees who were paid each time the owner or sex workers called on them for help with a particular situation.

After 2006, the backpackers' area of HCMC experienced a decline in bar clientele because of the economic downturn. Between 2006 and 2007, there were roughly twenty-five small bars that catered to foreign tourists. However, by 2009, this number had declined to eleven. The backpackers' area had become run down, with transient tourists looking to explore Vietnam as cheaply as possible. The clients I studied in these bars wanted to explore a "Third World" country as tourists who typically did not plan to return again. On any given night, they could walk into the bar and order a cheap beer that cost roughly two U.S. dollars while enjoying the company of one or two women at their table. The workers did not earn any money in tips or in wages from the bar owner. Instead, paid sex was the most common way workers earned money at Naughty Girls. These workers earned fifty to seventy U.S. dollars for paid sex and gave Tina a cut amounting to ten to twelve U.S. dollars, per sexual encounter, for using her bar as a space in which to procure clients. Some women also built longer-term relationships with clients to secure remittances after the backpackers had returned to their home countries. All the women in this niche market were factory workers and service workers before entering sex work.

The bar owner, Tina, was a tall, beautiful woman with a slim figure like a model. She started doing sex work at the age of sixteen and was able to open Naughty Girls with the help of a foreign boyfriend. The bar had a total of twenty-six workers, but only about fifteen worked there on a regular basis. The women were between the ages of eighteen and thirty-three. Half were from the Mekong Delta and half from HCMC, but all of them lived in District 4, an area known for housing the local mafia and sex workers. All the women spoke some English, which they picked up through working in the bar.

Nearly all interactions with the clients in the bar lasted roughly thirty minutes, during which time the men would consume one or two drinks before leaving with a worker for paid sex. The owner did not force the women to sit and talk with these men. However, because it was their main source of income, women in this niche market engaged in many more direct sex-for-money exchanges than the women in the other spaces. As in the other bars, no one forced the women to have sex with clients. In addition, these workers had the phone numbers of local men in the mafia whom they could call on to hunt down a client if he refused to pay or was too rough with their bodies, even though it was uncommon for women to experience abuse from their clients. On the rare occasions when a man tried to get away with "free sex" by refusing to pay, the women would cause a scene on the street, embarrassing the men until they opened their wallets. More often than not, women performed their part, and the men compensated them for their work.

Globalizing cities like HCMC are strategic sites where brokers of global capital and poor migrant women come into direct contact to both

TABLE I   THE COCONSTITUTIVE RELATIONSHIP OF GENDER AND GLOBAL CAPITAL

	Local Vietnamese and Asian Men	Viet Kieus	Western Expatriates	Westerners Budget Travelers
Capital involved	Asian foreign direct investment capital	Remittances through conspicuous consumption	Remittances as philanthropy	Remittances as philanthropy
Women's labor	Embracing pan-Asian ideals	Celebrating Vietnam's trajectory	Sexualizing Third World dependency	Exaggerating Third World poverty
Social contracts	Between men	Between men and women	Between men and women	Between men and women
Perceptions of Asian ascendancy and Western decline	Capitalizing on Asian ascendancy and Western decline	Claiming Asian ascendancy; contesting Western dominance	Recuperation of Western patriarchy to negotiate Western decline	Recuperation of Western patriarchy to negotiate Western decline

reproduce and contest hierarchies of desire and desirability. In Vietnam, inter-Asian circuits of capital from more developed regions to less developed regions have altered local perceptions of Asian ascendancy and Western decline. These broader political and economic transformations occurring in the globalized economy have become transparent in the (re)stratification of HCMC's contemporary sex industry.

While most studies of the global sex industry focus on individual niche markets catering either to Western men on romance tours or to local men, new capital flows in HCMC have fractured the Vietnamese sex industry into multiple niche markets that cater to demographically diverse consumers. In these spaces of leisure, powerful local elites, Viet Kieus from the diaspora, business executives, and marginal tourists enter into niche markets that never overlap. Instead, each niche market operates with a unique logic of desire that has important implications for how we think about the place of sex work in the global economy.

Table I outlines the four markets, along with their relationships to global capital involved, women's labor, social contracts, and perceptions of Asian ascendancy and Western decline. This frame explains how gendered relations and different forms of global capital converged to produce new forms of masculine privilege and performances of femininity. Local Vietnamese and other Asian businessmen were tied to Asian-based FDI, and elites depended on workers' embodied labors that projected pan-Asian modernity and the exuberant rise of the local economy in order to broker social contracts between men.

In the markets catering to Viet Kieus, Western expatriates, and Western budget travelers, relationships revolved around remittance money through social contracts between men and women. The remittance money, however, took on different meanings in each market. For Viet Kieus, relationships with local women hinged on the women's ability to embrace nostalgic Vietnamese cultural ideals of femininity that allowed Viet Kieus to feel a connection to their "motherland" while also embracing the rise of local elites and Asian ascendancy through conspicuous consumption. Western men's relationships with sex workers were tied to different trappings of economic capital as men practiced "philanthropy" tied to Western capitalist notions of Third World dependency. These philanthropic remittances hinged on women's embodied labors that racialized and sexualized their dependency, thereby enabling Western men to negotiate their sense of failed masculinity abroad. Together these niche markets illustrate how transnational capital flows and intimate life are linked in a circle of performative displays of consumerist distinction, hypermasculinity, and stylized femininity.

3

New Hierarchies of Global Men

It was noon, and I was sitting in the back room of Khong Sao Bar with about thirty other women. We were putting on makeup, fixing our hair, and eating a quick bowl of noodles before getting dressed. Hanh, the head mommy, walked into the dressing room and said to the women in general: "Hurry up and finish getting dressed. Dai Ca [Big Brother] Xanh just called and reserved a table. He will be here in an hour with nine other people." The women quickly slurped up their noodles, wiped their faces, and finished applying their makeup.

Hanh then said to me, "Your uncle is here; go sit next to him." She was referring to Chu Xanh, a key informant who had helped me gain access to the bar. She then turned to Lan, a twenty-year-old sex worker, and said, "Chu Xanh asked to sit with you too." Lan and I walked into the room and sat next to Chu Xanh. Nine men sat at the table: five local Vietnamese men (two political elites and three wealthy business elites) and four businessmen from Korea.

Chu Xanh introduced me as a hostess and his protégé who spoke English and Lan as his girlfriend. Two minutes later, the door swung open and twenty-eight women lined up on the dance floor. One by one, each man pointed out a woman to sit at the table with him. Over the next two hours, the women sang karaoke with the men, sat and talked with them, and played drinking games to break the awkward tension in the room. They helped Chu Xanh, their client, transition from a formal style of interaction with his Korean business partners to one that was informal, intimate, fun, and personable to help the men to bond. The clients went through eight bottles of Johnnie Walker Blue Label at a cost of U.S.$250 each before loosening up and laughing together. As the night came to an end, the bill came out and Chu Xanh pulled out a plastic credit card, jokingly placed it on the table, and then said, "Oh wait. These things don't work anymore. Americans broke the [global credit] system." He leaned back, grabbed his briefcase, pulled out a wad of cash, and instructed me to count out VND 42,000,000 (U.S.$2,100). Then he pulled out another wad of cash and tipped each woman two crisp VND 500,000 bills (fifty U.S. dollars).

After leaving that night, Chu Xanh revealed to me that he and his colleagues were negotiating a U.S.$60 million land development project to build a new commercial property that would include office space and a shopping center in HCMC. The Korean men at the table were potential investors, and the Vietnamese men were businessmen with strong ties to elites in Vietnam who could assure that the project would move forward quickly. Chu Xanh confided, "It's not just about trust, but about making the men feel confident that Vietnam is a nation worth their investment. They need to see that we are serious and that we can make money." The ritual of paying the bill and publicly tipping the women provided men like Chu Xanh with a symbolic vocabulary to critique the U.S. credit system and demonstrate Vietnam's ability to mobilize liquid capital to make deals in an increasingly Asian-centered economy. Chu Xanh went on to tell me that while the West was mired in the 2008 global financial crisis, Asia's economy was booming. "China is on its way to becoming the next global superpower," he said. "Vietnam is also ready to ride this economic wave."

This scene and countless others like it highlight the connections between the political economy and sex work in HCMC, the center of Vietnam's sex industry. Business deals such as this one were not merely about making money. Local Vietnamese businessmen also used them to redefine Vietnam's global economic position and its relationship to the West and East Asia. When Chu Xanh compared Vietnam to the economic powerhouse of China, he was asserting Vietnam's rise as a strong nation in the new global economy. In Vietnam's transition from a developing nation to an emerging market, HCMC has become an attractive destination for foreign investors from other parts of Asia who seek to underwrite ambitious projects in land development, trade, commodity manufacturing, and banking. These investments present Vietnamese elites with an opportunity to reconfigure their place in the global pecking order as a specifically Asian rising economic power.

While the relationship between gender and global capital in bars like Khong Sao revolved around local elites' ability to secure capital by brokering informal social relationships in hostess bars, Westerners operated at the other end of the economic spectrum in a context of relative global economic decline following the 2008 worldwide financial crisis. The next two vignettes provide some local context to situate Westerners both in the local business world and in the hostess bars. In a political economy that no longer recognized them as dominant, Western men turned to the bars to project their status anxieties onto their relationships with local sex workers.

One afternoon while playing card games in the back room with some of the sex workers, I received a phone call from Chu Hai, a Vietnamese entrepreneur who ran a local investment firm. Chu Hai's company had a diverse portfolio with investments in manufacturing, trade, and tourism, and he called to request my help as a translator in a meeting with a company I'll call Infinity Capital, a venture capital firm based in the United States. This group was interested in investing in a U.S.$85 million project that would include shopping malls, commercial properties, residential villas, luxury condos, and public parks on an exclusive beachfront property that would transform Vietnam's southern coast.

He instructed me to go home, change into a suit, and wait for his driver to pick me up around 5:30 P.M. I rode to the meeting in a black Mercedes with Chu Hai and two other Vietnamese men. On the car ride over, Chu Hai prepped me for the meeting by saying, "Westerners are formal, and they don't do business like Asians. They think our style of doing business involves too much uncertainty and unpredictability. So they will come with lawyers, translators, and thick contracts put together by their deal teams of researchers, analysts, appraisers, and brokers in the United States. We will meet them for dinner at the Sheraton, and then after dinner we will sit down in one of the conference rooms to listen to their offer. Don't smile, talk to them, or try to invite them out afterward. Keep a straight face and say as little as possible. They like to feel like they are making smart, rational calculations about their investments, not emotional calculations, . . . so the less you say, the better."

When we arrived at the hotel, Chu Hai introduced me to Kevin, Steven, and Howard—three American investors from the United States. As the only woman present at dinner, I sat at the corner of the table and spoke only when asked to translate as the men made small talk about their long flight, new restaurants that had opened up in the city, places where they could purchase tailored suits, and streets that sold local custom artwork. After dinner we made our way up to one of the conference rooms, where Kevin, Steven, and Howard handed us each a two-inch portfolio filled with charts and tables analyzing the potential costs and return on investments. The folder also contained computer-generated images with a set of architectural designs for the project, an estimated cost, and a strategy to reduce risk by selling the majority of units preconstruction.

Infinity Capital proposed to bring in U.S.$10 million (or 11 percent of the initial capital) to get the project started and promised to commit another U.S.$35 million, which would arrive in chunks at different phases of construction. They then told Chu Hai and his partners that they wanted a local Vietnamese bank to secure U.S.$40 million, along with a fifty-year land leasehold with a right to an extension, as part of a joint venture between a local Vietnamese entity and a foreign entity. I translated everything, moving back and forth between their PowerPoint slide presentation and my copy of the portfolio that each man held. Then I sat down and waited as the Vietnamese men sat in silence for nearly ten minutes. None of them said a word; they just sat in contemplation.

Then Chu Hai asked, "Can you bring in all $45 million in the next year? We cannot get a land leasehold with the kind of extension you're asking for without at least 50 percent of the capital." Kevin responded, "I am happy to bring this back to my team; but you will be wasting your time, because it will be hard to convince our investors to contribute another $25 million without a commitment from a local bank. If you want to close this deal over the next four weeks, I suggest we move forward with the contract so that we have something to show our investors."

Chu Hai and his partners sat for another ten minutes flipping through the portfolios and whispering with each other. Then he said out loud, "Thank you for coming here and pitching your deal to us. . . . But I have investors from Taiwan, South Korea, and Singapore who I know will bring in a larger share of capital in the first phase. We can't take any risks. . . . If you cannot raise the money, all we will have is an empty plot of land and an empty construction site with nothing but bulldozers." Without giving Kevin a chance to respond, Chu Hai stood up, shook their hands, and walked out.

During the car ride back to the bar, I asked Chu Hai, "Do you think they will come back with an offer to bring in more capital?" He responded, "No . . . Americans play with credit. . . . They're trying to

leverage too much out of a small investment. I brought them here knowing that I was going to turn down their offer." He paused for a moment,
pointed out the window to a high-rise, and explained, "See that building? If I told you that I wanted to get that building up in six months,
and that I could bring in only 10 percent of the funds, wouldn't you
look at me like I was crazy? That is how Americans are. . . . They think
they own the world. I want them to come here and see that Vietnam is
not a poor, backward country anymore. I want them to see these buildings and feel the energy on the streets. Then, I want them to know that
we don't need any of their money. They don't own us. They will feel the
pain when they have to go home with no deal in their bags." I asked
Chu Hai, "Why don't you build trust with Westerners in the bars? Then
they'll put in higher bids, and you can make more on the deals." Chu
Hai laughed and said, "Westerners don't do business in bars. They call
it corruption; we call it building trust."

Vietnamese businessmen were actively engaged in a project of contesting Western dominance by making Westerners feel their declining
influence even in a country as small as Vietnam. While all the Vietnamese businessmen in my study depended on Western finance capital in
some capacity, two-thirds of the Vietnamese clients in my study eventually told me that they purposefully met with Western investors to reject
their offers because they wanted Westerners to understand that Vietnam is redefining its place in the global economy.

After learning the importance of relationships to securing capital
deals in Vietnam, I began to ask why Westerners refused to engage in
the local practices of leisure and entertainment that would allow them
to compete with Asian bidders.[1] Almost all the Western businessmen
that I interviewed cited the Foreign Corrupt Practices Act—a U.S. fed-
eral law established in 1977 concerning the bribery of foreign officials—
as prohibiting their involvement in practices that mixed business with
leisure. In addition, the Western businessmen in Vietnam often worked
with less than 2 percent of their company's investments designated for
emerging markets. Thus, it was not worthwhile for them to engage in
informal business practices that could be construed as corrupt, because
there could be consequences, which would reverberate back to their
multinational corporation, negatively affecting its United States-based
investments. The perceived decline of the West, coupled with the incom-
patible business practices, made it exceedingly difficult for Westerners
to place competitive bids, particularly on land development projects
that involved a great deal of risk and potential reward.

However, although Westerners did not meet with business partners in spaces of leisure like karaoke bars, that does not mean they did not participate in the sex industry. But these men used the sex industry for very different purposes, and their relationships with women in the bars were tied to a different kind of economic capital. As Anthony, a fifty-three-year-old businessman from England, explained, "When I go to a bar with my coworkers, it's for fun, to have a drink or two and flirt with the women, . . . to get to know the women . . . [; whereas] when Vietnamese and Asian men go to a bar, it is usually about business and building a business relationship."

The niche markets that catered to Western men were not about establishing relations of trust among men that would lead to business deals. In these niche markets, the relationship between gender and global capital played out in the social contracts between men and women. That is, Western men engaged in relationships with local sex workers to mitigate their sense of Western decline through practices of benevolent Western patriarchy.

On a cool November evening in 2009, three men walked into Secrets and ordered a round of drinks. Business was slow that evening, and Lilly had just installed a dartboard on the back wall that a client had gifted to the bar. Lilly greeted them and then invited them to play a game of darts. She told them that none of us knew how to play and asked if they would be willing to teach us the game. The men obliged, so Lilly instructed six of us to watch. Before beginning the game, I introduced myself as an American researcher from the United States studying local bar culture. Alan, Derek, and Neil were all Americans in their midforties in Vietnam on a business trip.

The men worked for a boutique investment firm based in the United States that specialized in emerging markets. They had projects in Thailand, Indonesia, and Singapore, and this was their first foray into the Vietnamese market. The other workers began a game of darts with Derek and Neil while Alan, Lilly, and I chatted about the complicated nature of doing business in Vietnam. Alan refrained from discussing their particular business ventures in Vietnam, but he vented his frustrations to Lilly and me, saying,

> Launching a business here is so complicated because it's a country with jungle laws. . . . There are so many problems with corruption, and there's no legal infrastructure. . . . You would think a county like [Vietnam] would be jumping up and down for investors from the U.S., but they make doing busi-

ness here so difficult. It has been a nightmare trying to get land, dealing with construction permits, getting electricity, and trying to register a business. Everybody wants to get their cut [*rubbing his thumb and index finger together to signal money*]. It's a lose-lose situation here. If you bribe people to make them move faster, you have to deal with international laws around foreign corrupt practices. If you start paying people off, everyone here thinks you're a cash cow; and they will milk you for everything you have before you can even launch the business.

Although Lilly had no idea how to manage the world of international business ventures, she understood the local cultural style of doing business. To empathize with Alan, Lilly described her experiences with local officials in launching and maintaining her bar. Then, after allowing Alan to vent, she tried to help him de-stress by jokingly saying, "You come here to drink and forget about it. . . . Forget about business in here." Lilly called over nineteen-year-old Lan, one of the hostesses, and introduced her to Alan. Then she grabbed Alan's hand, placed it in Lan's, and instructed her to walk him over to the bar for a personal bar dance. Lilly turned on the song "Empire State of Mind," featuring Alicia Keys and Jay-Z, and turned up the music while Lan climbed onto the bar and began dancing. Neil and Derek left their game of darts and made their way to the bar to watch Lan. A few minutes later, Lilly slammed her hand down on the counter and in unison three other workers climbed onto the bar counter and began dancing. The men clapped and hooted as the women danced.

For the rest of the night the men drank, danced, played darts, and flirted with the women, dropping all talk of business. Over the next two months, Alan became a regular in the bar as he developed an intimate relationship with Lan. She became his go-to person, drinking with him after work and accompanying him on local vacations to the beach when he wanted to get away. We all referred to Alan, now a regular patron at the bar, as Lan's boyfriend—she provided him with a temporary escape and a feeling of connectedness to Vietnam.

Despite the dissimilarities between local Vietnamese men like Chu Xanh and Western businessmen like Alan, these two groups of men were embedded in the same political economy of sex work. However, they occupied different niche markets that rarely come into contact with one another. For Western men like Alan, relations with local sex workers had remarkably different social meanings in the local context, in comparison to those built around brokering capital deals with Asian investors. Importantly, Westerners formed relationships with local sex workers to escape from the daily stressors of their business dealings and to enact a form of Western patriarchy to negotiate their personal feelings of Western decline.

But, how exactly do different configurations of global capital structure new perceptions of self and nation in HCMC's sex industry? And how do the tensions between global imaginaries of Western dominance and of Asian ascendancy affect relations among men and between men and women in the hierarchical settings of the bars? A look at multiple performances of masculinities reveals how the spatial and symbolic boundaries of sex work in HCMC affirmed or contested Western dominance.[2] I draw on theories of intersectionality from the literature on postcolonial and global masculinities to unpack the processes through which men contest and affirm Western dominance.[3] The men in my study collectively drew upon intersecting classed, racialized, and gendered/sexualized relations to mobilize multiple masculinities hierarchically.[4] However, these masculinities were not simply based on men's individual subjectivity; instead, men constructed and asserted their masculinities according to their desire for a world order modeled on older tropes of Western global power or the rising prominence of non-Western nations in East and Southeast Asia.[5] This empirical data adds nuance to the analysis of an international hegemonic masculinity.[6] In HCMC's sex industry, men construct and compete within hierarchies of race, class, and nation in such a way that "Western ideals" and "pan-Asian ideals" transform our understanding of which racialized masculinities are inferior or superior.

"ASIA IS LIKE DISNEYLAND FOR [WESTERN] MEN": BUDGET TRAVELERS AFFIRMING WESTERN SUPERIORITY

Naughty Girls served Western budget travelers by appealing to men's desire to display Western superiority by drawing distinctions between the bodies of Western men, local men, and local women. Many tourists experienced a sense of failed masculinity in relation to women back home, as well as to other men worldwide who had the means to support women in the developed world. They affirmed their masculinity by constructing figures of poor exotic women, through intersecting relations of race, class, and nation. For example, Anthony, a retired fifty-eight-year-old white man from Arizona, explained the "sex scene" in Asia to a younger backpacker in this way: "I should tell you, man, you can bargain with these girls. The going rate is about 1 million Vietnamese dong [fifty-five U.S. dollars].[7] Some friends told me to go to Vietnam; they said the women were dark and pretty but thinner and had better figures. Asia is like Disneyland for retired men. You don't have to work hard or go far for sex." Men like Anthony came to bars like Naughty Girls not only for accessible women but also because they viewed Vietnam as "a retired man's playground," where men could fulfill their racialized desires for dark, thin, and cheap women. Sex workers who catered to this clientele were aware of this stereotype and strategically darkened their skin with makeup, bronzers, and an assortment of other beauty products (as described in greater detail in chapter 6).

Vietnamese male bodies were also central to clients' articulation of their racialized masculinity. Western men constructed a racialized masculinity in relation to women by describing their sexual prowess as better than Vietnamese men's. Westerners commonly asserted that women enjoyed having sex with white men more than with Vietnamese men. For example, Sam, a twenty-eight- year-old traveler from Australia, asked Thao, a nineteen-year-old sex worker: "You like having white men inside of you, don't you? We make you feel better than the tiny Asian guys, don't we?" Thao slid her finger up Sam's thigh, laughed, and jokingly said, "Show me [what's] in there." Such conversations were a nightly occurrence. Men based these assertions of white sexual superiority on the assumption that Vietnamese men had smaller penises and were sexually inhibited. By racially castrating Vietnamese men through stereotypes of penis size and libido, Western men conjured up stereotypes of racialized sexual relations between themselves and Vietnamese women, thereby asserting their masculinity.

Male clients also invoked class status as they asserted their masculinities in relation to the women. The majority of the men between the ages of fifty and seventy-five expressed the desire for a traditional marriage in which men were the economic providers and women took care of the home. Many could not afford to maintain such relationships in the United States, so they hoped to create them in less-developed nations. During a long conversation, Jason, a Montanan in his midsixties, told me,

> I grew up at a time in America when women stayed home and took care of the family while men worked. My wife and I were happily married for many years. When she died two years ago, my world fell apart. I didn't know how to cook, or clean, or take care of myself. I was depressed. I needed a wife . . . to take care of me. In Asia . . . some women still hold on to those traditional values. . . . I can afford to take care of a woman on my retirement fund [here].

Jason was not necessarily looking for a sexually submissive Vietnamese woman. In fact, sex never came up in my interview with him. Instead, he spoke mostly about finding a woman whom he could financially support on his retirement funds in exchange for care and domestic responsibilities. He was clear that, while he could not provide for a woman back home, he believed he could successfully construct a traditional heteronormative marriage based on a separate-spheres ideology (wife nurturing, man providing) in Asia.[8]

Sex workers capitalized on such desires by taking men to fake village families and creating fictive stories of crisis to procure large sums of money from clients. I listened as several sex workers told men like Jason stories about their dire financial situations in order to make the men feel like economic providers. After a few weeks, I asked the women why they lied about their lives. Xuan responded,

> A lot of the men here think that Vietnam is still a poor country. They want to hear that your family is poor and that you have no options so you came here to work. If you make them feel sorry for you as a poor Vietnamese village girl, they will give you a lot more money. We lie to them because it works. . . . We tell them that Vietnam is changing and growing so fast, and that the price of food and gas has gone up and people from poor rural areas cannot afford to live off of the rice fields anymore.

Such role playing speaks to the various ways that subaltern peoples can shape their presentation of self to appeal to humanitarian impulses. As scholars have noted, moments like these point to the aid industry that must wrestle with how it differentiates between the "truly" needy and imposters.[9] Reality tours, or trips to fictive rural homes, create narratives of non-Western misery to please charitable "rescuers."[10] Of the twenty women that I studied in this sector oriented toward Western backpackers, thirteen had received benevolent remittances from clients, ranging from U.S.$1,000 to $50,000. These women helped their clients feel like heroes, or superior Western men. Coming from strong nations, the men perceived themselves as engaging in charity projects that helped poor, desperate women in a developing country. In doing so, narratives of nation were mobilized to consolidate men's status as providers; while these men may not have been able to provide for a wife in the United States, in Vietnam they could not only support a partner but also save a village. This imaginary, therefore, turns not only on class but also on nation. In other words, establishing this relationship with local women allowed them to perform a class- and nation-based masculinity.

These men were not looking to contest global racial hierarchies. Rather, in line with much of the current literature on Western men, they hoped to maintain and exaggerate the status quo of normative gender roles by seeking sexual adventurism with exotic women who provided cheap intimate labor associated with a semiperipheral status in the world system.[11] These men tapped into a transnational market and capitalized on the cost-of-living differentials between developed and developing nations—or a world order where the West dominates global financescapes—to assert their masculinity. As such, clients and sex workers both engaged in a variety of practices and discourses that, as Hue, a nineteen-year-old sex worker, noted, allowed Western "men to be men" and to reaffirm Western superiority.

"THE GUYS WORKING HERE . . . COULDN'T MAKE IT IN NEW YORK": WESTERN EXPATRIATES ESCAPING THEIR FAILED MASCULINITIES IN GLOBAL CITIES

Expatriate men in Secrets constructed a nation- and class-based masculinity in relation to male clients who occupied the budget traveler's niche by describing themselves as men with more money who understood that HCMC was no longer Third World. These men's performances of masculinity were sandwiched between their local success and global failures. Calvin, an Irish man in his midforties, described this bar in relation to others, stating, "The backpackers' area is much more seedy. You cannot just go into a bar, sit down, and have a drink without the women insisting that you take them home. Anyone can walk into a bar and get a girl there. You see old white men there or stingy men who still want a Third World experience in Vietnam. This is a girly bar, sure, but the women here make you work harder. [*Long pause*] It's like the guys in here have to compete with each other for the girls' attention."

All twenty of the men I interviewed in this niche market had been to the backpackers' area at least once, and they often spoke of those establishments as the "poor man's" bars. Western businessmen avoided bars like Naughty Girls and instead went to Secrets, where hostesses helped men feel as if they had "won" the workers' attention. The expatriate men who frequented Secrets constructed a class-positioned masculinity in relation to men who occupied the budget traveler's niche, by describing themselves as having more money to build relationships with workers in high-end establishments. Further, they emphasized their understanding of shifts in the global economy by differentiating HCMC from the "Third World." For example, Michael, a thirty-eight-year-old IT consultant, stated that bars like Naughty Girls were "for men who wanted to see a poor Third World Vietnam that was static and undynamic. . . . But this is a dynamic country that is growing fast. The streets change just as fast as the people do, and those guys [backpackers] can't keep up."

Because world politics are increasingly organized around the needs of transnational capital and the creation of global markets, the superior masculinity in the current world order is associated with transnational business activity.[12] Research on global sex work often assumes that transnational businessmen are able to occupy superior positions in all local economies, overlooking the ways in which Western expatriates adapt and employ local cultural tools to construct their masculinity with varying degrees of success. In several in-depth interviews I had with Western expatriates, they revealed feelings of inadequacy in relation to peers who worked in global cities. In a conversation with six expatriates, Daniel, a client in his midthirties, turned to me and said, "None of the guys here will ever say this, but we all sort of know it. . . . The guys who are working here in Vietnam are men who for the most part couldn't make it in New York, Hong Kong, or Shanghai. We're all here hoping that we will get lucky, and that this market will grow as fast as everyone is predicting." Bernard interrupted and said, "It is easier to go from being a banker in New York to any place in Asia, but it's hard to go from Asia back to London or New York. The stock market here is tiny, and the fund that I manage is less than 1 percent of my company's total investments. Sometimes I get really depressed because I think to myself: if I can't even make it here, then I will never make it in a mature market."

Conversations with men like Daniel and Bernard revealed the relational construction of masculinity predicated on comparisons among multiple global financescapes, where transnational businessmen compare themselves unfavorably to younger, more successful businessmen back at home. Over half the men I interviewed had lost their jobs as a result of the 2008 financial crisis, and they expressed pessimism about their job and marriage prospects in developed nations. Jesse, a thirty-five-year-old investment banker from New York, stated,

> I was working on Wall Street making oodles of money. I bought a nice apartment in lower Manhattan with my wife, and we were trying to have a baby. Then I lost my job and she was supporting us for a while. . . . I couldn't handle it. I felt like less of a man. . . . After being unemployed for three months I started to pick fights with her and I said things that I just can't take

back. . . . A headhunter asked me to come to Vietnam to help develop the stock market here. I took the job, and my wife filed for divorce. I lost everything: my marriage, my job, and my house.

For Jesse, coming to Vietnam was an attempt to reinvent his compromised masculinity by capitalizing on his First World status in Vietnam's newly developing economy. This move was possible only because he had highly sought-after skills needed to help Vietnam establish itself as a player in the global economy. This move, however, was preceded by an unsuccessful search for a job on Wall Street. Keenan, a twenty-nine-year-old junior associate at an investment firm, described his situation to me:

> I lost my job in 2008 along with about thirty-five hundred other employees at Goldman [Sachs]. We all watched as the world of investment banking crumbled. I'll be honest: I was a first-year associate, which is near the bottom of the chain, so of course I was let go. . . . I couldn't find a job in New York for almost six months, and I was just burning through savings, so I went to Hong Kong and Singapore for a few months. I was literally broke when I met a guy who invited me to Vietnam. My MBA and the Goldman name landed me a great job at [a local investment firm]. We're working on some of the biggest joint ventures . . . [in] technology and media in the country by raising money through the international bond market. It's exciting.

For men like Keenan, moving to Vietnam was their only option to capitalize on their First World degrees, job histories, and skills that were no longer valuable in a constrained American market but which were highly sought after in Vietnam's newly developing economy. Todd, a thirty-two-year-old former investment banker who had worked at Lehman Brothers, said, "Most of the people that I work with were brought on right after the bank's collapse . . . to raise funds, with the goal of listing the company on the Vietnamese stock exchange." Dalton, a thirty-eight-year-old banker, added, "The market is not going to bounce back anytime soon. You have to move to Asia. You have to move to emerging markets, where the money is."

The move to Vietnam required these businessmen to swallow their pride, not only because of their lack of prospects in other markets, but also because of the challenges they faced adjusting to their new jobs. Most of the men I interviewed had to accept inferior positions in Vietnamese companies that were headed by Vietnamese CEOs and managing directors. They also had to quickly acclimate to local styles of communication that were often indirect. As a result, some men spent their off time in bars, joking and flirting with local hostess-workers, who would let them practice their Vietnamese language skills and new cultural styles of communication, in addition to giving them the chance to establish their authority as men.

Sex workers played a crucial role in helping expatriate men reinvent themselves in Vietnam. In this particular bar, women capitalized on the fact that expatriates lived and worked in Vietnam and were invested in long-term relationships. They rarely engaged in direct sex-for-money exchanges. Instead, women participated in drawn-out exchanges that made clients feel special or chosen in relation to other men in the bar. Nguyet, a twenty-one-year-old worker, explained, "Lilly [the bar owner] teaches us to be patient. The men here want to go into a bar and feel like all the girls want them. To make them feel like that, you have to play with them. You sleep with different men without telling anyone. When they ask if we have slept with their friends, . . . we lie."

While clients were well aware that women were not always honest about their sexual histories, many men described the bar as a space where they could engage in staged play. Alex, a thirty-two-year-old expatriate from England, said to me, "Here in this bar, it's like a game. You've got young attractive girls behind the bar and men vying for their attention. Everyone has a role they play. The women pretend like all of us are interesting and attractive, and we pretend like it's real. . . . It's like a show. After a while you become familiar with the script. It's the same script every night." This script allowed clients to construct a class-based masculinity in relation to men who occupied the backpackers' niche market, because it allowed them to demonstrate their ability to win women over in a context where men cannot win workers over so easily through direct sex-for-money transactions.

Like the men in Naughty Girls, the clients in Secrets also asserted their superiority over local women through racialized remarks about Vietnamese women's bodies. On one occasion, Nathan, a twenty-nine-year-old advertising executive, entered the bar dressed in a yellow T-shirt depicting an Asian woman in a rice paddy pulling her shirt up and her bra down to reveal her breast while coyly covering her nipple. In a three-hour conversation over a drink in the bar, he very bluntly said to me, "Let's call a spade a spade. We come in here because we want to look at beautiful women [who] are slender. The women back at home don't take care of themselves anymore, and they are just fat. I'm sorry, but none of the women back at home could even dream of competing with the women here. . . . And I like their small eyes and long black hair. I just find them very sexually attractive."

IMPORTANT QUOTE!

Western expatriates' desires for dark, slim Vietnamese women were distinctly tied to racialized notions of sexual desirability across transnational borders. White men constructed themselves as superior to local Vietnamese women by highlighting their desire for slim and exotic women. In short, whereas the backpackers thought about their masculinity in terms of their ability to be *providers,* the expatriates thought about their masculinity in terms of their *access to women,* which mobilized women in subtly different ways. As one client said to me, "Vietnam is great for men like me because, back at home, you're an 8 [on a scale of 1 to 10], I'm a 3—and here, I'm an 8 and you're a 2. Beautiful women fall at my feet all the time." Secrets provided Western businessmen with the space to recuperate a class-based masculinity in Vietnam that they had lost in relation to Western men and women at home, largely as a result of the financial crisis. Instead of contesting hierarchies of race, nation, and class in the global imaginary, these men were sandwiched between success in Vietnam and failure at home, and they used the space of sex work to situate themselves as superior Western men despite their loss in status.

"WHITE GUYS ORDER BEER, VIET KIEUS ORDER BOTTLES": VIET KIEUS CONTESTING WESTERN SUPERIORITY

Lavender provided overseas Vietnamese men with the space to distinguish themselves as better than Westerners through their public displays of alcohol consumption in bars that excluded Westerners. Viet Kieus often understood their consumption in bars as negotiating their superiority in relation to white men while simultaneously accepting their position of inferiority in relation to local Vietnamese elites. As Hiep, a thirty-five-year-old Viet Kieu from Texas, put it, "White guys order beer, Viet Kieus order bottles [of whiskey, cognac, or vodka], and well, Vietnamese—they order Blue [Label Johnnie Walker]!"

importance of alcohol

During the early period of my research between 2006 and 2007, transnational Viet Kieu clients in my study came to Vietnam with foreign capital from developed nations. Before 2006, Viet Kieu remittances had totaled more than foreign direct investments, and the West had yet to experience the 2008 economic crisis. These conditions allowed low-to-middle-income men from developed nations to convert their Western dollars into social status and respectability in Vietnam's developing economy.[13] However, by 2009, many Viet Kieus had experienced a loss of status in the local economy. Their U.S. dollars no longer had the same worth, because prices in HCMC soared and worldwide luxury brands like Gucci and Louis Vuitton were introduced into the Vietnamese market. As one client put it, "The Viet Kieu years are over in Vietnam. . . . Local [men] have all the money now." Expatriate Viet Kieu men who decided to pack up their lives and move to Vietnam to try to "ride the wave" of Vietnam's economic growth sometimes jokingly insisted, "I'm not Viet Kieu. I'm Viet Cong [local Vietnamese]" to disassociate themselves from the image of Viet Kieus as less cosmopolitan than affluent locals.[14]

Owing to Vietnam's booming economy and the crisis in the West, Viet Kieu men were no longer able to construct a local sense of superiority because of the visibly greater wealth of newly moneyed Vietnamese. Although many Viet Kieus experienced a decline in economic status in relation to rich local Vietnamese whose wealth derived from privileged access to FDI, they still figured prominently in the national economy through their remittances. Remittance money remained attractive across several niches because of the desire for hard currency. Moreover, Viet Kieus capitalized on Vietnam's rising position in the global economy to enhance their status and sense of self. In bars like Lavender, Viet Kieu men displayed a class-based transnational masculinity by consuming alcohol and sex in spaces that were often explicitly unavailable to white men.

This practice came into view when I spoke with Trung, the owner of a bar that refused service to Western men on busy nights. Trung explained, "It sounds backwards, doesn't it, that we don't let white men into the clubs. In the U.S., people would say we are discriminating. But in Vietnam, it is more about the business and how I can make money. White men are cheap. They order one or two beers and they stand and talk to each other for a long time, [taking] up space. I could make more money with Viet Kieus, who will order a bottle." Right outside the bar, a velvet rope kept guests standing in line, waiting for bouncers and security guards to escort them into the bar. Most of the Viet Kieus and young wealthy locals knew they would be automatically granted VIP access and easily skipped the lines to be seated at tables inside. Western men and other guests who had not preordered table service had to wait behind the rope.

On a few occasions, Western men were admitted entry as guests of the Viet Kieu clients. However, the sex workers rarely approached them or asked to sit next to them. While the women served food to and poured drinks for these clients just as they did for all the others, they made it clear that they preferred the Viet Kieu men over "white men" (*may ong tay*). Diem, a nineteen-year-old sex worker, explained, "This business is really complicated. Serving means that you have to be lower than a man. White guys do not know how to tip. You can sit there with them for two or three hours and walk away from the table with empty hands [*tay khong*]. Viet Kieu men tip more if you make them feel more special than white men."

That Western men were unfamiliar with the tipping rituals in spaces that catered to Viet Kieus was a reflection of the Westerners' perceived influence in relation to women. Many commented that they did not need to tip in Western bars and were not going to participate in tipping rituals elsewhere. However, their decision not to tip provided Viet Kieu men with an opening to assert their superiority, because it made them appear, to local sex workers, to have more disposable cash. Through their comments on the desirability of Viet Kieus relative to the Western friends of the latter, sex workers helped Viet Kieu men articulate a sense of Asian ascendancy. Thus, while both Viet Kieu men and white men were responding to perceptions of Western decline, they used their local affiliations and consumptive habits to assert superiority in different ways.

In the bars, Viet Kieu men engaged in a particular display of diasporic transnational masculinity by consuming alcohol and sex in ways unavailable to them in their home countries. Son, a twenty-eight-year-old Viet Kieu from New Jersey, said to me, "I don't go out much back at home, because it's expensive and it's not fun trying to awkwardly hit on girls in a bar. At Lavender, I walk in, order table service, and without having to say anything, there are girls ready to come sit at my table. In New York, [it] would cost thousands of dollars for a table without women."

After years of living in the United States, men like Son came to accept the discrimination that often excluded them from elite spaces in the West. While Son implicitly described his perception of Western superiority in the West, he also saw Vietnam as a place where he could contest that superiority by consuming in spaces that explicitly excluded Westerners. In that same conversation, Hao, a thirty-year-old Viet Kieu from New Jersey, elaborated, "No one lets a group of Asian guys into the clubs in New York. Just to get in, we'd have to bring ten really hot girls along with us." Son added, "In Asia its, like, flipped, you know? Everyone thinks white guys are cheap-asses."

In Vietnam's growing market economy, sex workers in local hostess bars played a critical role, through their embodied performances of femininity, in helping Viet Kieu men contest global racial hierarchies across national boundaries. Women strategically altered their bodies to look thinner, more feminine, and more desirable than Western and Viet

Kieu women; they also staged performances that appealed to their clients' nostalgia for a traditional Vietnamese femininity. Clients came to this bar precisely for women they felt were physically more desirable than Western women. Minh, a forty-one-year-old Viet Kieu from Germany, said to me, "Vietnamese girls are so much better looking than the white and Viet Kieu women back at home. The women back at home are fat and manly. They have big hips and squared bodies. Vietnamese women like the ones [in this bar] have nicer bodies, dress better, and they embrace their femininity. I feel sorry for Viet Kieu women like you, because local women [*biet chieu chuong*] know how to accommodate and please men here."

While working behind the bar, I watched women create an illusion of male dominance by feigning interest in the men's lives abroad, even though many believed that the men exaggerated their status in their stories. I asked several of the women I worked with how they felt about acting subservient to Viet Kieus. Duong, a twenty-two-year-old woman, stated, "I get paid to treat Viet Kieu men like men. If the guys in here [male service workers] had the money, I would treat them the same way too. I will be as submissive as a man wants if he pays for it. Viet Kieu men are spoiled here because there are so many beautiful women. If you want to compete here, you have to give them what they want." Whether women enjoyed acting submissive or not, all twenty-five women I interviewed in this sector told me that they *chieu chuong* (accommodated) men because they provided workers with access to U.S. dollars and a more urban/cosmopolitan standard of living. Huong stated, "[We] Vietnamese women . . . act like women so that they can act like men. If more Viet Kieu women knew how to do that, maybe their husbands would not come to Vietnam [for] it." Thus, while the West still cast its shadow in Vietnam, the HCMC hostess bars provided spaces in which men could play out their aspiration to shift racialized, classed, and nationally inflected hierarchies in relation to white men from Western nations with stagnating economies.

"THIS IS HOW THE VIET CONG PLAY!"—WEALTHY VIETNAMESE MEN CONTESTING WESTERN SUPERIORITY

The privileged access of local Vietnamese elite businessmen to Khong Sao Bar signaled their superior status in the social geography in relation to Viet Kieus and Westerners. They used that superior status to cement relations with Asian businessmen that would lead to lucrative capital deals and bring FDI into the country. In the bars, wealthy men enacted their masculinity through male bonding rituals, drawing on and reworking intersecting relations of class and race. To this end, groups of men always ordered Johnnie Walker Blue Label, a bottle of whisky worth U.S.$250, and they typically consumed four to eight bottles a night without ever asking to see the menu or inquiring about the prices. The choice of Johnnie Walker Blue Label, understood throughout Asia as an expensive, elite brand, conveyed their direct access to tremendous economic resources and their ability to consume Western luxury goods during a time of Western austerity.

Following the customs of Vietnamese and other East and Southeast Asian countries, sex workers in Khong Sao Bar learned to signal the implicit hierarchies among their male clients and assume subordinate positions in relation to all men at the table.[15] For example, only the mommies were allowed to sit next to the oldest or wealthiest men at the table (usually ones who consistently paid the bill). Implicit rules related to drinking also signified deference. First, when sitting at the table, a woman had to invite the men to take a drink before taking a sip from her own cup. It was considered rude to drink from one's glass without first toasting one's client and the other men at the table. Second, when refilling a clients' drink, workers had to hand men their glasses with two hands, one placed to the side of the glass and the other placed underneath. Third and most important, when clinking her glass against a man's glass, the worker had to cheer according to the man's status relative to other men at the table. It was always a rule that she had to clink her glass below the client's glass. For clients who were particularly respected in the bar, a sex worker would clink her glass toward the bottom of the man's glass, if not completely underneath it so that the bottom of the client's glass sat literally on the rim of the woman's glass. Although the women were often unaware of the men's positions outside the bar, clients would subtly inform women of the hierarchy between them through their use of honorifics and through the positions they used when clinking the others' glasses. Men in lower positions of power would clink their glasses below the glasses of their superiors, so it was the sex workers' job to figure out the hierarchy at the table by paying attention to how men clinked their glasses. These gestures were critical to helping foreign investors understand who had the most money or political connections. Vietnamese clients rewarded hostess-workers for acting out these subtle gestures that not only buttressed their sense of superiority in relation to their business partners but also helped to establish interpersonal hierarchies among the men in the bar.

When entertaining their Asian partners, local Vietnamese men often used cultural shaming techniques familiar among Asian businessmen to assert Vietnam's place in the global economy. For example, one night after Chu Xanh had spent about two hours drinking and entertaining eight Taiwanese clients in Khong Sao Bar, the lights went up and he asked Quan, the service worker, for the bill. He told Quan, "I paid the bill three nights now. Give the bill to one of the Taiwanese men but do not take their money. I just want to see the shock on their faces." Quan bowed and handed the bill to one of the Taiwanese men. The guest opened the bill and shuffled nervously in his seat because he did not have enough cash to cover the bill and the bar did not accept credit cards. After exchanging a few words in Mandarin, the Taiwanese clients asked to split the bill. Chu Xanh turned to me and said in Vietnamese, "Tell the men that the Vietnamese do not split bills." I translated what he said. In this space, women knew that it was their role to stay silent unless spoken to and orient their faces downward while looking upward to subtly embarrass the foreign men. By providing a female audience for shaming foreign businessmen, hostesses were critical to the Vietnamese men's displays of a classed-based masculinity.

Indeed, as the Taiwanese guests fidgeted at my comment and the women's subtle facial expressions, Chu Xanh turned to me and said, "*Viet Cong troi vay do con gai* [This is how the Viet Cong play]! Translate that." I translated while he picked up the bill, pulled out a wad of cash, and settled the tab. Then, in front of all the men, he produced a second stack of bills and handed each woman a VND 500,000 banknote (thirty U.S. dollars), for a total of U.S.$1,100 in tips. The women bowed and thanked him before leaving the room. After the men left, Chu Xanh turned to me and said, "I have to show them that we are serious and that we have money. I entertain them [because,] in Vietnam, you cannot do anything without relationships. I embarrassed them on purpose because I want them to know that Vietnam is not poor."

The backdrop for this scene was the global and local political economy. Vietnam's dynamism in an Asian-centered economy depended heavily on South-to-South (in this case Taiwan-to-Vietnam) investment relations. These dramatic performances in the bars alluded to men's economic performance in the new global economy. Further, just as the clients of Khong Sao displayed their wealth to their present Asian business partners through cash tips, they also used the tipping ritual to demonstrate Asian ascendancy in comparison the absent, inferior figures of Western and Viet Kieu men. At the end of the night, when the women lined up to receive their tips, it was not uncommon for the man handing out the bills to comment, "Have you ever seen white or Viet Kieu men tip like that?" Vietnamese men wanted local sex workers to understand both that foreigners were passé and that locals were the clients with the money.[16] Hostess-workers bowed their heads and thanked the men as they each took their bills. In front of the clients, Hanh, the head mommy, would always tell the women, "You see, Vietnamese men know how to take care of their women. They know how to tip. If you work in a bar with stingy [keo] white men, you would be lucky if they gave you a hundred thousand dong [six U.S. dollars]."

By consuming with cash, local Vietnamese men implicitly mocked Westerners who relied on the credit system. One night while I sat at a table with Chu Xanh and his Korean partners, he turned and said to me,

> What other place in the world plays like this? We take these men around in Bentleys worth half a million U.S. dollars paid in cash, and take them to high-end bars. Even in America, white men do not spend this much money on entertainment. It would be like driving a house in Little Saigon [Orange County, California] around on the streets of Saigon. And they don't even own their homes! The Viet Kieu years in Vietnam are over. Now it's the Viet Cong time. Asia is where all the money is now. . . . Vietnamese have a lot of money!

The 2008 global economic crisis in the United States and Europe provoked a major cultural shift in these men's imaginaries in relation to the West. All the men that I studied directly linked success in the capitalist economy to their own masculinity. They bragged that they owned their cars and homes outright, and that they paid a 100 percent luxury tax on their cars. Paying *more* for alcohol and consumer goods through luxury taxes became a means through which local men asserted a classed masculinity that trumped previous national and racial hierarchies.[17] Through conspicuous consumption with hard cash and at levels unavailable to foreign men, Vietnamese men contested dominant Western masculinities.

Sex workers also carefully worked to buttress their clients' class-based masculinity by talking openly about the many gifts they received from specific men.[18] For example, one night, a Malaysian businessman in his midforties, Aqil, pointed to hostess Yen-Nhi's iPhone (a cellular phone that cost U.S.$700 in the local market) and asked her where she purchased it. She responded in English: "My Anh Hai [eldest brother/ Vietnamese client] give to me. Vietnamese [men are] rich, they buy me a lot of present. All my sister have phone [pointing to the other women at the table]. All gift from Vietnamese customer." Aqil looked over at

Xin, his Vietnamese business partner and said, "These girls [are] rich, yeah?" Xin winked at Yen-Nhi and said to the client, "Girls get bored. They play [with] this toy and want a new one all the time." Xin's comment insinuated that Vietnam's economy was doing so well that even sex workers had constant access to new commodities.

 With the help of women workers, Vietnamese men used cash and conspicuous consumption to cement their relationships with business partners and to establish their superiority in relation to Western men. This work was possible in the gendered space of the bar because masculinity is not always performed in relation to femininity.[19] Rather, men also achieve their masculinity in relation to other men, in this case, through displays of wealth. Hostess bars provided their clients with the space necessary to engage in male rituals that constructed them as Vietnamese men of a certain class who were succeeding in the midst of rapid economic restructuring and a turbulent global economy.

Though hostesses typically played a supporting role to buttress men's performances of superiority in relation to other men, women occasionally became the uncomfortable object of a man's attempt to perform masculinity. Because Khong Sao was one of the most expensive bars in HCMC, not all who entered could engage in conspicuous consumption. Middle managers who came to the bar without the large sums of cash that their bosses threw around relied on relations with women to perform their masculinity. Rather than through economic transactions, these individuals asserted their masculinities in relation to sex workers by trying to kiss them, grab their breasts, or otherwise touch them inappropriately. For example, one night while Vietnamese clients were showcasing their Vertu cellular phones (worth U.S.$10,000 to $20,000), Tin, a twenty-six-year-old local Vietnamese man without anything to show off, grabbed a sex worker's breasts and, in front of everyone, proclaimed that he had two rocks of gold (*hai cuc vang*). In another instance, Dao, a thirty-two-year-old local Vietnamese man who had trouble drinking large quantities of alcohol, grabbed a woman under her skirt and pinched her until she squealed, thus diverting attention away from his drinking habits and onto the worker's body.

Four middle managers I interviewed over a late-night snack spoke openly about how they did not enjoy work after hours because they had to endure public ridicule. Hung, a thirty-six-year-old man, explained, "If you don't have money and you can't drink, everyone will call you weak [*yeu ot*] or gay [*be de*]. When bosses push me down, I grab onto women to get back up. That's their job." Backstage, workers often warned each other to be careful around men who did not have as much disposable cash, because those men were much more prone to be aggressive with women's bodies. The women were not impressed by such displays. They developed strategies to dismiss these men from the bar. They would, for example, drink at a faster rate to get the men so intoxicated that they either passed out or went home. Nonetheless, these clients' actions served as an affront to the class-marked masculinity deemed appropriate in this context. When they reached for women's bodies, they attempted to compensate for their otherwise emasculated status in relation to the other men.

By asserting their superiority through cash, shame, and embodied practices, local elite men capitalized on Vietnam's rising economy to assert a new place in the global order. Writing about capitalism in a postideological world, Slavoj Žižek suggests that "when individuals use money, they know very well there is nothing magical about it—that money, in its materiality, is simply an expression of social relations."[20] In Khong Sao Bar, however, men's use of money was not simply an expression of social relations in their current state. It was an expression of what they imagined and aspired social relations to be and a tool by which they enacted those social relations. That is, while conspicuous consumption—especially paid for in cash—allowed very wealthy local Vietnamese men to display their superior status by showing that they could consume at levels unavailable to foreign men, the wealthiest Americans were still significantly wealthier than the wealthiest Vietnamese.[21]

Despite this reality, HCMC hostess bars like Khong Sao gave local Vietnamese men a space to assert, and possibly even realize, Vietnam's potential as a new international force. The global imaginary shared by men and buttressed by women filtered very real political and economic processes of rise and decline through aspirations, fears, and desires about men's masculine identities. Local elite men's masculinity and their desire for Asian ascendancy were inextricably linked, making these bars central to the (re)production of masculinities in a dynamic global context. Thus, as Matthew Gutmann argues, by framing culture not simply as a space of distinctions but as a space of difference and struggle, where the masses of men who are underdogs are inspired by a will to form a certain identity, one can see how the rich local Vietnamese men as global underdogs actively worked to contest the meanings of superior masculinities.[22]

The dynamic global political and economic context has created new elites and new status inequalities in Vietnam. These shifts were reflected in the world of investment banking and finance and in the gendered relations and cultural practices of sex work. Across the four bars, powerful Vietnamese local elites, Viet Kieus from the diaspora, Western business executives, and marginal Western tourists were uneasily poised between globalized cultures. All men drew on intersecting relations of race, class, gender, sexuality, and nation to construct their masculinities in relation to other men and to women, but their particular strategies reflected their positions in the contemporary geopolitical moment. Thus, whereas Western budget travelers and expat businessmen worked to *reaffirm* Western superiority, Viet Kieus and local elite Vietnamese businessmen mobilized new hierarchies to *contest* Western power through styles of consumption that expressed Asian ascendancy. Importantly, men relied heavily on the bodies and labor of women to help them achieve their desired masculinity. This was especially the case when they perceived that their performances of masculinity in relation to other men, through classed and racialized relations, had failed. In the two highest tiers of sex work, Viet Kieu and wealthy local Vietnamese men contested existing hierarchies of race and nation by engaging in acts of conspicuous consumption that displayed a financial dominance tied to conceptions of Asian ascendancy.[23] With the help of local sex workers, Viet Kieu men articulated a transnational masculinity by converting their Western dollars into luxury, social status, and dignity. For local Vietnamese elites, conspicuous consumption demonstrated distinction to potential investors from Taiwan, Hong Kong, and other East Asian countries.

In contrast, Western budget travelers and Western businessmen worked to affirm the status quo by affirming their superiority as white men. Western budget travelers enacted a classed and racialized masculinity in relation to women through benevolent forms of patriarchy. However, both groups of men also experienced status anxieties linked to the financial crisis and their sense of Western decline, and they negotiated these anxieties through sex workers' bodies and labor. Thus, despite previous research that highlights the superiority of transnational Western businessmen, transnational businessmen compared themselves unfavorably, in the context of HCMC's sex industry, to more successful investment bankers in global cities and used the space of sex work to reinvent themselves locally rather than asserting their universal, global superiority. Together, these four niche markets of HCMC's sex industry show that as the source of foreign capital being directed into Vietnam shifted from the West to Asia, men on the ground constructed new symbolic positions.

Importantly, although the global context is such that wealth is still concentrated in the United States, local elites seized upon this shift in global relations to show that they no longer depended on the West. The increase in Asian FDI provided these men with the opportunity to disentangle themselves from Western-based capital and the historical legacy of colonialism and Western intervention that came with it. In this new political-economic landscape, men's participation in HCMC's sex industry involved much more than the purchase of sex. Men purchased status, dignity, and protection for their precarious positions in the global order.

4

Entrepreneurial Mommies

Several years ago, my family learned that we might be next
in line. We never knew for sure, but based on my great-
grandfather's influence and my grandfather's connections,
people predicted that one of the men in my family would
come to power. So ten years ago, we started to put things in
place so that we would be ready when the day came. . . . We
knew that we would need a safe place to entertain our guests,
so we started looking around for girls we could trust and
train. . . . Without the mommies, money would not move as
fast. Understand?

—Nam, a forty-nine-year-old local Vietnamese businessman

In response to my question "Could local Vietnamese businessmen
secure business deals without karaoke bars?" Nam, like many other
clients in the high-end niche market, told me that hostess bars were
responsible for much of the country's recent economic growth. The
mommies provided local elite Vietnamese businessmen with crucial
space in which clients could build trust to secure business deals with
Asian investors. Although local Vietnamese men entertained foreign clients in fancy restaurants, in lounges of luxury hotels, and on golf
courses, these were not spaces of intimate bonding. The trust-building
necessary to securing inter-Asian foreign direct investments occurred
primarily in high-end hostess bars.

In these bars, local Vietnamese men relied heavily on the mommies
to train their workers and facilitate male bonding rituals.[1] Likewise, in
Lavender, Secrets, and Naughty Girls, the clients relied on the mommies
to help facilitate relationships of intimacy between clients and hostess-
workers. Mommies are crucial brokers who connect capital flows into
Vietnam—through FDI and overseas remittances—to gendered rela-

tions in sexual commerce. Their involvement in commercial sex work shapes their own personal trajectories of economic and social mobility. A close look at seven women who were either mommies or bar owners in the places where I worked (three from Khong Sao, two from Lavender, one from Secrets, and one from Naughty Girls) reveals how the mommies trained workers to establish and facilitate different kinds relationships with their clients, relationships tied to different forms of foreign capital.

In high-end bars like Khong Sao, local Vietnamese and other Asian businessmen engaged in _business-oriented intimacy_ that was crucial to facilitating business deals that brought foreign direct investments into the country. Mommies played important roles for clients like Nam by providing men with the space in which to engage in male rituals and make specific allusions to their ability to perform in the global economy. In this way, mommies helped men establish the trust required to attract FDI into the country. Mommies who catered to Viet Kieu men in bars like Lavender, on the other hand, were responsible for providing clients with the space to engage in _fantasy-oriented intimacy_ that allowed men to feel desired by women across transnational borders. Fantasy-oriented intimacy occurred around the indirect movement of a portion of the overseas remittances brought into the country. Workers in Secrets and Naughty Girls, who catered to Western businessmen and Western tourists, helped clients engage in _philanthropy-oriented intimacy_ built around developing intimate relations with clients critical to attracting overseas money framed as charity projects through benevolent remittances. Thus, while Khong Sao Bar was important for helping to attract FDI into the country, the three bars that catered to overseas Viet Kieus, Western businessmen, and Western tourists were tied to different logics attached to remittances.[2]

If the mommies in these four bars differed in the kind of capital they attracted and in their main job duties, they also had different trajectories into sex work. All but two of the mommies started off as village girls and grew into shrewd entrepreneurs with multiple investments and properties. Their relationships with male clients and their involvement in the sex industry transformed their lives over the years, allowing them to capitalize on their social ties to wealthy local Vietnamese men, Viet Kieu men, and Western men, in different ways, in order to diversify their income-generating strategies. Mommies served as role models for the sex workers because they were living embodiments of economic and social upward mobility. Young women with few other resources tried to emulate these women's ability to create and facilitate social networks.

ENTICING FDI IN KHONG SAO BAR VIA BUSINESS-ORIENTED INTIMACY

At the age of twenty-nine, Hanh, the top mommy of Khong Sao Bar, was highly sought after by HCMC's most affluent men. Everyone referred to her as one of the most well-networked women in the world of high-end commercial sex. She had established strong ties with some of the country's richest businessmen and most powerful political officials. She carried herself with poise and had clearly invested a considerable amount of money in plastic surgery, clothing, and accessories to maintain her image. One afternoon, while rummaging through her clothes for hand-me-down dresses to give to me, she told me how she had entered the sex industry. As she looked at herself in the mirror, she said,

> Looking at me [now], you would never know that I was a poor village girl. I started working in a karaoke bar in my village when I was sixteen. A group of men came in for drinks. I knew they were from Saigon but not much else about them. They liked my voice, and they kept coming back to the bar to hear me sing. Then Chu Thach asked me if I would be willing to move to Saigon to work in a bar that his friend owned. I was scared, so I kept refusing.

She told me that Chu Thach had been stubborn, and that he had kept coming to the bar for six months so that she would trust him. He also understood the fears that many mothers have about their children getting kidnapped, abused, or forced to have sex against their will. So he had told her that she could bring her mother with her to the city and try it out, and if it did not work he would put her and her mother on a bus back to her village. She went on:

> I was really shy, and it was hard because I did not know anything. He kept saying that he has been looking for someone like me, and that he knows that I will one day run a bar that serves the richest, most powerful men. Looking back, I was also very lucky. When I moved to the city, I did not know anything, but for some reason I got called to every single table. . . . I was making a lot of money and I did not know how or why. Everyone says that I am lucky because I was born in the year of the golden pig.

Like Hanh, many of the sex workers I studied spoke in great detail about how "lucky" they were because they were able to thrive in this business. However, Hanh's social mobility also depended a great deal on the social networks that men like Nam and Chu Thach mobilized on her behalf as she transitioned from the village to the city, as well as on the connections she later established as a result of her work inside the bars. For example, she said,

> I met a lot of different men who treated me well and tipped me well. I even fell in love with some of them and had my heart broken. But I always say that I have been lucky. Sometimes at night, I would lie there thinking, Is this really happening to me? When I turned eighteen, Chu Thach told me that he was opening a new bar and he wanted me to be the mommy there. I didn't know this at the time, but he was watching me and training me to run a bar that catered to very powerful men. I started small with local officials and businessmen that Chu Thach worked with on business projects, and then it grew and grew.

For almost four years, Hanh had no idea that Chu Thach worked for a man named Nam whose family had strong political and economic ties and was preparing to move into a position of political power. Their connections were key to many of the joint business ventures that would take place between Vietnam and foreign investors from other nations. Chu Thach set up Khong Sao Bar so that Nam would have a safe place to entertain clients where no workers would recognize his family's prominence. Now, about ten years after Chu Thach recruited Hanh from her village, she is comfortable associating with men whose names are on buildings, high-level party officials, and overseas Asians. She reflected, "I know who they are, and some of them rely on me to help connect them. I owe a lot to Chu Thach, because they worked with me for ten years now, making me into the mommy I am now. They taught me how to save my money and invest it so that I would have something to fall back on when I am too old for this business." For Hanh, even though she is embedded in a patriarchal social structure where men direct capital and the women provide entertainment, becoming a mommy enabled her to establish local, translocal, and global connections with people in positions of economic and political power critical to her long-term financial success.

Hanh had been groomed for her role as mommy for about ten years, and she had relied on positive working relationships with men to gain her training for the sex industry. Much like discovering a model or a recording artist in the world of legal entertainment, Chu Thach had recognized Hanh's potential and, without telling her what he and his partners hoped she would become, had thrown her into the mix in a karaoke bar to see if she could survive. Her trajectory was not only a matter of "luck" but also a result of these men's active role in promoting her and trusting her, which had enabled her to achieve fame among a coveted network of high-powered elites.

While all her clients brought business contacts into the bar, few were as well connected as Nam. Therefore, many of the clients came into the bar hoping to tap into Hanh's network of clients established by these well-connected men. By serving as a conduit who sometimes introduced men to key economic and political elites, Hanh positioned herself so that some of her clients relied on her as much as she relied on them. Hanh's job was not only to provide men with a space for entertainment but also to help men establish business relations with one another. She operated in a liminal space, connecting relationships established in the informal economy to those in the formal economy. Compared with the other niche markets in HCMC, in Khong Sao Bar the relationships between well-known clients and the mommies seemed to involve more reciprocity, as well as exchanges of equal status.

As the right-hand man of Nam, the wealthy local businessman I quoted at the beginning of this chapter, Chu Thach was charged with developing a safe space for business deals to prepare for the day when Nam's family would move into a position of political power that would provide them with direct access to land and certain business ventures controlled by the state. Chu Thach began the preparations to secure the space for Khong Sao Bar and to recruit and groom a mommy to run it. I asked Chu Thach directly why Nam needed a space of sex work to conduct his business deals, and after nearly a year of talking in circles around this question, Chu Thach finally opened up and told me his side of the story:

> This is a sensitive [*nhạy cảm*] topic. The Women's Union and many people want to get rid of the [commercial] sex industry in Vietnam, because they do not want Vietnam to become like Thailand. . . . But without the sex industry, we cannot build business relationships. We need them to help us bring business to Vietnam. . . . This is the way we have been doing business since the 1980s. Asian men expect this service. We cannot get around it. When I met Hanh, I knew that she was the one. I spent a long time looking for [someone like] her. I never told her that we were training her to work with powerful men, because I was not sure that she could handle all the money that would come to her. A lot of women get into gambling, drugs, or [get] addicted to money because they are lonely. . . . And I did not know if the family was really going to move into that position. Nothing is ever for sure. Sometimes you have to rely on fate to bring the right people together at the right time. . . . We knew that we were going to need a place to entertain, because we would have access to a lot more projects, land, and investors [both local and foreign]. We needed someone born in the year of the golden pig. It was Hanh.

The Chinese-Vietnamese belief that individuals born in the year of the golden pig will experience prosperity may have influenced Chu Thach's choice of Hanh, but luck was not the only source of Hanh's success. Chu Thach also played an active role in helping her establish the necessary connections to run a successful business. He did not do this for altruistic reasons; theirs was a mutually beneficial relationship. Chu Thach depended on Hanh's skills to run a stable business that would provide him with the space to entertain his guests. Hanh knew how to manage her clients, the sex workers in the bar, and the flows of money that kept the bar open. Chu Thach clearly viewed these skills as an important part of the country's recent economic growth. High-end hostess bars did not emerge as a response to global economic restructuring; rather, with the help of mommies like Hanh, men like Chu Thach strategically established high-end karaoke bars to facilitate the movement of FDI linked to land development projects into the country.

Neither Chu Thach nor Hanh could have predicted that their businesses would grow so rapidly, or that Vietnam would become an attractive destination for foreign direct investment from Asia. A combination of luck and strategic planning eventually shaped their involvement in the sex industry and the development of the nation's economy. This is because in Vietnam's rapidly developing economy, it is often difficult to trace direct capital flows. Anh Minh, a sixty-year old Vietnamese businessman, explained the lack of transparency in this emerging Asian market:[3] "There are many layers to the way we do business in Vietnam. We never assume that the guy we are dealing with has the cash. He may just be the person representing the project; but there could be three other investors behind him whom we don't know about. That is why everything is about trust and connections. When you look at a new commercial property, there are people involved in those projects whose names are not on the paperwork, because they don't want people to know that they were a key investor."

Anh Minh was one of many men in the high-end niche market who described the complicated relationships that businessmen had to establish in order to take the lead on major development projects. Hanh, he explained "is the main person connected to all these men," but even she might not understand all the pieces of the puzzle or the different men involved in the business dealings. Her job was to provide the necessary entertainment so that men could establish deep relationships of trust. As in China, these relationships were sustained by emotional bonding and affect-based—rather than instrumental, cognitive-based—trust that characterizes business networks in the United States, Europe, and Japan.[4] Through this trust-building, Hanh became a key figure who facilitated the flow of foreign investment capital in and around HCMC.

The reciprocal social debt built between Hanh and men like Anh Minh and Chu Thach was critical to their working relationship. Chu Thach told me, "You might not understand this as an American girl, but in Vietnam everything is give and take. She does favors for me and I return the favor." She relied on him to bring business into the bar, and he relied on her to help him establish informal working relationships with his potential investors or local Vietnamese entrepreneurs. Some male clients felt the social debt they owed the mommies was substantial and helped maintain the moral codes that governed men's interactions with sex workers in the bars. In a long conversation I had with Anh Phat, a fifty-year-old businessman, he explained to me why it was important to tip the workers well and treat them with care and respect:

> On the outside, it looks like play and fun, but nothing is ever what it seems. Without these bars, we could not gain trust; without trust, we cannot secure deals. There are many men in the middle because it is hard to get direct access to people with power. You have to make connections with a lot of different people in order to get to the top. . . . Nobody wants to think about prostituting [their] own women to develop the country, but what choice do we have? We tip them well because we want them to know their value. They are making deep sacrifices for their families and for us. They help us build relationships with [the middle men].

While most scholars of gender and sex work write about the sex industry as a consequence of economic restructuring or neoliberal marketization, conversations like these reveal how relations in the formal economy actually depend on the informal, and in this case illegal, service economy. In other words, the informal economy helps drive growth in the formal economy. Without these women, it would have been difficult for men to attract the investments that were critical to Vietnam's development.

Hanh's Personal Trajectory of Upward Mobility

Hanh's ability to provide men with the space to attract foreign investments into the country through the informal economy of high-end commercial sex shaped much of her personal, social, and economic upward mobility. Her story is compelling because she defied the common perception that sex workers only think about acquiring fast cash in the short term and do not have long-term career plans. Hanh made a career in the sex industry by building a network of powerful men who visited her bar, which is similar to the ways that men and women network in other, legal occupations. Her ability to manage a strong network of political elites and businessmen in an informal economy was critical to her own personal success. Although her clients could never acknowledge her in the spaces of the formal economy, they provided her with a great deal of money and business advice in exchange for introductions within her network of men.

Both Hanh and Chu Thach told me that, over the years, she slowly learned how to save and invest her money. Chu Thach said, "It is hard to last a long time in this business. I did not want her to fall hard, so I taught her how to save and invest so that she could have something else to work on when the family stepped down from power." Hanh capitalized on the social networks she had established in the bars to maintain her new standard of living. She followed clients' advice on how to save and where to invest her money, and she now had two homes in newly built complexes in HCMC. She owned a condo in a high-rise located in District 4, a short distance from work, along with a second house in District 2. The latter was farther out—about an hour's commute to work—but she bought it because of a sentimental attachment to owning land. She also owned two vacation homes, in Dalat (a mountainous region) and Da Nang (a beach town), as well as three restaurants. Her estimated net worth at the time was close to U.S.$1 million. She also took home a monthly average of U.S.$20,000 to $30,000 in profits from the bars and restaurants. The sex workers looked up to Hanh because of the money and other assets she held, and when three of them eventually left sex work because they were either too old or had decided to get married and settle down, they became full-time managers in Hanh's restaurants. In this way, Chu Thach helped Hanh carve a pathway out of sex work and into more legitimate businesses that were then passed down to her own staff, creating a structure of mobility that lasted much longer than the short-term career in sex work.

Failed Mommies and the Choice to Leave

Hanh's story was characterized by extreme economic and social upward mobility. She served as an ideal type of someone who "made it" in the sex industry. However, there were many others who came before her who were not as successful. Although I was unable to speak with "failed mommies," because they did not frequent the bars where I conducted my field research, I asked both Hanh and Chu Thach about women they knew who did not make it. One night while eating noodles at 4 A.M. after a late night of entertaining a group of foreign businessmen, Chu Thach said to me,

> I have been going to these bars for over twenty years now. I have seen a lot of girls come and go. Few make it. . . . Only one out of every ten women I know saved enough money to start a small business. Most of them were not as savvy [*kheo noi*] with words as Hanh. They did not know how to manage the customers or take control inside the bar. Women who are smart with their words can control any man. [Hanh] earned their respect. . . . [*Laughing*] She has even slapped a few men, and they kept coming back. The other girls were not as smart. They never saved any money, so they went back to their villages, married a local boy, and settled down. I still see some of them when I visit the villages. . . . Some have kids who are old enough to be bar girls now.

Chu Thach acknowledged that in the twenty years he had spent in bars, he saw few women who were as lucky as Hanh. However, it was not merely about luck. From his perspective, Hanh's success had a lot to do with her ability to maintain her relationships and carefully manage her networks with powerful men. She provided men with the space to engage in *business relations* that were deeply embedded in the world of commercial sex. In a conversation with me, Hanh told me why she thought many workers never rose to become mommies: "This is a business, and some girls forget that. On the outside, when girls come in here, you think it is fun because you drink and play with the men. Play is our business, but it is a business. You cannot fall in love with anyone, and you have to be smart about how you manage your relationships. My relationships are everything." Hanh provided her clients with a space to enjoy themselves and entertain their business partners. In this way, she was a critical player in formalizing sex work as a business with its own institutional roles and expectations. Hanh had to stay single because, if she fell for one client, she would burn her bridges with all the other men in their network. She was in the business of building and maintaining relationships, and the only way she could do so successfully was to remain single.

One afternoon while business was slow, I sat in the back room of Khong Sao and talked with Xinh and Hong—the two junior mommies—about how long they planned to stay in this business. Xinh was thirty-four years old and Hong was twenty-eight; both women had been hostess-workers with Hanh in her village and were now too old to work full time as hostess-workers. Therefore, Hanh had recruited them to help her manage and train hostess-workers and to serve as key brokers for her clients. However, neither Xinh nor Hong had as many regular clients as Hanh or the level of respect that Hanh had earned from her clients. Xinh said, "Ten years ago, I wanted to be a mommy. I am one now. . . . Not as big as Hanh . . . , but I have been a mommy for four years. I have a house, and a restaurant where people go eat after the bars close. I come here at night after the bars close. I have a way out of [the bar] business when I want to leave. Right now, the money is good, so there is no reason to leave."

I asked, "Why would you want a way out if you can make so much money here?" Hong interrupted and explained, "Very few people will understand this, but if you want to be a top mommy like Hanh, you have to make a lot of sacrifices."

Kimberly: Like what?

Hong: You have to accept a single life. Hanh can never fall in love or marry anyone. If she chooses one man, she betrays all the others, and that is a dangerous choice. Hanh is very careful [*kheo*] with her words. She knows a lot of her clients' secrets; and if they ever feel threatened by her, they can destroy her. If you want to make a lot of money like her and have a lot of businesses, you have to be willing to play with fire and hearts [*troi voi lua va tim*]. . . . Hanh tells both of us that if we are not strong enough to live [independent lives], then we should plan a way out. . . . Hanh has all the material things a person could want, but without the girls in this bar she would be lonely. She can have sex with men, but she cannot climb into bed with the same person every night for the rest of her life. She will never have someone to worry about her or take care of her.

In her conversations with the junior mommies, Hanh consistently reminded them to carefully plot their way out of the bars if they had dreams of having a family and living a life with a romantic partner. Aside from keeping company with the women who worked for her in the bars, Hanh led quite a lonely and solitary existence because she could not confide in any one man about her own personal feelings of love and loss. As a result, she constructed the realm of family and intimacy with her sex workers, since she could not do so with the clients. Hanh did not pressure her junior mommies to stay in the bar business, because the moral codes that guided her business practices revolved around providing her workers with the freedom to choose to work. The *business* side of her work involved carrying many of the clients' secrets and helping men secure business deals. When those deals failed, workers also provided men with the space to deal with their feelings of anxiety and failure, emotions that clients hid from their wives and families to maintain their image as successful economic providers. Hanh embodied the importance of gendered relations to economic development. Vietnam's economic growth brokered through informal deal-making involved the tremendous labor and sacrifices of women like Hanh.

Clients and sex workers in the highest-paying niche market of HCMC's sex industry were all involved in business-oriented intimacy. That is, the bar provided men with the space to build rapport with potential investors and maintain those ties with the help of women like Hanh. I will never know the full extent of Hanh's social network, mainly because keeping her relationships a secret was important to her ability to keep her business up and running. Hanh played her cards close to the chest and rarely revealed the true identities of her clients, even to the workers in her bar. As I discussed in chapter 3, high-end clients wanted to maintain a degree of anonymity because many were public figures who worried that public exposure of their business practices could result in corruption charges. These men relied on Hanh to procure women from rural villages who could sing karaoke, dance, drink, and help men bond but would not be aware of men's business relationships or political ties. This way of conducting business was very different from the approach of the mommies who catered to Viet Kieu men or that of the bar owners who catered to Western businessmen and tourists.

ATTRACTING VIET KIEU REMITTANCES IN LAVENDER VIA FANTASY-ORIENTED INTIMACY

Among the mommies I interviewed, only two came from relatively wealthy urban backgrounds, and they ran bars that catered to Viet Kieu men. In 2006, the women who worked in this niche market either were highly educated, with bachelor's or trade school degrees, or came from families with successful businesses.[5] At that time, none of the bars that catered to Viet Kieu men employed a group of women to work exclusively at their bar. Bar owners relied on women who moonlighted to attract customers. However, by 2009, the organization and structure in these bars had altered. Bars like Lavender began to employ promotion girls, or "PG girls," to work as hostesses. By 2009, many of those women who used to moonlight in the bars had quit working in the bars altogether because they were pushed out by PG girls willing to work for much less money, or they had become mommies to manage the new crop of workers. Once they became mommies, these women worked closely with male bar owners, who depended on women to establish order among the sex workers and to manage the competition with other bars.[6] Anh Nguyen, the owner of Lavender, told me,

> Running a bar in Vietnam is very complicated. A lot of people are involved, because there is so much money. Last Saturday, we made thirty thousand U.S. dollars, so you can imagine how complicated it is. Other people, maybe the mafia, used to send girls in here to start fights or plant drugs in the bar so that we would get caught and have to shut down for weeks. I needed to find a way to manage the girls in my bar, because we need pretty girls to get men in here but we do not want trouble. . . . I hired Tho and Huyen to manage the girls.

While Hanh was specifically groomed by powerful men in high-end bars, Tho (thirty-five years old) and Huyen (twenty-nine years old) were freelancers who groomed themselves by adapting the skills they developed in the formal advertising world to the informal sex trade. Both women grew up in HCMC and had college degrees. They had worked together at a day job for an advertising agency, where they managed a group of promotion girls who advertised an alcohol brand for a foreign distributor. During that time, they also moonlighted as independent sex workers in bars that catered mainly to Viet Kieu men. Tho and Huyen ended up in this particular niche market because the alcohol company they worked for sent promotion girls out to a number of different bars and restaurants to introduce and advertise the product to new customers on site. Before becoming full-time mommies, Huyen and Tho worked together during the day training a group of women at the advertising agency in how to manage their image, advertise the product, and implement strategies to increase sales. At night, they made their rounds among the various bars to build informal relationships with several bar owners so the bars would promote their alcohol as a personal favor.

At the time, Tho and Huyen made, respectively, roughly U.S.$1,300 and U.S.$900 a month through their day jobs. In addition, they each generated an income through informal sex work. However, as they spent more time working two jobs, their bodies started to break down from stress. Huyen said, "I was greedy. If I could make money, I worked. I worked all the time. I felt like I was working morning to night and night to morning. I would come home when the sun was coming out, shower, and go back to work." Huyen fainted one day as a result of severe dehydration, lack of sleep, overconsumption of alcohol, and improper nutrition. She told me that going out at night was crucial, however, because it allowed her to expand her network by establishing ties with various bar owners in town and because she was able to double her income through nighttime sex work.

In 2008, Anh Nguyen's bar was shut down after local authorities found drugs inside. While the bar was closed, Huyen spent weeks joking with Anh Nguyen about running his bar for him. She talked extensively about "branding the bar" so that clients could expect a particular kind of service from the women who worked there. Anh Nguyen took her offer seriously, and they agreed to an arrangement in which he would assume all the liability as the main owner of the bar, while she would earn 5 percent of all alcohol sales as a silent partner. He agreed to allow her to bring in a friend, and he gave her three months to get the business back up and running. Huyen decided to quit her job and work full time building up Anh Nguyen's bar. She brought Tho, her former coworker, onto the project with her a few weeks later. Huyen took 3 percent of all alcohol sales and Tho took 2 percent. Tho and Huyen agreed to work seven nights a week to manage the flow of women who entered the bar. Two weeks before the bar's grand reopening, Tho and Huyen recruited promotion girls they had managed at the alcohol company. Huyen also recruited a number of her bar friends. They designed sexy uniforms for the workers modeled after the uniforms that promotion girls for the alcohol distributor wore. Within the first ten days, word spread that Lavender Bar had beautiful hostesses, and the bar reached full capacity. Tho and Huyen introduced their customers to the women they managed, and they encouraged their customers to tip generously. The women earned tips from customers at no cost to the bar. The mommies also earned tips from the clients that were often double the amount the workers received. Huyen said to me,

> We started about seven months ago, and business has been up and down. I remember the first month, we were taking home about 2 million [one hundred U.S. dollars] a night in tips alone. I watched the alcohol sales and recorded everything at the end of each night. In the first month, Tho and I each made six thousand U.S. dollars. The owner likes this because he does not have to come in to work all the time—because we are here. I was so excited, I went and bought this [*pointing to a colorful Louis Vuitton handbag*]. We went out with the girls and partied after work. It was fun.

Tho and Huyen told me that after the first month, they made roughly U.S.$4,000 per month between alcohol sales and tips from the Viet

Kieu clients. At the end of 2010, their sales dropped to roughly U.S.$3,000 per month. In an unstable economy, Lavender depends on certain types of clients—namely, Viet Kieu men who come to Vietnam looking for a particular brand of alcohol that they can purchase and label as high-class consumption. To maintain a steady income, mommies such as Tho and Huyen had to build networks among men linked to overseas remittance money.

Conspicuous Consumption Based on Fantasies of Celebrity

While thinking about the Viet Kieus' impact on the local economy in the realm of commercial sex, I asked Huyen about her role in branding and promoting the kind of bar with promotion girls who double as hostess-workers. She responded, "When I worked for the [alcohol] company, we were taught to promote a brand. We were selling a brand and a type of woman who represented the brand. Now we take that concept and apply it to the bar. We have a certain kind of girl who represents the bar. When Viet Kieu men come to the bar, they want to be around pretty girls who will stand at their tables, serve them, and drink with them. We're selling a brand."

While the concept of a "promotion girl" inside these bars was taken directly from a new model of advertising introduced into the local market by advertising agencies, the mommies created a brand and a service that specifically catered to the tastes of Viet Kieu men. I pressed Huyen to more fully explain the "brand" that she created for the bar:

> *Huyen:* Viet Kieu men come here to receive VIP treatment. They want to have the prettiest girls from Saigon wrapped around their tables, and they want five-star service. They want to be kings. We make them feel like kings.
>
> *Kimberly:* What do you get in exchange?
>
> *Huyen:* [*laughs*] You are so naive [*kho*] . . . U.S. dollars!
>
> *Kimberly:* I still do not understand.
>
> *Huyen:* It is a fantasy [*ao tuong*]. The lights, music, alcohol, VIP service.

The "product" created by Huyen and Tho was fantasy, the type that Katherine Frank describes as rooted in and circumscribed by everyday life through past experiences, beliefs, prohibitions, and social interaction.[7] In the countries where Viet Kieu men reside, luxury is often a distant dream for them. By incorporating the advertising concepts they learned in their day jobs, Huyen and Tho created a space in the bars that enabled Viet Kieu men to act out their fantasies of high-class luxury. To create a celebrity experience for their clients, the bar hired professional photographers to post photos of clients and hostesses on Lavender's website. Over the course of the night, the bar would spotlight various tables with flashing lights, which made the clients feel like stars at the center of attention in the bar. The purpose of having PG girls in the bar was to create the experience of VIP service that—as Huyen put it—made men "feel like kings. . . . Like local stars."

When I asked Anh Nguyen what he thought of having PG girls in the bar, he said to me, "The bar scene in Vietnam is changing now. A lot of places have PG girls to draw men into the bar. It is a win-win situation. Sex workers make their money from tips from the clients, and [from] sex if they feel like it, so I don't have to pay them. They use my bar to meet [Viet Kieus], who are willing to spend more money on vacation; and I use them to get men into the bar."

Anh Nguyen did not pay the workers to entertain his clients. Instead, he depended on the clients to tip the workers in the bar. PG girls typically received between U.S.$12 and $20 per table in tips for drinking with the men. Clients almost always left proper tips, because they worried that workers would publicly humiliate them if they tried to leave without tipping. Shame was a powerful tool that sex workers employed to get money from their clients. For example, Duy, a twenty-six-year-old Viet Kieu, said to me,

> Everyone in Saigon knows that you cannot really trust these girls. They all lie to you, and you lie to them. It is a fantasy—they play their part, and we play our part. It's like [pause], like [pause], an escape, you know? I know that they have multiple boyfriends, and that they make up stories about their lives. But it is a game, those are the rules, and that is how you have to play. . . . They come and flirt with you, make you feel good; you pay them a tip and you leave.

I asked him how he learned the "rules" of this game, and he said, "By watching other people, or making mistakes." He described one of his mistakes:

> The first time I came to Vietnam, I was very naive. I remember going into a bar, and all these pretty girls came to drink with me. I was like, "Oh shit! This is cool, yo!" We took them out to eat late-night food, and then one girl came home with me and another one with my boy. We did our thing, you know. . . . And then in the morning, she started crying, telling me how poor her family is and shit. I did not know what to do. The same thing happened to my friend, and so he gave the girl money. But I did not want to give her

money. So then she asked me to take her down and get her a cab, and when the cab came, she started screaming and crying on the street in front of all these people. I was embarrassed, so I slipped her a hundred dollars. . . . So now I know, if I take a girl home from the club, I need to give her "taxi money" when she is on her way out. That way I don't have to make her ask and she does not have to embarrass me in public.

The male clients with whom I spoke often learned the "rules of the game" or the "appropriate behaviors" through the mistakes that they made with workers, who sometimes corrected them in subtle ways or, as in the case Duy described, through highly public displays. The slippages where clients made mistakes or failed to meet sex workers' expectations actually helped create boundaries and reinforce norms around appropriate and inappropriate behaviors in clients' interactions with sex workers. These norms also allowed workers and clients to maintain the fantasy that PG girls went home with Viet Kieus because of mutual attraction, and that Viet Kieus were big spenders who could easily drop a hundred dollars on a "taxi fare."

Remittance Relationships Based on Fantasies of Return

While several scholars have documented remittances sent from overseas Vietnamese to family members living in Vietnam, they have overlooked the flow of capital from clients to sex workers as another remittance source.[8] Tam, a fifty-four-year-old man from Texas, described how the blurring of fantasy and reality in Viet Kieu bars facilitated the movement of overseas remittances into the country:

It feels strange telling you this, because back at home [in the United States], you are young enough to be my daughter, but in Vietnam, I call you *em* [honorific for younger woman/girlfriend] and you call me *anh* [honorific for older man/boyfriend]. . . . I came to Vietnam and I met this girl, Lien. She made me feel respected and important. She was very submissive, because she spoiled me and did everything I asked her to do. [*Long pause*] . . . I took out a line of equity on my house in the U.S. without telling anyone, and I sent it to her to buy a house in Saigon.

With advice from the mommies in the bar, Lien convinced Tam to take out U.S.$150,000 and give it to her to buy a three-bedroom home in District 4 of HCMC. Tho and Huyen were able to procure similar funds from male clients and taught their promotion girls to do the same. When I asked Tam whether he ever stayed in that house, he told me that the house was extremely crowded, which did not allow him to maintain his privacy, so he generally stayed in hotels when he came. Even though he admitted that he worried because the house was in Lien's name and not his, the house came to symbolize a plan to retire in Vietnam with someone who made him feel important, unlike his wife and children in the United States, who were furious upon discovery of the equity loan.

The fantasy of retiring with a young, beautiful mistress or of living the life of a celebrity in Vietnam allowed men like Tam to escape the difficult reality of immigrant life in the United States. Although Tam was an exception among the male clients in this niche market with respect to the amount of money he remitted to Vietnam, many clients I interviewed reported remitting between U.S.$10,000 and $70,000 to women they met bars, so that these men could either retire in Vietnam or test the market with small business ventures.

Huyen and Tho's trajectory of upward mobility was very much tied to their ability to cater to Viet Kieu men who were spending their U.S. dollars in Vietnam's local economy. The two women were able to capitalize on their social networks to expand and diversify their income-generating strategies. Both Huyen and Tho saved their earnings to reinvest in other business ventures. Huyen opened a shop selling clothes purchased from Hong Kong, and Tho combined her resources with those of a family member and opened a seafood restaurant in District 6 that catered mainly to local Vietnamese men and women. Through networks established among bar owners, they received business advice on how to start small before growing big. Moreover, these women did not have to deal with the added costs of rural-to-urban migration: when they were ready to take on new projects, they had the support of relatives who already resided in the city. Their business ventures started in a place where they already had considerable social, economic, and spatial capital. When I asked them what they planned to do in the next five years, both women said they would like to have multiple businesses. Huyen said, "Vietnam is changing so fast. There are so many people who come here, and I think that in ten years Saigon will look like Hong Kong or Singapore. I want to open more businesses and try. It is a risk, but I think I can do something big. I am lucky because my family has a nice house, and they do not need my help; so I do not have to worry about taking care of them. They help and give me ideas about what kinds of things to [invest] in."

Tho and Huyen's involvement in Lavender enabled them to expand their social networks and tap into a sizeable Viet Kieu population, which provided them with a venue in which to explore other entrepreneurial opportunities. They expanded their businesses and sought ways to generate more capital, experiencing economic upward mobility by generating a higher income and taking advantage of investment opportunities. However, their trajectory of economic mobility was steady and cushioned by the financial stability, support, and proximity of their family members. This is because the women brought their skills in branding from work in the formal economy to their endeavors of commercial sex work in the informal economy. The other five mommies and bar owners discussed in this book were also able to maintain their upwardly mobile trajectories; however, their pathways were much more dramatic because they all came from poor rural backgrounds. By using their creative skills to brand Lavender as a bar that provided luxury service, Huyen and Tho were engaged in a business that revolved around fantasy-oriented intimacy. This fantasy indirectly encouraged Viet Kieu men to spend their U.S. dollars in local bars and remit large sums of money with the hope of maintaining their fantasy "celebrity" status in the long term.

SECURING WESTERN REMITTANCES IN SECRETS AND NAUGHTY GIRLS VIA PHILANTHROPY-ORIENTED INTIMACY

While Tho and Huyen capitalized on their relationships with Viet Kieus to tap into the existing flows of overseas remittance money and expand their business ventures, Lilly, the owner of Secrets, and Tina, the owner of Naughty Girls, tapped into networks of Western men who viewed Vietnamese women as the deserving beneficiaries of Western largesse. As a result, not only did the source of remittances differ, but also the clients marked and framed this money differently, based on their relations with local sex workers.

Philanthropy through Long-Term Investments: Lilly

Lilly was twenty-four years old when I first met her. At the time, she owned four bars and had a net income of roughly U.S.$20,000 per month. One day while we visited the construction site of a bar she planned to open, Lilly described her pathway toward extreme upward mobility: "You do not know, Kim. I used to be so, so poor. I remember when I was a kid, saving potatoes to put in our soup because we could not afford to buy rice. I remember that my stomach used to hurt so much because we did not have enough food, and I used to cry, dreaming of a bowl of soup with some meat. I wanted to take care of my parents, so when I was thirteen years old I went to Saigon to work as a maid."

Lilly worked as a maid for two years, but because she did not earn enough to support her parents, she began sneaking out of the house at night to find work in a bar as her mother had when she was young. Lilly worked in what she called a "hooker bar" in the backpackers' area, because a girl in her neighborhood told her that was where all the white men went. After a few months, she fell in love with an older man, who gave her enough money to move out of the home where she worked as a maid and to live on her own. However, after a few months, he left her, and Lilly experienced heartbreak for the first time. She returned to sex work in a different bar. She reflected,

> I was sixteen and shy, but for some reason, the men really liked me, so I made a lot of money as a working girl [sex worker]. So many men asked me to marry them, but I kept saying no because I was afraid that over time, they would get bored. Then one day, this man named Mark came in. He told me that he was married and would not leave his wife, but that he was doing business in Vietnam and he wanted to have a local girlfriend. He was very sweet. He stuck money in my purse all the time, and he was okay with me working. He paid to put a toilet and shower in my parents' house out in the village. Then, when he found out how cheap it was, he paid to renovate the whole house. A year later, he bought a house in Saigon under my name and paid to move my parents into it. He lived upstairs on the top floor, and my family lived on the other floors.

Lilly's relationship with Mark began as a simple sex-for-money exchange, but over time it grew into a relationship. However, after having learned through her first relationship to protect herself romantically and financially, Lilly strategically chose to establish long-term relationships with multiple men. These relationships allowed her to ask for large sums of money that she used to renovate her family's village home and eventually buy a new house in the city, among other things. In addition, she sought security for herself and her family by leveraging gifts to begin new business ventures, borrowing U.S.$16,000 from Mark to open a bar that catered specifically to the growing number of Western expats she saw as regulars in other bars. She explained, "I wanted men to have a bar they could go to that was not all about sex. It is a relationship bar with [long-term] girlfriends. I made the money back in three months. When I tried to pay Mark back, he told me to take that money and do something else with it. It was all happening so fast. Six months after opening my first bar, I opened a second one around the corner from here." Between December 2010 and August 2012, Lilly launched two more bars and a new restaurant selling Western food. Across these five businesses, she had over sixty employees. Unlike Hanh, who relied on a local network of men to help build her career and investments, Lilly relied on the help of white Westerners like Mark, whom she provided with relationship-based intimacy in exchange for loans.

Lilly approached these relationships not as a naive romantic but as an entrepreneur seeking capital. For example, she dated a man named Trent, whom she caught cheating. Even though she herself was not being monogamous at the time, she ended the relationship and presented Trent with a bill for U.S.$40,000 for all the dates she had gone on with him, all the dresses she had bought during their relationship, and all the time she had spent with him. When Trent refused to pay, Lilly called on a few of her friends with police and mafia connections and threatened to kill him, to scare him into paying. Over the course of three months, Trent paid Lilly U.S.$20,000, which she used as a down payment on the restaurant she opened in 2010.

After launching her first successful bar, other Western men approached Lilly and asked if they could partner with her to open other bars. These men framed this kind of investment as a form of charity work that was a better alternative to NGO-backed microfinance projects. Kelly, a fifty-six-year-old man from Texas, explained,

> If you look around this country, you can see that people here have a very entrepreneurial spirit. They know what it means to work hard and build a business. There are markets at every level from street hackers to small bars. I have been watching Lilly for two years now, [and] she is a smart woman. She teaches her girls how to make their money grow, . . . by teaching them to think about the bigger picture. . . . All the bars in this area are partnerships between local sex workers and their Western boyfriends. People in the West—they don't understand. I would rather give money to these girls, who know how to hustle, than to NGOs who squander it on stupid microfinance loans that don't support business growth.

Kelly framed his remittances to Vietnam as a charity project supporting small businesses. He and other Western clients/investors believed that their money had a direct impact on the local economy by providing enterprising women with jobs and long-term opportunities beyond commercial sex work.

Like Hanh, Lilly invested in multiple businesses. As she explained to me, "People in Vietnam lived through a war, so they know how to hustle. If one business idea does not work, then you have to be ready to try something new, because nothing is for sure." Lilly's ability to take on multiple projects, design a Western-style restaurant based on Internet photos, and train a staff allowed her to take advantage of business opportunities outside of sex work. On several occasions, she spoke reflexively about her own mobility, and she was always generous with street children who sold flowers, gum, and lottery tickets. One night, while we sat on the street eating Vietnamese-style escargot, Lilly said, "Some nights I climb on my rooftop and lie on a hammock looking up at the sky, thinking about how lucky I am to have this life. I think of the girl who used to eat potatoes instead of rice, and I tell myself that I will never go to bed hungry."

Lilly did not have the good fortune of Hanh, who had a wealthy local businessman seek her out and train her; instead, she relied on her networks of Western businessmen to support her entrepreneurial endeavors. Lilly was an anomaly, since few women in sex work were able to achieve her success. While she referred to her success as a streak of luck, it is clear that her family history and her social networks helped shape her trajectory of extreme upward mobility. Lilly's mother had been a prostitute servicing American GIs during the Vietnam War, leading Lilly to seek work in a niche market that catered to Western men. However, in the contemporary economy, the forms of capital in this niche market that Lilly had access to were different from those she would have had during the era of U.S. intervention.

When the Vietnam War ended, Lilly's mother resigned herself to marrying a man from Cambodia because the Vietnamese men in her hometown all saw her as "used" or "damaged" goods left over from the war. In contrast, Lilly was able to use spaces she established as "relationship bars" to capitalize on men's desire for philanthropy-oriented intimacy. These men did not come to Vietnam to wage war like American GIs, to do business like Asian businessmen who partnered with Vietnamese elites, or to fantasize about an opulent return to Vietnam like Viet Kieus; instead, Western transnational businessmen needed a familiar place that made Vietnam feel more like a home away from home, and they needed sex workers who made them feel like savvy philanthropists investing in Vietnam's development. In this niche market, mommies like Lilly and some of the hostesses who worked for her capitalized on long-term relationships to facilitate "charitable" remittances that enabled a lucky few women to establish businesses and build large, modern homes in their villages.

Philanthropy through Short-Term Gifts: Tina

Tina, the twenty-two-year-old owner and mommy of Naughty Girls, migrated to the city when she was fourteen and worked in a variety of service sector jobs as a maid, manicurist, hairdresser, and factory worker. As in the case of Lilly, Tina's economic mobility was tied to her ability to establish remittance relationships with her clients. However, her bar differed from Lilly's in that the women who catered to Western tourists traveling on a budget engaged in more direct sex-for-money exchanges that involved short-term relationships. Tina taught the hostesses at Naughty Girls how to facilitate the flow of similar kinds of overseas remittances by performing poverty that pulled on men's heartstrings. In doing so, she helped the men in Naughty Girls frame their financial gifts as a particular form of charitable giving.

When I asked Tina how she moved from menial labor to owning a bar at such a young age, she laughed and said to me, "Fate. I quit my job at the shoe factory where I was working twelve hours a day for eighty U.S. dollars a month. I could not find work, so I got desperate and went to a fortune teller. The woman told me that I would be rich and have a lot of money in the next year. She told me to try sex work because a [client] would change my life."

At the time, Tina had friends who were working in a bar that catered to Western men; so following her visit to the fortune teller, she asked her friends to introduce her to the bar owner. The woman who owned the bar explained to Tina that she would not pay her, and that Tina's earnings would come only from her sexual encounters with the clients. In exchange for allowing Tina to use the bar as a space to procure clients, Tina would have to follow some rules: she would come to work on time, ask for days off, and try to get men to buy drinks in the bar. Tina was not allowed to have sex with a client for less than VND 1 million (fifty U.S. dollars), because doing so would ruin the price for everyone else. She also had to pay the bar owner VND 200,000 (ten U.S. dollars) for every client she left the bar with, and the same amount if she wanted a day off. Tina explained how sex work provided her with the only viable pathway to becoming an independent entrepreneur:

> I only had to sleep with two men to make what would take me a month to make [at the shoe factory]. I met this man from Switzerland who told me he was a photographer. . . . He asked if he could take some photos of me. He paid me two hundred [U.S.] dollars for a whole day of taking photos [with my clothes on]. Then we had sex and he paid me another two hundred U.S.

dollars. He left and I did not hear from him for seven months. When he returned . . . , he told me that he wanted to help me get out of the bar life. I wanted to open my own bar, and he [asked] me to show him a business plan. I wrote it out on paper with a pen like a child. He asked me to find the place. I did, and then he paid for things every step of the way, because he was afraid that I would run away with ten thousand [U.S.] dollars.

Tina opened a bar in the backpackers' area, and in five months she broke even. After paying rent and the utility bills, she made about U.S.$3,000 per month between profits from alcohol sales and the kickbacks that her workers paid her following sex with a client. While Tina had not set out on other entrepreneurial ventures like Lilly or Hanh, she was able to capitalize on the short-term relationships in her bar to get multiple men to provide her with small charitable gifts every now and then.

These onetime charitable donations allowed her to renovate her parents' village home and make it the largest in the area, purchase a small flat in HCMC, and renovate her bar. To ask men for money, she told me (in English): "I tell them I love to work. I love my job. My job help people, many people. This bar, see, . . . I have many people work here. If you give money to other people they no work. They no make money back. I make money, help my family, help other people."

Indeed, the men I spoke with who were close to Tina framed their investments as charitable work. Like Lilly's investors, they often framed their donations as investments that generated a financial return for the sex workers and an emotional return for them because it made them feel like they had a direct impact on the local economy. Phillip, a thirty-five-year-old backpacker from Georgia, explained to me, "I know that once Tina takes the money out of my hands, I will never see it again, but when I look at everything she has done with the money, I can take a step back and say that I played a small part in giving to those who are less fortunate." In a later conversation, Phillip elaborated on this "giving":

> Back at home, you always see those signs at the grocery store asking you to donate a dollar to a poor village somewhere in Africa. It sounds like a good thing, . . . but I'm not a fan of that. The problem is that you don't feel a personal connection to that dollar. I also don't like to give people free handouts. I'm a Republican who believes in rewarding hard work. Here in Vietnam, everyone has a hustle. Five-year-old kids [in Vietnam] are on the streets selling candy, gum, flowers, books. . . . You can feel the entrepreneurial spirit here: . . . everyone wants to own their own business because that is how they know how to survive.

Men like Phillip who gave Tina gifts to improve her business felt a direct connection to their donation. These gifts were not merely personal; they allowed men to feel that they were serving a greater good. As Phillip explained, "This is not just about Tina and her own success; it is about the success of a small business [and] a whole village, . . . [because] she is providing jobs for all these girls, the maids who clean, and the men who help with construction." And indeed, their remittances influenced Vietnam's development and the transformation of the urban and rural landscapes as Tina used the money to improve her business and her family's standard of living.

Most of the men in this niche market critiqued what they thought of as conspicuous consumption, or wasteful spending on luxury items; but during the months in which I conducted research in Tina's bar, Phillip willingly helped Tina shop for a car. He said to me, "Tina is a very strong woman. This is a girl who used to work in a factory, who has sold her body, and who clawed her way here. She is a fighter who knows how to run a successful business. She should buy a car. . . . It's her money. She worked hard for it."

After looking at a variety of Hondas and Toyotas, I said to Tina, "I cannot imagine buying a car in Vietnam, because you have to pay 100 percent tax and in cash." Tina said, "My father used to pedal the *cyclo* bikes [three-wheel taxi bikes]; now, I am buying a car. Vietnam is not the same anymore. Before, you saw motorbikes slowly replacing *cyclos*. [Now], the only *cyclos* on the streets are the ones for tourists. There are a lot more cars on the streets. I want a car because, now, only the rich can afford them. [Soon] they [will] start making cars cheaper and everyone will have one. I want to be the first."

Tina's desire to purchase a car was symbolic; the car would be a tangible marker of her extreme upward mobility. Indeed, she went from being a factory worker to a sex worker and then to owning her own bar. By capitalizing on short-term relationships with her clients and pulling on these men's heartstrings, she was able to acquire overseas remittance money framed as philanthropic or direct charitable giving. In less than ten years, her entrepreneurial spirit enabled her to go from owning a bicycle to owing a car that enhanced her physical mobility and symbolized her newfound economic and social status.

In each of the bars, the mommies played different roles in facilitating business-, fantasy-, and philanthropy-oriented intimacy that was linked to different forms of capital brought into the country. These mommies actively worked to create an infrastructure in the underground economy of sex work tied to different kinds of economic capital—FDI and overseas remittances—and different logics of intimacy. The mommies embodied the kind of success in Vietnam's commercial sex industry that most of the sex workers hoped to achieve.

In the high-end niche market that catered to wealthy local Vietnamese and other Asian businessmen, Hanh spent nearly ten years preparing to assume the responsibility of providing wealthy businessmen and powerful elites with a safe space to establish relations of trust that would attract FDI into the nation. Although Hanh's birth in the year of the golden pig allowed her to attribute her success to good fortune, Chu Thach played a deliberate role in shaping her pathway toward upward mobility. In addition, Hanh herself actively cultivated skills that enabled her success in commercial sex work.

Hanh and her two junior mommies played a critical role helping wealthy local Vietnamese businessmen establish relationships of trust through sex tied to business transactions. Chu Thach worked to prepare various women for the mommy role, but Hanh emerged as the most savvy. Hanh's life story illustrates both her own agency in developing this reciprocal relationship and Chu Thach's deliberate, long-term strategy to capitalize on the possibility of his employers' future political power by creating a space for safe networking among businessmen.

Tho and Huyen, on the other hand, used the skills they had learned in the formal economy—as promoters for alcohol distributors—to turn a profit in the informal service economy tied to Viet Kieu remittance money, and they did so by introducing the concept of branding to Lavender. The PG girls in their bar provided overseas Vietnamese men with the opportunity to participate in fantasy sex, in which they could convert their U.S. dollars to social status in Vietnam and act like "kings" in the bars of HCMC. In effect, the workers who catered to overseas Vietnamese men manipulated their clients' fantasies of local celebrity status in order to tap into the flows of overseas remittances brought in by Viet Kieu men.

In the Western bars, men created their own illusions by framing their gifts to sex workers as a form of charity. This process was possible because both Lilly and Tina found ways to carve out their own space in niche markets that catered to Western men. By being bold enough to escape service work and factory work and step into sex work, these women were able to tap into overseas remittances that are tied to both pleasure and philanthropy. These mommies/bar owners served as models for workers looking to escape poor labor conditions and low pay as maids and factory workers and find success in entrepreneurial activities tied to sex work that produced real opportunities for economic and social mobility.

Contrary to common assumptions about the status of sex workers, participating in HCMC's sex industry transformed some of the mommies' lives, allowing them not only to escape poverty but also to launch multiple entrepreneurial projects crucial to their long-term security. These mommies' trajectories of upward mobility by means of their relationships in the sex industry reflect the dynamism of Vietnam's economy as the women capitalized on HCMC's transformation into a global, cosmopolitan city. These women were not victims of global economic restructuring but creative agents with an entrepreneurial spirit who played a vital role in developing their nation by facilitating the flow of major sources of capital—FDI and remittances—thereby transforming much of the country by means of the world of commercial sex work.

Autonomy and Consent in Sex Work

Western men hear about girls who are sold and forced to sell their bodies, but no one here is forced to do anything. I come to the bar to work, . . . and if I want to have sex with a client, I have sex with him. If I don't, then I won't. No one forces me to do anything I don't want to do. [NGO workers] come here trying to give us condoms or save us, [but] how can they help me when I make more money than them?

—Vy, twenty-two-year-old hostess in Naughty Girls

Can you go back to America and tell all your friends that I do NOT want to be rescued? All these Americans and Viet Kieus who come here thinking that they need to save us are so stupid. If you had to choose between working in a factory for twelve hours a day with bosses who don't let you rest and [who] look at you like they are raping you with their eyes, or working in a bar where you have a few drinks and sometimes spread your legs for a man, which would you choose? Why don't people go rescue factory workers? We are the ones who were not scared to leave factory work for sex work. We are smart hustlers [*nguoi chen lan*], not dumb, scared factory workers!

—Trinh, twenty-four-year-old hostess in Lavender

In the U.S. popular media, advocates like Nicholas Kristof and Sheryl WuDunn frequently suggest training in factory work as a form of rescue for women they view as either trafficking victims forced into sex work or coerced, impoverished women without training or options for their labor.[1] However, the women in my study asserted the opposite. These women experienced sex work as an escape from the low pay and harsh working conditions in other sectors of Vietnam's economy. Remarkably, given the negative tone in many previous studies, all fifty-six of the female workers I spoke with in 2006–2009, along with the ninety women I later interviewed in 2009–2010, described their relationships with their mommies and bosses in a positive light. That is because, in these bars, the actual practice of sex work operated according to strict moral codes oriented toward freedom and consent rather than forced labor. Their work in the sex industry allowed women workers to imagine themselves as citizens of a vibrant contemporary political economy in Ho Chi Minh City, rather than as poor, Third World victims.

Several studies suggest that bar owners and the madams who run the bars exploit their workers.[2] However, recent works by Christine Chin, Rhacel Parreñas, and many others analyze the complex social structures that shape the range of choices available to women in their relationships with clients, club owners, and brokers.[3] Rather than treat women as victims of global poverty who are kidnapped and forced, or duped, into the sex industry, sex workers across all four markets offer a different perspective from which to examine the sex industry. Like Vy and Trinh quoted in the chapter epigraphs, many sex workers were frustrated with media images and NGO narratives about trafficked victims, because they saw themselves as fearless women who stepped out of the factories and into sex work, where they had much more autonomy over their labor and their bodies.[4]

The majority of workers from Khong Sao Bar came to sex work directly from their family homes in rural villages, while many of the women from Lavender, Secrets, and Naughty Girls had worked in factories producing textiles or in the service sector industry as maids and housekeepers. All these women were, however, careful to distinguish *sexual commerce*, in which women view sex work as skilled labor and their chosen occupation, from *sex trafficking*, described by governments, NGOs, and activists as forced sexual labor.[5] Key to this distinction is a labor process that depends heavily on workers' consent and the establishment of trust in relation to both the clients and the madams/bar owners who regulate the workers' labor.

While research on sex trafficking speculates on the kinds of problematic relationships that might emerge between brothel owners and pimps who *force* women to have sex with their clients, to my knowledge none of the women in my study were ever forced to have sex with a client.[6] In contrast, the bar owners and mommies worked within a strict moral economy tied to a labor structure that depended on workers' consent.[7] This moral order shaped the mommies' actions, the actions of sex workers, and the meanings that all of them ascribed to the work they did. Specifically, the mommies worried that forcing a woman to have sex with a man was bad karma that would result in the failure of their businesses. Theirs was a business predicated primarily on the ability to secure free or low-cost labor because workers' earnings were generated primarily through client tips or sex work. As a result, the mommies adopted a maternal model of care to motivate the workers to return to work. This model of care involved not only strong relationships among women but also protection from aggressive men, since hostesses relied on the mommies to help them regulate men who touched women's bodies inappropriately, tried to coerce women to leave the bar for sex work when they did not wish to, or failed to pay women for their sex work.

In short, the sexual commerce that took place in all four bars hinged on a strict moral code that inhibited the bar owners and madams from forcing a woman to have sex against her will. To illustrate this process, I draw on Erving Goffman's concepts of "frontstage" and "backstage," which describe the roles *social* actors (that is, individuals in everyday life) play in relation to various audiences. According to Goffman, one's performance on a frontstage is open to judgment, and actors perform there in a way that adheres to conventions that have meaning to the audience. Meanwhile, the backstage is a place where the audience is absent and actors can let their guard down and discuss or refine their performances without revealing these strategies to their audience.[8] The process through which consent shapes the moral order of the workplace comes to light when we look at how madams and workers establish trust on the frontstage in relation to their clients, and on the backstage through what James Scott calls "hidden transcripts."[9]

The mommies and bar owners carefully managed the labor process and worker relationships through their frontstage performances and backstage conversations.[10] On the frontstage, I witnessed several moments when male clients tested the mommies' moral codes about refusing to force sex workers to have sex against their will. Mommies and sex workers often worked collectively to defend themselves against these aggressive men. Backstage, the women in my study developed strong bonds with each other and with the mommies who helped them manage their clients. The moral codes that supported a woman's ability to consent to the labor of sex work enabled workers to develop a sense of autonomy and worker collegiality, rather than the fierce rivalries and competition between workers that others describe.[11] The bonds of collegiality allowed the bars to operate in a peaceful manner, and instances of confrontations or fights between women were rare.

Global discourses of vulnerable sex workers in need of rescue clash with the local possibilities that emerged in the bars as many women escaped factory work and entered into sex work. While women's mobility hinged a great deal on their ability to appeal to their clients' intimate desires, workers ultimately drew boundaries limiting clients' access to their bodies. The moral codes guided worker-client relations and embedded workers' agency in complex webs of emotional care bound within male patriarchy and desire in the everyday interactions among sex workers, mommies, and clients.

"GO SAVE FACTORY WORKERS!"—CONSENSUAL LABOR IN SEX WORK

One afternoon when the bar did not have many customers, three NGO workers walked into Naughty Girls with pamphlets informing the workers of centers where they could get tested for HIV/AIDS and packets of information on local NGOs working to save victims of sex trafficking. All three of the aid workers were local Vietnamese women hired by an international organization to target sex workers and drug users. As the aid workers walked through the bar, the hostesses openly mocked their looks and commented that they wished the NGOs would simply leave them alone. After the outreach workers left, Truc, a twenty-nine-year-old hostess, told me,

> I got arrested three times after the police found me making a deal with a client. The second time, I was sent to this [detention] center for eighteen months, and they made me learn how to sew. I told them that I worked in a factory for two years before working in the bar, and that I already knew how to sew, but they didn't care. The third time, they told me that if I told people I was forced to sell sex, I could leave and go to a rehabilitation center. . . . A Viet Kieu woman from the United States ran that center. That place wasn't any better. There was a strict curfew, and she wouldn't let us leave at night. We couldn't call anyone, and we spent our days taking English lessons or learning how to sew or cook.

For Truc, the training that she was forced to go through in both the detention center and the rehabilitation center was isolating and demoralizing. She could not understand why these places were so focused on teaching the workers skills in the very trades that they were trying to escape. Life in the factories, she told her coworkers, was much worse than life in the bars.

In that same conversation, Mai-Lan, a twenty-eight-year-old hostess, turned to me and asked, "Do those Western and Viet Kieu women who come here thinking that they are going to help us know that we are sleeping with their husbands? We are not the ones they should save." Vy-Van added, "When you go home [to America], tell people that this is a job just like any other job." Truc jumped in, saying, "Tell [the NGO workers] they should go save factory workers who are forced to work long hours for little pay, [are] beat by their bosses, and [who] sometimes have to offer sexual [favors] to get higher pay."

Sex workers made a clear distinction between force and choice and were incredibly articulate about the paternalistic approach of the state's rehabilitation centers and NGOs looking to "rescue" them. Because organizations needed to show their donors that they were indeed "rescuing and reintegrating" trafficked victims, they often ended up working with women who had been free agents and who were arrested on the streets. NGOs required these sex workers to reframe themselves as "trafficked victims" in need of aid, rather than as "criminals" who engaged in illicit sex-for-money exchanges, before they could get out of the detention centers. Though the sex workers did not see themselves as in need of rescue, they often capitulated, adopting NGO narratives to avoid the eighteen-month sentence in a detention center. These arrests, though rare in the bars where I did my research, demonstrate the contemporary frictions within the state, which attempts to appeal to the interests of NGOs and the U.S. Department of State while simultaneously turning a blind eye to critical spaces of entertainment for Western tourists.

In conversations with me, workers in Secrets and Naughty Girls provided articulate critiques based in their personal experience of factory work, domestic work, and other forms of service work, which they saw as far more exploitative than sex work. The women in my study almost always contested my questions about forced sexual labor. Vy-Van explained,

> I have had many jobs in my life. I have done everything. When I was thirteen, my aunt introduced me to a family in Saigon who needed a maid. I worked for them for three years. I was their slave. I worked fourteen hours a day, seven days a week, [and] I made only 1 million dong [fifty U.S. dollars] a month. I woke up every day at 4:30 A.M. to cook three meals a day, do all the laundry, run errands for the kids, and give the wife massages. They kept all my money and sent it straight to the village, because they said that

I would not know how to manage my money. They told me that Saigon was very dangerous, and if I left the house alone someone would kidnap me and sell my virginity. It didn't matter, because when I turned sixteen the husband raped me and took my virginity anyway. He told me that he was preparing me for life as a wife and was teaching me how to please my future husband. I hated him but I was afraid to say anything, because I was embarrassed.

One day [the wife] caught us. She did not say anything. The next day she found me a job in a local factory making clothes and told me that I had to move out. The factory, she told me, would pay me 2 million dong (one hundred U.S. dollars) a month. She said it was a better job for me. In the factory, the bosses were cruel. They fed us only one meal a day of porridge and fish; and if you did not work fast enough, they would come around with a skinny stick and hit our hands. My fingers hurt and my back was always in pain. I was desperate to get out, so I asked to work in a bar, first as a bartender and then later as a sex worker. It was the only way out.

Like Vy-Van, many of the women in my study described domestic work or factory work as far more abusive and less autonomous when compared with sex work. As maids, not only did the workers have to work long hours, but some were also vulnerable to rape by their bosses. As factory workers, women often felt coerced into performing undesirable labors at impossible speeds and were victims of wage theft, making them feel less free or less in control of their labor. Thuyen, a twenty-five-year-old worker at Naughty Girls, told me that her friends who also worked as maids never told anyone about their sexual relations with their bosses, because they were afraid that they would lose their jobs or, worse, their places to live in the big city. In the factories, workers were constantly racing to produce goods in a timely manner. If they could not keep up, their bosses did not hesitate to publicly humiliate them or physically abuse them. Hue, a twenty-two-year-old hostess in Lavender, clearly annoyed by my inquiries about why she chose sex work, snapped at me, saying,

> People judge us. . . . To them, either we're poor, stupid, weak girls who were forced into the sex trade, or we're immoral people who don't believe in hard work and just want hot [fast] cash. I worked hard in the factory and did everything to make the bosses happy, but I felt like a robot. . . . We went in every morning like cattle. They treated us like animals. At least in this bar, I can [develop] a personality and talk to people. This is a skill. Only the ones who are fierce enough, only the girls who know how to fight, have the [courage] to leave factory work for sex work.

In the conversations that I had with the women about why they entered into sex work, many described their sense of freedom and the relationships of intimacy built on trust and consent that enabled them to be innovative and flexible in their work. The madams were key to supporting this trust and consent because they made sure that sexual relationships between clients and workers were consensual. These mommies felt morally bound to support workers' desire to fight back at moments when clients overstepped the women's boundaries.

LABOR AND THE MORAL ORDER OF MOMMIES AND BAR OWNERS

Over the year and a half (2009–2010) I spent in Khong Sao Bar, Lavender, Secrets, and Naughty Girls, I learned that the relationships between mommies and bar owners and the hostesses who worked in the bars were guided by a strict moral code entrenched in a labor system that relied on free or cheap labor. The women in Khong Sao Bar and Lavender all earned their money through client tips and sex work. As a result, they were essentially a pool of free labor for the bar owners and the madams in those bars. While workers were required to drink, sing, and dance, none of the women I worked with were ever forced to have sex with a client. Hanh, the head mommy in Khong Sao Bar, described the moral order that governed her relations with workers in the bar in this way:

> If you have *dao* [faith or religion] without *duc* [morals], you have nothing. You have to have both *dao* and *duc*. If you decide to have sex with someone for money outside the bar, you can. I will never take any money from what you make from having sex—it is not moral to take that money. I do not want to live with those sins when I die. When a client asks if they can take a girl out of the bar, I always say that they have to ask the girl and negotiate with the girl themselves. I am just here to help the ones who are having a hard time getting clients.

The moral compass that Hanh described as stemming from her religious beliefs provided her with practical guidelines that she used in her work. She earmarked the workers' earnings from sex with a client as a special kind of money—the kind of money that Zelizer describes as having a particular social and moral meaning.[12] While Hanh did not believe that it was a sin for a worker to have sex with a client for money, she did consider it a sin for a mommy to take any of the money women earned from sex. Central to Hanh's moral compass was a worker's right to freely engage in sex work on the worker's own terms.

In my time at Khong Sao Bar, Hanh held firm to the principle of not forcing workers to have sex with any particular client. For example, on one of several occasions when a worker refused to leave the bar with a client, I watched the client turn to Hanh and urge her to convince the woman to leave with him. Hanh responded by smiling and saying, "All I can do is make sure that you are having a good time in the bar with the girls here. I cannot control what happens outside the bar. If something goes wrong, I don't want to be responsible for it. It is her choice. I cannot force any of them to go, because I do not want to worry about them outside of this bar."

After this, Hanh walked to the back room where the women sat when they were not at a client's table. She pointed to the cross that hung on her necklace and said, "I have morals. These men think that they can push me to make you go with them. I will not do it. If I do it one time, for one person, they will think that I treat some people more specially than others. God will never forgive me if I do that." Hanh stood firm in her belief that forcing women to have sex with clients was a sin and even actively defended her workers against customers who tried to insist on taking women out of the bar against their will. However, it was not simply Catholicism or Hanh's religious beliefs that drove her to take a moral stance. Rather, her religious beliefs reinforced a labor process here, where the need for worker consent also pushed her to adopt this morality. Neither she nor the bar owner paid the workers a wage for working in the bar; if she did not cultivate a trusting relationship with her workers by making them feel completely free and in control of their labor, she would lose their consent to her management.

Anh Nguyen, the male owner of Lavender, and the bar's two mommies, Tho and Huyen, also believed that forcing a woman to have sex with a client against her will was bad for business. Anh Nguyen said, "These girls have rough lives, and most of them can fight hard if someone pushes them too far. I see them as part of my family. When they are in the bar, their job is to drink and sell alcohol, but I do not make them have sex with clients for money. If I did that, it will bring bad luck into my business and we will shut down fast." While Anh Nguyen framed his comment in terms of profitable business management, he also used a language of safety and morality, saying he wanted to avoid instances where workers were raped or forced to do anything against their will. Tho reiterated this concern with safety, saying, "People think that in this business we force women to have sex with our clients. But if you ask anyone in here, they will tell you that we do not do that. We want them to bring in business, not take it outside. [Because,] when they are in the bar, we know they are safe. We cannot control what happens outside." Fears that bad karma would circulate in the bar led the owners and the mommies to follow a strict moral code that prevented them from forcing any woman to have sex with a client against her will. This was a common sentiment among most other bar owners and madams in the area, as well.

In Secrets, Lilly placed an altar next to the bar with a Buddhist statue decorated with offerings and incense. At the start of business every day, she would light incense and pray to Buddha and her ancestors to support her business. She encouraged the workers to pray for their own safety and health. Lilly's religious beliefs were so strong that she made it a point to pay her workers a monthly salary as well as nightly wages for every drink they consumed with clients. When I asked her why she adopted such practices, she said, "I believe that when you are generous with your money, when you give, money will always return to you. If the girls in here get paid every month, they at least know they have a choice. They can sleep with someone if they want to, but if they decide that they do not want to, they will not starve." Lilly's model of paying her workers indeed allowed them to be much more selective in the men with whom they developed relationships. Secrets was the only bar that paid workers a wage. By paying them nearly double the amount they would earn in a factory, Lilly made sure the hostess-workers never felt desperate enough to have sex with clients as part of a survival strategy. The workers' ability to be selective empowered many of the women to refuse clients who were overly aggressive in seeking sexual services.

While the money that hostesses earned through tips or wages at Khong Sao Bar, Lavender, and Secrets enabled them to make clear choices in their sex work, this was not always true at Naughty Girls. Like other owners and mommies, Tina, the owner of Naughty Girls, believed that forcing workers to have sex with her clients would bring bad karma. However, Tina took twelve U.S. dollars from the women for each bar client they left with in order to have paid sex, as a fee for using her bar as a space to solicit clients. The women who worked in the niche market that catered to budget travelers earned all their income from sex with clients rather than from tips, payments for drinking, or other wages. As a result, the women sometimes felt financial pressure to leave with clients with whom they did not feel completely comfortable. This increased the riskiness of sex-for-money exchanges at Naughty Girl, and it meant that workers' choices, while not forced, were at least somewhat constrained. Likewise, whereas workers in the other bars rarely complained about clients who did not pay them after sex, workers at Naughty Girls often had to deal with clients who refused to pay. As budget travelers, the men who came into Naughty Girls often left town without paying the women for sex because they knew their transience would make them difficult to find and punish. This was one reason Tina developed strong ties with members of a local mafia, who would chase down clients and scare them until they paid. Tina said to me,

> I do not like that I have to deal with them [the mafia], but I have to make sure that I have a good relationship with them because I need to know that if something happens to one of the girls, I can pick up the phone and in five minutes they will be here on their motorbikes, ready to go. There are a lot of assholes [*ca chon*] out there who think that they can have sex for free. So we pay the mafia four hundred thousand dong [twenty U.S. dollars] if they can get the money from the guys. . . . I have to protect the girls here, because if you do not protect the women in the bar, who will work for you?

The bar owners and madams at all four bars believed that they had a duty to care for their employees. By ensuring that workers felt they had complete autonomy over their sexual labor, as well as protection against aggressive clients, the mommies established a sense of community in the bars. This maternal care was bound within a labor structure that relied heavily on the mommies' and bar owners' ability to ensure that workers felt they had control over their own bodies, and that they could rely on the mommies to offer them an extra layer of protection against aggressive clients. Workers' consent was crucial to the social and moral order within the bars. It was the key factor that made sex work seem like a viable option, in sharp contrast to the beatings and the withholding of wages that workers experienced in factories.

In response, hostesses looked to the mommies for advice about men and believed that the mommies looked out for the workers' best interests. This was especially true among the hostesses and Hanh, the head mommy in Khong Sao Bar. Duyen, a nineteen-year-old worker, said to me, "People think that mommies are bad people because they force you to have sex or they force you to drink. In [Khong Sao] Bar, you have to drink because that is part of the job, but Hanh always notices when someone is not getting in to [sit at] tables, and she will always try to bring them in so that no one gets left behind. She has a heart." Tram, an eighteen-year-old worker, said, "When I first came from the village, Hanh told me to come live with her. She did not charge me for the first month, and she gave me some of her old clothes. After that, she charged me one hundred U.S. dollars for rent [approximately 5 percent of Tram's monthly earnings]. She does not believe in taking money from us. . . . She is a person with morals [*duc*]."

The appreciation of Hanh's "heart" and "morals" expressed by Duyen and Tram was echoed by other women as well. Many of the women felt indebted to Hanh for fostering their upward mobility and helping transform their lives. Describing an emotional bond with her that made them feel tied to the bar, they stated that she nurtured them without force. When I asked the women whether they felt comfortable quitting, Bi, a twenty-year-old worker, said to me,

> Hanh will not force anyone to work. If you want to work, you have to come in every day at the right time. If you do not come on time and follow the rules at work, she will stop bringing you in to tables. But if you want to quit, she will let you go. . . . I met a man who wanted me to quit and live with him as a *gai bao* [paid girlfriend]. Hanh told me not to do it, because he would get bored and leave me with nothing after a few months. She warned that I would lose my customer base, and if I were to come back to work it would be hard to start over. . . . I was stubborn, so I quit, and she was right. After two months, he left me. I came crawling back here for work, and it is hard. I am lucky if I get in to one table per night. I used to *chay show* [run around] and sit at three or four tables per night.

When I asked the workers if they ever had a negative experience with Hanh, the only bad thing they had to say about her was that if she was upset with them, she would not work hard to bring them in to tables. If she was not on their side, they had to work harder to get clients to select them in a lineup. I also asked them if there were any consequences for quitting, and every worker told me that they were free to quit whenever they chose. When they were no longer able to attract clients or bring in men, most workers quit on their own. Those who were on Hanh's bad side were sometimes forced out because she would not go out of her way to connect them with her clients.

Lilly and Tina, the owners of Secrets and Naughty Girls, respectively, went to great lengths to incorporate workers into their bars by occasionally treating the women to late-night food and drinks and by sponsoring group trips to visit a nearby temple or the women's villages. I accompanied the women on these journeys and was amazed at how much they bonded on the bus ride and at the destination. I watched as the women prayed and lit incense at temples and paid their tributes to the monks. The trips to the villages put many of the workers' families at ease because the parents could develop relationships with Lilly and Tina, which allayed their fears that their daughters were trapped or abused by their employers. This protective relationship established a bond of trust between the workers and the mommies that revolved around feelings of mutual respect and care.

Unlike the other mommies, Tho and Duyen did not cultivate close relationships with their workers outside the bars. The relationships between the mommies and women in Lavender were much less maternal because most of the workers in this bar had a community of family members and friends outside the bar scene. The vast majority of the women in these bars were urbanites who did not have to build a new community as a result of rural-to-urban migration. Still, none of the women working at Lavender reported ever feeling forced or afraid to quit if they felt uncomfortable. Chinh, a twenty-two-year-old worker, said to me, "There are all these stories about women trapped in brothels in Cambodia or village women who get kidnapped and sold across the border. That does not happen in this bar. No one forces anyone to work, and no one takes the money I make from sex. This job is better than a lot of other jobs, because we make more money and do not have to work as hard." These women spoke openly and frequently about the freedom that sex work afforded them compared to work in other occupations, such as manufacturing or service-sector work.

While the moral compasses and religious beliefs of the owners and mommies guided their relationships with their workers, their maternal acts of care were not simply acts of generosity. In all four niche markets, meeting their moral obligations was central to the mommies' management of the labor process. If the mommies could not provide a safe working space and allow the workers freedom to manage what happened to their own bodies in relation to the clients, the workers would not consent to providing free labor in Khong Sao Bar, Lavender, and Naughty Girls or cheap labor in Secrets. The mommies' moral obligations and maternal duty to care for their workers ultimately kept the bars open and their workers readily available to meet their clients' desires.

FRONTSTAGE BONDS: MATERNAL DUTY TO DEFEND WORKERS' CONSENT

The positive relationships between mommies and hostesses fostered a dynamic of respect and mutual reciprocity among hostesses. In each bar in which I worked, the mommy regulated the work atmosphere by making it very clear that if a worker violated these norms, she would be fired. On the frontstage, workers brought each other along to tables or introduced their coworkers to clients. At Khong Sao Bar, if a woman was left behind, the other workers would try to get her seated at a table or set her up with new clients who entered at the end of the night. Workers also collectively shared responsibilities related to drinking and serving the clients. Women who served clients drinks and food often did so to free up other workers who were strong performers to sing or dance. In all four bars, workers established a shared culture related to drinking. Each time a woman poured a shot, she poured one for each person at the table, so that no worker had to consume more alcohol than another at the table. And each time a woman raised a glass to her clients, the other women also raised a glass, so that each woman matched her drinking pace to that of the other women at the table. This way, no worker drank more than any of the other workers. In sharing the work of drinking, the women also actively protected each other from sexually aggressive clients or clients who became belligerent after they had too much to drink.

One evening, a group of men became aggressive in Khong Sao Bar after two hours of drinking, and a client began to grab Nhung's breasts; he then sat on top of her and pressed her against the couch. Almost immediately, Tram, one of her coworkers, picked up her glass and insisted on toasting the client to distract him. He drank with her while the other workers turned on loud techno music, pulled Nhung onto the dance floor, and began dancing to distract the men in his group. As everyone danced, the women signaled to each other that they were going to begin drinking quickly and heavily in order to push the bar tab up so the men would leave. When the table had almost finished its fourth bottle of whiskey, another aggressive client asked Nhung to go home with him. She politely refused by smiling and telling him that she had to work. When the client refused to take no for an answer, the other workers chimed in and said that Nhung had to attend her brother's birthday party later that night. After he continued to insist, the workers called on the mommy.

Hanh walked into the room, picked up a glass, and began toasting the men. They all drank with her, and then she turned on the karaoke machine to sing a song for them. Everyone listened as Hanh sang, and when the song was over she had the service workers bring in the bill. The client told Hanh that he wanted Nhung to leave with him, and Hanh firmly supported Nhung's decision to remain in the bar. The client got upset and decided that he was not going to tip Nhung or Hanh. Hanh turned to him and said, "I have never had to deal with someone as aggressive as you. This is a high-class bar with respectable women. You need to treat them with respect." The man turned and grabbed Hanh's breasts in front of everyone. She responded by slapping him twice. He was stunned and ashamed in front of his friends, so he tried to slap her back, but his friends stopped him and apologized profusely. Finally, his friends tipped Hanh on behalf of the aggressive client before they left the bar.

This interaction illustrated the solidarity that workers shared on the frontstage. By singing and dancing, workers were able to distract clients from touching hostesses' bodies in ways that made the workers feel uncomfortable or violated. The strategy of drinking at increased speeds was a common one that served two purposes. First, it forced clients to quit before driving the bill up too high, and second, sometimes it got the clients so intoxicated that they would pass out and leave the workers alone. Importantly, by slapping the client in an especially tense interaction, Hanh established her power in relation to the men in the room and set boundaries around clients' sexual aggression. In this way, although Hanh and her workers engaged in performances of deference in their everyday interactions, they also drew strict boundaries that men could not cross.

Hostesses faced moments of sexual aggression in Secrets and Naughty Girls as well, although, as in Khong Sao, these moments were the exception rather than the rule. One night, a client forcefully grabbed the genitals of one of the workers at Naughty Girls; when she squirmed, he picked her up from her seat and tried to carry her out of the bar. Tina, the owner, quickly grabbed a thick stick and began to twirl it between her two hands, screaming and chasing after him as he left the bar. The man dropped the hostess and started to run. Tina yelled, "Don't come here and think you can fuck with me. You no scare me! Come here! You want to fight? Come here!" Tina went back inside to call her mafia friends, who arrived five minutes later with machetes. They rode around the block several times to see if they could find the man, but he was nowhere to be found. This caused a scene on the entire block as crowds of workers, store owners, and tourists gathered around Tina's bar. Several of the Western tourists joked that one should "never fuck with these women unless you want the entire neighborhood to chase you down with machetes!"

When the commotion settled, it was clear that the bonds these women shared revolved around a particular form of dealing in desire. Although workers were in the business of catering to their male clients' desires, there were limits to how far men could go in expressing their sexual desires. Moments like this established the mommies' strong support of workers' freedom to choose when to leave the bar with a client and when to stay. This was a far cry from the images that portrayed women as helpless victims in need of rescue. Moments like these allowed sex workers to fight back against violent clients not only with the support of the mommies and bar owners but also with the support of the local mafia and regular citizens. This system of safety and security reinforced the reality that sex was a negotiated relationship in these bars, not simply something that men could take. Regardless of how much money clients had in Khong Sao Bar, they could never force a worker to leave the bar against her will. Moreover, moments like the one in Naughty Girls set limits to Western men's ability to assert their superiority in relation to local women through acts of violence.

The workers' ability to draw boundaries and establish their agency by fighting back when necessary was crucial to forming the long-term relationships that brought remittances or foreign direct investments into the country. The moral and social order of the hostess bars was crucial to their long-term stability and success. Hostess-workers' ability to provide clients in Khong Sao Bar with a safe space to broker Asian-based FDI deals, and their ability to develop long-term remittance relationships with their clients in Lavender, Secrets, and Naughty Girls, hinged on workers' ability to protect themselves from the kinds of relations that could make them vulnerable to abuse. Without this ability, they would quit, as they had quit their jobs in domestic and factory work. Without the regular presence of skilled hostesses, men would not have a space to broker business deals or develop the emotional attachments that fostered remittance relationships.

BACKSTAGE BONDS OF FRIENDSHIP

While solidarity on the frontstage makes intuitive sense as a strategy for women to protect one another from clients by spreading individual risk across the group, I anticipated that the women would have fierce rivalries backstage, where they interacted outside of clients' view. However, during my first week at Khong Sao Bar, while I was getting dressed at Hanh's house, she said to me, "When you go in to work, you work for yourself. Do not compete with the other girls or get jealous because they are making more money than you. If I see you competing, I will tell you to leave." At first, I assumed that her words were hollow, but on my first day in the bar all the women gathered around me to help me dress properly and teach me how to get seated at tables. This rite of initiation set the stage for all new workers to build relationships of mutual respect and reciprocity with the other women in the bar.

In all the bars in which I worked, I found myself in a "drama-free" environment, interrupted only rarely by conflicts between women. During the fifteen months that I conducted fieldwork, I witnessed only one fight between the women. This fight was over a client at Khong Sao Bar, and it resulted in the mommy telling both women that she did not want them to return to the bar for at least one week. Instead of rivalry, women's relationships were characterized by mutual support. Workers regularly shared advice on how to dress to accentuate their particular bodies, because they believed that if their coworkers looked attractive, the bar as a whole would regularly attract more clients.

Perhaps more surprisingly, workers rarely expressed anger or jealousy when clients moved from one worker to another. For example, Nam, a regular client in Khong Sao Bar, had been sitting with Diem for nearly three months when he requested a lineup and picked Phuong. Initially, Diem was upset, and she asked him why he chose someone else. When he ignored her, she went to the back room and sat in frustration. The next day, however, I listened as Diem provided Phuong with tips about Nam. She told Phuong how he liked his drinks mixed, saying, "He likes to have one shot of whiskey with half a cup of soda, but he likes the soda from the bottle not the can. . . . He will give you a stack of bills to tip the girls at the end of the night; make sure you do not overtip them, because he will notice if one bill is missing." Diem then helped Phuong get dressed because Nam text-messaged her to say that he would be coming to the bar in an hour.

When Nam arrived, Phuong went to his room, and I asked Diem, "Why aren't you mad at Phuong for stealing your client?" Diem said angrily to me, "We do not work like that in this bar. That is a stupid question. If you think that you are going to come in here and compete, you are in the wrong bar." I sat in silence, completely puzzled, when Na added, "We all have to drag our legs into this bar. We are all doing the same thing. If we compete with each other over men, we will have nothing. You cannot get jealous or fight with each other." Nhi jumped in and said, "If you had to come to work every day and deal with a tense environment, would you want to come? We all have to live in here." I stayed silent as they lectured me, the new worker, about the ethical codes that guided their interactions. In all the bars I studied, workers frequently lost their clients to other workers; but it was a normal part of the routine and did not create tension between the women.

Backstage at each of the bars, I also listened as hostesses helped each other cope with feelings of pain, loss, anguish, and undesirability. They coached each other on how to deal with clients, giving advice that ranged from small things like how to respond to a text message to bigger issues like how to subtly ask for money. When new workers entered into the bar's culture, the older workers usually refrained from providing advice. If a new hostess turned out to be competitive, the older workers would isolate her and make her work life unpleasant. However, if the new worker was humble and noncompetitive, then after a few weeks she became part of a familial environment where women shared stories, clothing, tips, and advice.

The strong bonds that tied workers together allowed the women to create a positive working environment. Many of the hostesses looked forward to coming to work because the workspace provided them with a sense of community in a stigmatized profession. In fact, the women felt so closely tied to their workplaces that they came into work on their days off simply to spend time with the other women backstage. The bars were also a place where hostesses and former hostesses celebrated their birthdays, held bachelorette parties before getting married, and cried through heartbreak and grief. The bonds created at work extended beyond the workplace, since many of the women traveled together to each other's hometowns when a family member passed away or to escape the hectic pace of city life.

Over time, I came to understand that the bars provided the workers with a place to build bonds and create a sense of community that rural migrants missed in the city. The bonds among women in these bars created an orderly work environment where women shared the bulk of the responsibilities, both frontstage and backstage. These strong bonds further created a situation in which male clients understood that when they entered a bar, there was an established set of boundaries and norms that would guide their interactions with the women.

BOUNDARIES OF LOVE, SEX, AND ROMANCE

In addition to providing workers with protection and community in the bars, mommies also helped them cultivate the skills necessary to cater to their clients' desires. For these women, escaping the long hours and harsh working conditions they had experienced as factory workers or maids, and gaining autonomy in sex work, hinged on their ability to develop what Parreñas terms "emotional capital," the naturalization of flirtation in their mannerisms and actions. This crucial skill allowed them to maintain the emotional attachments of customers and keep them coming back to the bars.[13] Like the Filipina hostess-workers in Parreñas's study, the sex workers in Vietnam cultivated emotional relationships with various clients to gain greater control over their labor in the bars. To do this, they relied on the mommies to help them draw boundaries and establish a kind of intimacy predicated on the workers' consent to having sex with their clients.

The mommies in all four niche markets held similar moral philosophies with respect to worker-client relationships. They trained their workers in how to dress, walk, talk, and carry a conversation in order to keep their clients interested. One of the most important skills that the mommies tried to teach their workers was how to maintain boundaries around their emotions and to differentiate between emotional labor as a performance and real feelings of love. While all mommies cautioned their workers not to fall in love with their clients too easily, they differed in their views about the possibility of long-term relations.

The mommies in Khong Sao Bar and Lavender, which catered to local Vietnamese men, other Asian businessmen, and Viet Kieu men, all had strict rules about dating and relationships. Hanh, Tho, and Duyen all believed that it was acceptable to have relationships with men outside the bar, but that a worker should never devote all her time to one man. They also warned workers that falling in love with a client would lead them down a difficult path. Hanh, for example, said,

> In this business, you cannot fall in love. Do not be stupid and fall in love. These men are married already, and they have a responsibility to their wives and their wives' families. It is bad karma to break up a marriage. You have to respect the wife and her place by knowing your place as always second. Many men loved me and they wanted to marry me. They promised to leave their wives for me. But if I did that, I would be stuck to him. I am free now to do what I want; no one controls me.

Tho and Huyen expressed similar sentiments about falling in love. One evening, while business was slow, I listened as Tho lectured the sex workers in the bar. She said, "Viet Kieu men will always flirt and have fun. They come here to play, and then they will leave. They will tell you that they want to marry you, so they can use you for free sex. Some will marry you, but most of them will marry a girl they met through their families. You can have fun with them, but do not fall in love, because you will fall hard and it will hurt."

Although some workers in all the bars indeed fell in love with their clients, most found themselves back in the bar within a few months following their heartbreaks. Many of the women who worked in Khong Sao Bar and Lavender often referred to their work as part of a business in which they each served as the mistress of many men. Thi, a twenty-year-old worker at Lavender, said to me, "Sometimes I dream about meeting the right person and falling in love, but right now I care more about money than love. The men I work for will never marry someone like me; they have wives and women who their families know and accept. If I fall in love with one person, I cannot have many men take care of me."

In her relations with the men in the bar, Thi understood her place as a mistress or a lover and never the wife. She also knew that falling in love would limit her ability to generate an income, and at that time she was more interested in income than romance. Like Thi, many of the workers often spoke of making an active decision to hold off on love and marriage in their quest for wealth. None of these women described a clear image of what their long-term futures would be like or seemed sure of whether they would eventually settle down. The moral boundaries that related to emotions of love and care meant that workers in Khong Sao Bar and Lavender had short-term exchanges with their clients that were intimate, sometimes lasting several months to a year. Such relationships rarely evolved into long-term marital partnerships. Moreover, most women working in Khong Sao Bar understood that the time they would spend with their clients was limited, and that eventually the men would move on to someone else.

The structure of relationships was different for women who catered to Western men. Lilly, at Secrets, opened what she called a "relationship bar," which was distinct from a "hooker bar" because the workers did not engage in direct sex-for-money exchanges. In opening the bar, Lilly hoped to target Western expatriates living and working in Vietnam on a long-term or recurring basis. On several occasions, I listened as Lilly advised the women working in her bar: "I pay you to work here so you do not have to sleep with men for money. Men out there are all the same. They play and then they get bored. If you are too easy, they will say okay, then play with someone else. You [should] date many men, and then fall in love later." Lilly advised her workers to date many men and then decide later so that they could take their pick among a variety of men. She wanted the workers to engage in long-term relationships with men who were committed to them and who were willing to help them experience upward mobility.

Secrets was the only bar strategically set up to promote the development of long-term relationships. Lilly encouraged her workers to be patient with the men and invest in long-term relationships rather than quick, direct, sex-for-money exchanges, because doing so would allow them to ask their clients for more money. While sitting in the bar late one evening, she said to me (in English), "This is a relationship bar. Smart girl will have a longtime relationship with a man and get him to help her set up a business, help her family, or build a house. I don't like the dirty backpacker or the Viet Kieu who lie and pretend to have a lot of money." The logic behind workers' investments in long-term relationships is that they allowed women to relax and not feel as though they needed to hustle to get money from their clients. Lilly, who had previously worked in a bar in the backpackers' district catering to Western men traveling on a budget, recalled the feelings of desperation that had compelled her to engage in sex for money to help her family. She did not want her workers to experience that desperation and preferred that they had a base they could rely on in times of need—their monthly salary. If they wished to build on that base and earn more money, women could invest in longer-term relationships. Lilly pointed to a number of workers who had multiple boyfriends and were able to spend thousands of dollars rebuilding their families' village homes. She also pointed to the numerous boyfriends who had helped her former workers open small businesses and venture out on their own. Lilly helped her workers focus on the longer-term gains they could reap by having multiple boyfriends, rather than on the short-term gains of direct sex-for-money exchanges.

During my time working in Secrets, the clients talked with one another about how they "knew" that the women in the bar had "boyfriends" or relationships outside the bar. They understood that these relationships sometimes involved direct sex-for-money exchanges and at other times involved longer-term commitments. However, the men rarely learned who the workers did or did not have relationships with. This mystery enabled workers to capitalize on the clients' anxieties by leading multiple men to believe that they were the "only" man a particular worker cared for. While men associated care with emotions, sex workers often associated care with money. That is, if a client provided a women with a comfortable standard of living, or was willing to help her family financially, he did so because he loved or cared for her. Many of the workers talked about how clients bought them small gifts, took them on trips throughout Southeast Asia, gave them small amounts of money to pay for small purchases, and sometimes gave them lump sums of money to help their families.

All the women told me they wanted to hold out for the client who could take the best care of them. This meant women had multiple boyfriends while in the process of selecting long-term partners. During my time working in the bar, two of the women who had been employed there for over a year had long-term relationships with multiple men and decided that it was time to quit working in the bars and settle down with only one of them. I went to their bachelorette parties and attended their weddings. The work culture at Secrets created a structure where workers saw men not merely as clients but also as potential boyfriends and even husbands.

Women who catered to Western backpackers in Naughty Girls were much more direct than workers in Secrets. The workers in this niche market engaged in the most explicit sex-for-money exchanges with their clients. Because their clients were tourists, encounters were necessarily fleeting, requiring workers to engage in direct conversations about sex-for-money exchanges rather than using the more subtle methods of women in the high-end niches. Women in the tourist niche market did not make a salary, so there were days when they spent ten to twelve hours at work without making any money. Thus, they were much more likely to have sex with men whom they did not find attractive. However, women in this niche also had both a short-term and a long-term strategy for acquiring money. While they certainly engaged in direct sex-for-money exchanges, the women in Naughty Girls also worked hard to develop long-term remittance relationships with their clients, using text messaging, instant messaging, and email.

Like the women in Secrets, those I met in Naughty Girls worked hard to maintain multiple "boyfriends" who would send them remittances to help them quit sex work and find a more "respectable" occupation. Women asked for money to take English classes and sewing classes or attend beauty school. Their clients sent large amounts of money via Western Union to help pay for expenses that were part of the women's everyday lives. I observed that clients also sent money to help pay off workers' debts, care for an ailing family member, or help them start a business. However, the men were not always easily duped. Workers had to establish long-term relationships in order to build ties and establish trust. They needed clients to sympathize with their fate as Third World subjects caught in global poverty, because this empathy would motivate clients to send large remittances.

The moral compass the women used to establish boundaries around "love" created different structures of intimacy within the bars. The workers who catered to local Vietnamese men and their Asian business partners in Khong Sao Bar, and the workers who catered to Viet Kieu men in Lavender, engaged in intimate relations with their clients that involved short-term encounters. Those who became hired girlfriends did so knowing that they would have to return to the bar in a few months when their clients decided to move on to other women. Women who catered to Western men in Secrets and in Naughty Girls engaged in intimate relations that involved both short-term and longer-term committed relationships.

Unlike women in popular-media accounts of human trafficking, most of the women I interviewed entered sex work because the labor conditions in the bar were much better than labor conditions in the factories or in homes where they were employed as domestic workers. When we move beyond sensationalized media accounts and take a deeper look inside the bars, it is clear that there was a moral order to the organizational structure inside each bar. The moral codes guided (a) how the mommies managed the workers in the bar, (b) frontstage relationships with clients, (c) backstage relationships among workers, and (d) the emotional boundaries around love. In contrast to findings in previous studies that describe sex work as dangerous labor rife with competition, the vast majority of the workers in my study believed in and succeeded in creating a collaborative work environment. Workers shared clothing, tips on how to engage with clients, and life stories that nurtured strong ties among them. These bonds led workers to come into the bar on their days off to celebrate birthdays and engagements and to mourn the deaths of family members.

Sex workers also cultivated skills that allowed them to establish emotional boundaries that guided interactions in the bar. These skills were crucial because they provided clients with a sense of comfort and predictability, allowing men to feel as though they were partly in control of the interactions, when in reality the women exercised considerable collective power in structuring these interactions. Moreover, the varied structures of bars that served different types of clients led to different types of emotional intimacy. Workers who catered to local Vietnamese men, other Asian businessmen, and Viet Kieu men all engaged in intimate relations that were short-term intimate encounters. Workers who catered to Western expatriates and budget travelers engaged in intimate relations that involved both short-term interactions and long-term committed relationships.

In short, most women across all niche markets felt that sex work offered them better financial security compared to other types of work. However, sexual consent in these relationships formed the bedrock of the dynamic capital flows tied to local perceptions of Asian ascendancy and Western decline.

Constructing Desirable Bodies

On my first day at work in Khong Sao Bar, I arrived in what I thought was an appropriate outfit—a long, black, low-cut V-neck dress and a pair of three-inch open-toed high heels. However, as I walked into the room, Hanh, the head mommy, immediately said to me, "How are you going to get in on any tables if you look like that? You look like a poor village girl!" She placed a phone call and asked her maid to hand deliver a dress for me. While we waited for the dress, she said to the women, "This is Ca Xanh's girl. [Ca Xanh was one of my main informants.] He brought her in here, and she is going to work here for as long as he wants. She is new to the business, so help her get dressed." Five women descended upon me with tote bags full of makeup and clothing and immediately set to work on my appearance. One woman started with my hair and said, "Since your hair is short, you need to pull it up and do it every day. Leaving it down will make you look too old." As this woman pulled my hair up, Yen-Vy, a twenty-one-year-old woman, came over, handed me a mirror and said, "Look into this as I show you how to do your makeup."

I watched as she applied various layers of foundation, blush, and mascara to my face and listened as the women offered opinions about what she should do to improve my appearance. She said to me, "Tomorrow, you need to go to the market and buy some makeup." She took out a piece of paper and made a list of things I needed to buy and the cost of each item so that I could bargain properly. Then she said,

Your skin is very dark, so you need to buy a foundation that will make you look lighter. Apply that foundation to your whole face and neck. Then put some white baby powder on your face, neck, and shoulders so that your skin looks lighter. Draw your eyebrows in thick so that they shape your face and make you look younger. . . . You are lucky because you do not need surgery. You have a high nose bridge and a double eyelid. That's what men like. They like girls who look like pop stars from Hong Kong, Japan, or Korea. To make your eyes look even bigger, you need to apply a white eye shadow around your eyelids and right below your eyebrow along the bone of your brow.

Several other women agreed, complimenting Yen-Vy on her makeup application skills. Because Yen-Vy had fake eyelashes permanently glued to her eyelids and kept no spares in her makeup bag, she asked to borrow a set from someone else. Khai-Thu handed her a box and said, "Take a pair from here. Make sure that you save them after today, because the best eyelashes are the ones that have been reused by you. They look more natural." I closed my eyes as Yen-Vy applied a set of fake eyelashes. She then took a small angle brush and applied black eyeliner along my eyelid to make my eyes appear large and round.

An hour later, Hanh walked into the room carrying a short black tube dress and a pair of clear six-inch high heels. I put on the dress and heels and she said to me,

You cannot wear long dresses, because you are short and chubby. You need to wear short dresses and very high heels so that it makes your legs look longer. When you are short, you have to remember to sit and stand up tall. Women who look expensive get tipped more. I'm going to bring you in to every table tonight and introduce you to all the clients. You will make at least three million dong [U.S.$150]. Tomorrow morning, I will take you and three other girls makeup shopping at 9 A.M. Then, I will call the tailor to come and make you some dresses and bring you some shoes with the money that you make tonight. Later tonight, a lady will come to do some of the girls' nails. Tell her to do yours.

This embodied transformation that I had to undergo made me hyper-aware of the aesthetic ideals in Khong Sao Bar and, later, in Lavender, where I quickly learned how to embody a sought-after beauty ideal modeled after Korean pop stars. The practice of learning how to do my own hair and makeup and dress my body appropriately opened my eyes to a world of hidden aesthetic and bodily labor that I otherwise would have never paid as much attention to.

After working in Khong Sao Bar and Lavender for several months, I thought I had mastered the aesthetic necessary for me to succeed in

HCMC's hostess bars. But as I transitioned to Secrets and Naughty Girls, I was surprised to learn that I would have to construct an entirely different look in order to appeal to Western men's racialized and sexualized aesthetic desires. To work at Secrets, I had to conform to the Orientalizing uniform of a modified traditional Chinese- and Vietnamese-style dress that was short and low-cut for sexual appeal. I also had to completely change my makeup techniques to fit this entirely different aesthetic.

In my first week at Secrets, my coworkers rummaged through my makeup bag and told me what to keep and what to get rid of. Ly, a twenty-four-year-old woman, said to me,

> Get rid of the baby powder. It is going to make your skin look too pale, and under the lights in this bar you are going to look like you are sick. You do not want to look dark, but you don't want to look too light either. . . . You can't use pink blush in here; it makes you look like those Japanese or Chinese play dolls. You have to go buy a brown, orange, or darker color to use on your cheeks. It will make your face look smaller and narrower instead of round.

The women replaced the baby powder with a self-tanner that they used to make their skin look darker. And I was told that, instead of wearing very little eye shadow with heavy mascara, I should apply darker eye shadows to create the smoky-eye effect to make my face look more exotic under the dim yellow lighting. While working on my eyes, Vy-Van, an eighteen-year-old sex worker who was relatively new to the bar, explained the process to me:

> Take a nude color that is a little bit lighter than your skin color and apply it on your eyelid all the way up to the bottom of your eyebrow. Then take a darker color and brush it right above your eyelash line, slowly blending it toward the brow bone. Get another brush to blend the colors so that it doesn't look messy, and then finish with a dark eyeliner [before] gluing on the fake eyelashes. Since your skin is not too dark and not too light, start with purple colors; but as your skin gets darker, move to the grays and blacks.

Although I never asked the men what they thought about this smoky-eye effect, the women in the bars were convinced that the look appealed to the men in the bar. As Uyen, a twenty-one-year-old sex worker, explained, "It makes you look very sexual. You want turn them on."

These divergent, embodied ideals reflected the different circuits of capital and culture in Asia. Sex workers altered their physical embodiments to appeal to their male clients' differing perceptions of Vietnam's place in the global imaginary. The multiple terrains of women's altered embodiments show that sex workers strategically altered their bodies to construct and reinforce ideas of Vietnam's place in the global imaginary.

COMPETING TECHNOLOGIES OF EMBODIMENT

Much of the research on gender and nation examines how *cultural* transformations inform the expression of varied national ideals in non-Western contexts.[1] We know less about *economic* transformations that inform variations in the gendered expression of national ideals within the space of HCMC's sex industry. In order to examine the tensions between different perceptions of ascendant pan-Asian, and declining Western, cultural influences, I've pinpointed embodiment as a key site where diverging ideals are projected.[2] In paying particular attention to economic and geopolitical shifts in Asia, I discovered that women's embodied representations of nation and performances of femininity varied in the different niche markets.[3]

Although some might presume that all women in developing nations aspire to a Western aesthetic, a comparison across the multiple niche markets of HCMC's sex industry illustrates that women may in fact alter their appearance to satisfy men's desires based on specific, diverse perceptions of national progress. When niche markets catering to local Vietnamese and transnational Asian elites are compared with those catering to Western businessmen and budget travelers, it becomes clear how individual agents in the developing world actively project their nation's place in the global imaginary through their embodied practices.

To describe microlevel practices and interactions, I turn to theories of body work and body capital.[4] *Body work* refers to labored modifications that individuals inflict on their own bodies or the bodies of others; the resultant *body capital* describes how the bodies that are worked on become valued as a means of production in competitive consumer contexts.[5] Drawing on Foucault, I introduce the concept of technologies of embodiment, which refers to the process through which women produce, transform, or manipulate their bodies through particular kinds of body work that signify divergent perceptions of national progress.[6] These technologies are tools existing outside the user's body that allow her to manipulate or alter her embodied performance of femininity as she interacts with the world around her. Like other technologies, technologies of embodiment are rapidly evolving and quickly consumed and can swiftly respond to evolving standards of beauty to instantly reshape the user. Specific technologies include but are not limited to skin lightening creams or tanning lotions/bronzers, natural-looking eye makeup or heavy makeup, and plastic surgery to alter one's face or chest, as well as clothing that makes one look more modern and fashionable or deliberately impoverished. These technologies of embodiment do not exist in a vacuum; their development and consumption signify and are shaped by a nation's shifting place in the global economy.

By linking the micropractices of body work to a broader narrative of modernities, the concept of technologies of embodiment adds another layer to theories of how *differences* between women's embodied ideals vary within one nation.[7] In the hierarchical niche markets of HCMC's sex industry, competing technologies of embodiment represent divergent projections of Vietnam's uneasy transition into the global economy. The point is not how women in different niche markets compete with each other; rather, technologies of embodiment compete with each other to establish the appropriate way to reflect the aesthetics of the nation for different audiences.

A comparison of the multiple niche markets of HCMC's segmented sex industry illustrates how sex workers reflect male clients' different projections of Vietnam's place in the global economy by means of three competing technologies of embodiment: pan-Asian modernity, nostalgic cosmopolitanism, and Third World dependency. In the case of HCMC's high-end niche market, sex workers help wealthy elite Vietnamese businessmen attract foreign direct investments from Asian investors by constructing themselves as pan-Asian modern subjects whose femininity conveys a deliberately exuberant projection of Vietnam's new position as an emerging economic player within the globalscape. Vietnamese businessmen's ability to convey a new global configuration hinges on women's well-groomed bodies that adopt a pan-Asian aesthetic ideal as a counterpoint to representations of Western feminine ideals.

In contrast, sex workers who cater to Viet Kieu men construct themselves as nostalgic cosmopolitan subjects, altering their bodies to make themselves more desirable than Westernized white and Viet Kieu women while also catering to their clients' desires to relive a nostalgic past in which women buttressed male superiority and patriarchy.

Sex workers who cater to Western expatriates and tourists employ technologies of embodiment that are deeply embedded in discourses of Western paternalism, to attract benevolent remittances. These women project Third World dependency by embodying virtuous Third World subjects, holdovers from an era when the "sun never set" on Western dominance. These workers play into their clients' racialized desire to imagine Vietnam as a poverty-stricken Third World country in need of Western help. Within their distinct niche markets, sex workers employ competing technologies of embodiment that in turn reveal how desire reflects and constructs different national formations in the global imaginary.

PAN-ASIAN MODERNITY IN KHONG SAO BAR

Whoever said that money can't buy love doesn't know where to shop. In Saigon, girls go under the knife. . . . They get nose jobs, boob jobs, liposuction, or whatever, just so rich men will pick them in the lineup [inside high-end karaoke bars]. . . . To get picked in the lineup, they have to transform themselves to look like Korean pop stars.

—Nguyen, a thirty-eight-year-old Vietnamese plastic surgeon

Sex workers and their clients played a critical role in contesting hierarchies of race and nation by constructing new, distinctly non-Western ideals of beauty through the workers' technologies of embodiment. Although their methods of asserting superiority remained in tension with Western modes of dominance, they reflected the ideological repositioning that accompanies shifting political economic alignments.[8] These new configurations did not merely depend on the ways in which men wielded capital in the bars. They also hinged on the women who worked in these bars, through the symbolic etchings of modernity and progress displayed on well-groomed and surgically altered bodies that were highly desirable under an aesthetic of pan-Asian modernity.[9]

The workers in Khong Sao Bar did not want to look Western. Instead, conforming to regional Asian standards of beauty, they wanted to look like the women from Hong Kong, Korea, or Japan. Women lightened their skin, accentuated their eyebrows, and worked to look like Korean pop stars. A small economy thrived in the space of the women's dressing room. Backstage, Korean and Japanese fashion magazines littered the dressing table and the television was always tuned in to a Korean soap opera dubbed in Vietnamese. Over fifteen tailors came through the bar every couple of days to measure the women's bodies and take their orders. These tailors shopped for fabrics, sewed clothes, and designed dresses like those depicted in Korean magazines and hand delivered the items to the bar. The highest earners always ordered the most expensive fabrics, like silk and chiffon. Manicurists and pedicurists stationed themselves in the back room during the early afternoon, providing women with on-site nail services. Makeup artists came in to help women groom their eyebrows and glue on permanent eyelashes. Tattoo artists came to the bar with equipment to put permanent makeup on many of the women's faces. An array of services groomed women's bodies in such a way that, over time, the women looked increasingly similar.

Hostesses were clear that blonde hair and blue eyes were desires of the past; they believed that the East and Southeast Asia region was emerging as a new global center of beauty—much as it had had become a global center of finance—as a result of its economic rise and the declining significance of the West. Sex workers pointed to the Wonder Girls, a famous group of five female singers from South Korea, as their ideal of femininity. Vy, a nineteen-year-old sex worker, gestured to a photo of the pop singers and explained, "You see that the women are light skinned and their makeup looks natural. . . . They do not wear a lot of eye shadow, [but] they accentuate their eyebrows, thicken their eyelashes, and wear blush that highlights their cheekbones."

It is often argued that the bodywork performed by Asian women—building nose bridges, constructing double eyelids, and lightening their skin—creates changes associated with Western standards of beauty.[10] However, rather than looking to the West for a model of beauty, less-developed Asian countries like Vietnam look to East Asia to represent modern cultural ideals. Even as European body features have been integrated into the beauty ideals of Korea and Japan, the resulting beauty standard is not simply a European white ideal; as the women quickly pointed out to me, some Asian women, too, are also born with light skin and double eyelids.[11] Furthermore, the *meaning* that these women ascribe to their appearance is that it is a modern Asian look, not a Western look. Tang Ha, a twenty-one-year-old sex worker, explained to me, "Western models are big boned and muscular. They look like men. . . . Asian women look like real women." Unlinking whiteness from European whiteness, the women were explicit about not wanting to look like Western women.[12] Dai, a nineteen-year-old hostess-worker, explained skin lightening as a project distinct from emulating Western whiteness:

> When women use skin lightening creams for the face and body, people think they want to look like white people in America or Europe, but actually the true skin color of women in Asia is white. When a baby is born in Japan, Korea, or Vietnam, what color is their skin? It is fair and white, right? Dark skin is from going out in the sun a lot. We are just trying to bring

out our natural beauty. . . . No one wants to look Western here anymore. People come to Asia for beautiful Asian women, not for women who look Western.

In this comment, Dai describes a regional standard of beauty that is much more nuanced than a simple aspiration to Western ideals. The tone of Dai's comment illustrates how sex workers used distinctly Asian standards of beauty to resist ideals of the West. Sex workers' deliberate avoidance of Western standards illustrates how local, regional, and global ideals converged in their practices. Sex workers in this niche market engaged in practices of bodily modifications in which strictly European features were eschewed in favor of a pan-Asian ideal type that included some features that may appear typically Western—light skin, eyelid crease, and eyelid shape. But this ideal type was in fact a specific East Asian ideal: round face, thin body, and even an untanned skin tone.

Moreover, the women in this niche preferred Korean and Japanese skin-care products to Western ones. Anh Minh told the sex workers that products from South Korea "are about twelve years ahead of the U.S. in terms of their skin-care technology." South Korea, he said "has become the new France." These new technological developments enabled women to craft themselves as modern yet distinctly pan-Asian. By claiming that whiteness of skin was a "natural" Asian feature, sex workers actively contested the racial and aesthetic geographies of beauty in relation to white (European) women.

In addition to emulating pan-Asian standards of beauty, workers tried to differentiate themselves from rural women, whom they viewed as poor, backward, and unsophisticated. Several of the mommies worked hard to build a network of young beautiful village women they could teach to reconfigure their bodies to look like cosmopolitan subjects. In order to feel desirable and be desired by men, workers engaged in a variety of disciplinary practices to transform themselves from village "bumpkins" into modern urbanites. For example, the women in the bar regularly monitored their weight. Most ate only one meal a day, which usually consisted of a bowl of ramen noodles and two eggs. They consumed pills to curb their hunger, and they routinely made themselves vomit at the end of the night to purge the alcohol from their systems to avoid weight gain. Women who were heavier than others were subtly reminded by the mommies and the other sex workers to purge at the end of the night. On several occasions, the women joked about how, in their villages, women used to take pills to gain weight because having a larger figure was a sign of wealth and prosperity, but in the city everyone wanted to look slim because that is how modern, urban women looked on television and in magazines.

The highest earners at Khong Sao Bar had subjected their bodies to a great deal of change both because investing in their body capital required financial resources and because women who altered their bodies received more attention and bigger tips from male clients. When women began working in the bar, they made aesthetic changes to their bodies by altering their makeup, rubbing whitening creams and powders on their bodies, and learning to wear appropriately fitted bras and walk in six-inch heels. According to Hanh, the head mommy, the highest earners were women who "made smart business choices by knowing when to buy new clothes or invest in plastic surgery." While sitting in the back room playing card games, I listened as Hanh advised the women:

> When you are new, it's better to invest in cheaper dresses and save your money, since men will bring you in to their tables because you are a fresh face. After you've been here for a couple of months, you need to do things to stay fresh [tuoi]. You can buy new dresses, and that will help, but you should save your money and use it only if you think that it is going to make you more money. Like with Diem: after four months she saved over one hundred million dong [U.S.$5,000]. I told her to take three hundred dollars and get a nose job. After she got a nose job, men pulled her in to all their tables. They wanted to see her new face, her change. She went from looking like a poor village girl to looking more modern [hien dai].

Surgical alterations permanently changed both how women looked and their ability to interact with the clients who came through the bar. In addition to focusing on surgery, women spent a lot of energy on the proper presentation of their breasts. Big breasts were not the primary goal; rather, most women worked to move their breasts so that they were positioned firmly together. One afternoon, Xinh, one of the junior mommies, walked into the back room with a bag of new bras. As the women tried them on, Xinh said, "We bring in the richest men in all of Saigon, and you need to look like you are worth a lot of money. There are millions of country girls [nha que]—men can go anywhere to get them. They come here to be around women who *look* modern [mo-den] and worth a lot [sang]. . . . You do not have to go out and spend a lot of money on expensive dresses all the time. It is about the little things, like the bra and how you wear it."

Breast size did not differentiate urbanites from rural women entering the bar; rather, women in the city distinguished themselves through the knowledge of how to purchase the proper bras and pull their breasts up into a bra so that it had a firming effect. This was because it was more important for them to appear aesthetically appealing than sexually desirable. Mommies like Hanh relied on workers' ability to portray themselves as modern subjects whose bodies were worth a lot of money, because that image allowed the bar to maintain its status as one of the highest-status bars in HCMC. Claiming such a modern subjectivity through consumptive practices displaced an understanding of modernity as embodied in the West. Rather, the women's practices of negotiating, appropriating, and challenging Western beauty ideals reflected the multiple hierarchies signaling Asia's relation to the West.

Compared to women in other niches of HCMC's sex industry, the women in Khong Sao Bar underwent the starkest and most rapid bodily transformations during the course of their employment. The bar had connections with two separate plastic surgery offices that hired doctors trained in Singapore, Thailand, and South Korea to perform rhinoplasties that would make the Vietnamese women look like Korean pop stars. All the women I worked with had undergone rhinoplasty, and roughly 80 percent of them had had double eyelid surgery.[13] Less than a quarter of the women had saline breast implants, and 20 percent of the women had undergone liposuction. These modifications complicated the women's claims about natural, feminine-looking Asian bodies as they actively worked to pursue a supposedly innate ideal.

Technologically and surgically altered bodies became symbols to elite businessmen that reflected the nation's economic progress. Male clients also played a crucial role in mediating workers' sense of self worth. Whenever a group of men entered the bar, the mommies would greet them and order the women to line up so the men could select the ones they wanted at their tables. During the lineup, men regulated women's appearances by complimenting them or critiquing their style of dress and body parts. Male clients rewarded women they found aesthetically pleasing by inviting them to sit at their tables. It was not uncommon to see men play with women's noses or ask questions about their various surgeries.

In fact, local Vietnamese men often acted as representatives of the nation, showcasing the nation's beautiful women to their foreign investors. One evening, a few days after Diem returned to work following her rhinoplasty, Quang, a thirty-nine-year-old client, pointed to her nose and asked everyone at the table: "What do you think of her nose? She doesn't look like a poor country girl anymore, does she? This face looks modern [*Mat nay nhin tay thiet*]!" Everyone laughed as he kissed her nose, raised his glass, and cheered everyone at the table. Diem shyly covered her nose and looked down as the men complimented her. For these men, Diem's nose represented not only her own transformation but also the progress of the nation.

These bodily modifications, which highlighted the women's malleability and mobility, were crucial to local Vietnamese business elites because they signaled the nation's progress and economic development. Dong, a sixty-year-old businessman, explained to me, "When you look from the outside in, it seems like they [the women] need our money, but we need them just as much as they need us. When you bring in businessmen from Asia, you can say, 'Look, this country is growing and developing so much that even the poorest village girls can afford to get plastic surgery.' It shows them that we're a nation growing very rapidly, and that there is a lot of potential in our market. They [the women] represent Vietnam to the most important people, our investors!"

For foreign investors making large speculations in Vietnam, women's enhanced bodies provided figurative reassurance that Vietnam was a dynamic market where they could expect to see returns on their investments. Sex workers' altered bodies projected Vietnam as a nation on the move, where even the poorest of the poor were beginning to reap the rewards of economic development.

Deferential Performances of Femininity

Although sex workers at Khong Sao Bar were made to look like modern Asian women, they also had to engage in performances characteristic of a "traditional" Vietnamese woman. Hanh repeatedly told the women that she felt a special affinity with rural women because she could alter their bodies and make them look modern, but they would never have a problem performing deference and showing respect to her clients. In explaining her preference for rural women, she said, "It is harder to teach women how to act like a traditional Vietnamese woman than to look modern. . . . I can tell you what to wear and how to do your makeup, but I cannot always tell you how to act." Sex workers engaged in a gendered strategy of mobility, and male clients rewarded successful performances with generous tips and punished those who failed to perform their gender correctly.[14] There were subtle rules for how to signify deference and respect that women quickly learned on the job from the mommies, in conversations with clients, and by observing more experienced workers.

New workers did not undergo formal training in workplace conduct. Instead, they were sent to sit at tables with clients to be socialized in the interaction styles of the bar. Usually, if a client elected to sit next to a new worker, he took it upon himself to teach her the rules and norms of the job. For example, Tai, a man in his midfifties, instructed Uyen on her first day on the job: "Before you sit down, bow and greet everyone at the table from eldest to youngest with a glass. Watch how you clink your glass. If you don't know where to clink your glass, it is always better to go lower or watch how the man you are sitting next to clinks his glass."

Sex workers also had to learn their place at the table. Women whose bodies were beginning to show the signs of age were always told to sit with the eldest man at the table and to play the role of mature big sister to the other workers. Older or more experienced women bore the burden of reminding their younger sisters to refill their clients' cups, serve men food, light their cigarettes, and sing a song for their companion. More experienced women were also better at gauging men's feelings. If a client seemed bored, or if it seemed as though he wanted more attention from his hostess, other workers would encourage her to dance, sing a song, or ask if her companion was hungry.

As discussed in chapter 3, women learned detailed but implicit rules related to clinking glasses to signal deference. Women also signaled deference through body language. When sitting next to a client, it was common to see a woman cross her legs and place one hand on her lap and the other over her client's thigh while leaning in so that her head was below his. Women subjected their bodies to men's sexually charged gaze by diverting their eyes and looking down at the ground or by pretending not to notice when clients subtly ran their fingers across the women's breasts.

Some men would ask if the worker's breasts were real as an indirect way of asking if they could touch them. For example, one night Son, a man in his early sixties, turned to My and asked, "Are those real?" To which she replied, "Why don't you see for yourself?" He ran his fingers between her cleavage and said, "They are soft. They feel real to me." She then grabbed his hand, folded it into hers, smiled, and picked up her glass to toast him. By allowing Son to run his fingers across her chest, she subtly deferred to his request while simultaneously managing it so that he would not act overly aggressive toward her body. Subtle acts of deference such as this one communicated to men the boundaries around permissible behavior without shaming or embarrassing them in front of their friends. Women maintained their place as sexualized subjects, and they deferred to their clients' desires as a traditional Vietnamese woman might.

In this high-end niche of sex work in HCMC, new definitions of modern subjects hinged on both regional and local conceptualizations tied to pan-Asian standards of beauty. Women engaged in two simultaneous projects—embodiment and performance—which positioned them in constant tension between modernity and tradition. There are limits, therefore, to how "modern" women could be before losing their unique qualities as Vietnamese feminine subjects. The performances of a particular Vietnamese femininity hinged on the workers' abilities to perform a "localized" femininity by assuming their inferior positions in relation to local and global men. The tension that played out on women's bodies reflected Vietnam's state of transition as it worked to find its place in the global order.

The reputation of Khong Sao Bar depended on hostesses' ability to develop and maintain a certain look coupled with a performance that constructed pan-Asian progress in a global market economy as an embodied ideal. Put differently, the technologies of embodiment and the performances of a distinctly Vietnamese femininity seen in Khong Sao Bar projected a shift in FDI, from the United States and Europe to major Asian economic powers. Not all women, however, embodied pan-Asian modernity: Viet Kieu and Western businessmen and tourists had different perceptions of Vietnam's place in the global economy, thus illustrating the substantial variation of embodied ideals within one nation. The competing technologies of embodiment employed by women in these distinct niche markets illustrate the competing tensions within an emerging market that influence Vietnam's economic viability in HCMC's sex industry.

NOSTALGIC COSMOPOLITANISM IN LAVENDER BAR

In Vietnam, almost everything is fake—clothes, CDs, DVDs, food, alcohol, boobs, noses, and even love. The only thing [that is] real is the money you spend on these items, assuming the bill you are using to pay for it is not also fake.

—Tuyen, thirty-four-year-old from New York

Female sex workers who catered to Viet Kieu men embodied Vietnam's schizophrenic attempt to emerge as a powerful country in the global economy while striving to hold on to nostalgic cultural values and traditions that made Vietnam unique. For Viet Kieu men, women's physical embodiment came to represent Vietnam as a modern nation on the rise, while women's performances of femininity simultaneously represented nation-as-home to their nostalgic desires.[15] For local sex workers, modern ideals meant looking more cosmopolitan than Western and Viet Kieu women. However, these women also had to embody nation-as-home to present Vietnam as a place where overseas men could find women who spoke a similar language, shared similar cultural values, and engaged in nostalgic performances of femininity.

Women in Lavender Bar typically spent two to three hours applying their makeup, fixing their hair, and getting dressed upon arrival at the bar. Like the women at Khong Sao, these women tried to find ways to make their bodies look like those of Korean pop stars or supermodels. One evening as we dressed together, I listened as Van, a twenty-two-year-old woman, talked about the new set of face creams that she had purchased. She pulled the jars out of her purse and said, "I spent two million dong [U.S.$110] on these creams yesterday. They are supposed to make your skin whiter and softer. It is a Korean company that makes it, and they are expensive, but one of my friends is using it and her skin looks really good. . . . I think it's better to buy Korean and Japanese creams, because Western brands like Estée Lauder and Lancôme do not work."

She passed the jars around and promised the other women that she would pick up three more sets and bring them to work the next day. Out of curiosity, I asked Van why it was important to have lighter skin and whether she wanted to look white. She said, "I don't want to look like a white woman. No one thinks that white women are pretty." I asked, "So what is it then? Why do you all care so much about your skin color?" She replied,

> Viet Kieu men want to be with beautiful women. They did not come here to be with women who look like they are from the rice fields. They want to be with Vietnamese women who look like they are worth a lot of money. . . . Times have changed in Vietnam. Five years ago, no one cared about fashion or their looks. . . . But now, Vietnamese women are some of the most fashionable women. We all look better. We dress better. Vietnam is not a poor country like it used to be. We have a lot more money now, and Viet Kieu men want to be around women who look like they are worth a lot of money [*tuong sang*].

Like the women in Khong Sao Bar, workers at Lavender purchased whitening creams not to look Western or European but to embody their social status as part of a rising privileged class. The whiter workers looked, the less rural they seemed, and they wanted to embody Asian wealth. Living in a country undergoing rapid economic restructuring, the workers were keenly observant of the changes taking place around them, and they wanted to capitalize on these changes to ride the wave of prosperity and economic progress. The purchase of skin creams allowed them to literally transform their bodies from those of poor country girls into those of modern women at the frontier of a globalizing economy, women whose livelihood was no longer tied to the land.

Women's bodies bore the signs of high-end modernity as they began to acquire a taste for designer clothing and handbags. Workers referred to these purchases as attempts to become modern women. In 2006, global luxury brands like Gucci and Louis Vuitton made their debut in the Vietnamese market. By 2010, Marc Jacobs, Chloé, Jimmy Choo, Burberry, and Versace, among many others, had also entered the market. Middle-range brands (like Gap, J. Crew, and H&M) that were popular elsewhere in the world were, however, not available in Vietnam. Thus, luxury brands became part of the local imaginary defining what it meant to be global and cosmopolitan. Clothing and fashion became important markers of women's access to modern goods. Although few women in this niche could afford real luxury items, many paid hefty prices for high-quality fakes from China and Hong Kong. These fake handbags ranged anywhere from one hundred to four hundred U.S. dollars. The replica market was a marker of status among workers, as Thao informed me: "The cheapest purses are the Louis Vuitton, Gucci, and Burberry purses. They are low-quality fakes. You can tell when you look at them from far away that they are not real. With the good fakes, you can put them right next to a real purse and you cannot tell the difference. They make high-quality Chanel and Versace purses. Those are 4 million to 8 million Vietnamese dong [two hundred to four hundred U.S. dollars]."

Sex workers' knowledge of luxury items and keen attention to detail signified their newly acquired taste for and access to brands that were well known around the world. The women coveted accessories such as replica designer handbags, belts, and shoes because these signified economic upward mobility, change, and progress. They allowed women to feel that they could take advantage of the new flows of global capital that had transformed the city landscape with high-rise buildings, luxury cars, and a new taste for leisure.

The main difference between women in Khong Sao Bar and Lavender was that women in Khong Sao Bar, which catered to wealthy Asian men and their business partners, compared themselves to women in other parts of Asia, while the women who worked in Lavender explicitly compared themselves to Viet Kieu women as well. In order to make themselves appealing to overseas Vietnamese men, sex workers in this niche market had to contrast their bodies to Western and Viet Kieu women's bodies by highlighting their feminine but modern embodiment.

Most women in Lavender had transformed their physical bodies by investing in their body capital through plastic surgery. Among the twenty-five women I studied in this niche, twenty-three had had nose jobs, ten had had double eyelid surgery, and four had breast implants. In my conversations with the women about their choices to alter their bodies, Phuong commented, "If you are a girl in Vietnam, people will judge you for your looks first. I fixed my nose [*xua mui*] in two parts. I got a nose bridge, and then I made my nostrils look smaller. After I had my nose done, I felt prettier. People noticed me more. When I walk around outside, I do not look like a normal Vietnamese girl. I want to look like the Girls' Generation [a group of Korean pop singers]." As with the women in Khong Sao Bar, workers at Lavender believed that noses differentiated rural women from modern urbanites. Sex workers associated flat noses and large nostrils with Third World rural poverty, whereas high nose bridges and smaller nostrils were markers of economic prosperity. Women wanted to look modern, and sex workers who had cosmetic surgery that looked "natural" were highly sought after by male clients.

Men rewarded these women with higher tips. For example, in a conversation I had with Chuyen, a Viet Kieu client from Denmark, I asked him what he thought about women with plastic surgery. He replied,

> I don't mind that they have had plastic surgery. If you look around the bar, all of the women have fake noses. All of them do. But they look good. They also wear a lot of makeup, and sometimes I joke with my friends that these women look very different during the day than what they look like in here with makeup on under these lights. It's all a show; none of it is real. That's part of the fun. . . . Look, times have changed in Vietnam. These girls aren't poor anymore. I mean, most of these girls own cell phones that cost over a thousand U.S. dollars. They have to hustle when they get here. No one wants to stand around cheap-looking village girls.

Like Chuyen, many Viet Kieus boasted of their ability to win over hostesses they perceived as highly sought after. Women who had had plastic surgery and could afford expensive phones were women who appealed to a large number of men. Clients invited women who looked like modern urbanites to sit with them at their tables and tipped well to compete with other men for their company.

Sex workers who catered to Viet Kieu men worked constantly to make themselves more desirable than Viet Kieu women. One important way in which they accomplished that task was by constantly comparing their bodies to those of global Viet Kieu and Western women. Almost any time a Viet Kieu woman entered the bar with a group of Viet Kieu men, the workers would comment to each other about how fat she was. For example, one evening, a group of Viet Kieu men brought three Viet Kieu women into the bar with them. The women all wore summer dresses with flip-flops, wore very little makeup, and had their hair pulled up in either a bun or a ponytail. It was clear that they had been walking around outside in the heat for some time before entering the bar. Hang went over to serve their drinks and then walked to the table where I was standing with Kevin, a thirty-two-year-old Viet Kieu from California, and said to the two of us, "Why did those guys bring those women in here? They look so messy, and they do not take care of themselves. Vietnamese women are meant to look small and slender; their frames are not built to carry around a lot of weight. Why do these women let themselves get too fat?"

Kevin turned to me and said, "I can't stand Viet Kieu women. They come to Vietnam and they think that they are so hot. Well, I've got news, bitches—you ain't got nothing on girls in Asia." I stood in silence because, as a Viet Kieu woman myself, I was slightly mortified. Kevin went on: "When you look at Viet Kieu women in Vietnam, it is like times have changed. It's all about Asia now. This is where the money is at; the economy is growing so fast here, and the women are so much hotter than the women back at home. It's like, why would I try to get one of those fat and ugly chicks when I can come here and take my pick of all these hot girls who actually know how to treat a man and act like a woman?"

Local sex workers who catered to Viet Kieu men altered their bodies and carefully managed their self-images to embody Vietnam's changing position in the global economy and its emergence as a modern nation. While this quote highlights the physical changes that women go through to alter their bodies, it also brings our attention to the *performances* of a particular femininity that is contextually and culturally specific. The vast majority of the men described these interactions as fake or unreal, yet most of them went along with it because they felt like they were around "familiar strangers" who spoke a similar language and shared similar cultural values. That familiarity, which was key to making the fantasy feel partly real, had a lot to do with the sex workers' ability to perform for Viet Kieu men a nostalgic femininity that represented nation-as-home.

Nostalgic Performances of Femininity

Although sex workers in this niche market performed acts of deference to clients that were similar to those used by women working in Khong Sao Bar, the logic of these performances was different. Sex workers' performances of femininity for Viet Kieu clients were almost always set in contrast to Viet Kieu women's inability or unwillingness to exalt men's masculinity. That is, rather than highlighting the unique qualities of a "traditional" village woman, the women in this niche played on Viet Kieu men's desires for a Vietnam the men had left behind, or a Vietnam of the past, thereby tapping into a different kind of money— nostalgic remittances that hinged on sex workers' ability to make themselves more desirable than Viet Kieu women by playing into Viet Kieu men's fantasies of feeling rooted in, tied to, or connected to Vietnam.

One night while I sat around an empty bar with a group of sex workers, we began talking about how women consciously play into men's nostalgic desires. I asked the other women, "How does it feel to always have to defer to the men when you serve them?" Chi replied, "If I were a Viet Kieu woman, I would never let my husband go back to Vietnam alone, because he will cheat. In Vietnam, there are so many women, so many beautiful women who all want to change their lives by making money. We all want it. So we spoil [*chieu*] Viet Kieu men. We give them whatever they want. We make them feel like kings in Vietnam because we know they cannot get that back at home. It sells." Minh-Thu added, "It is easy to get hurt in this business if you are not careful, because you give and give a lot of yourself because you have no choice." Diep said, "You have to spoil them, serve them, pretend like you do not know things, make them feel smart while trying not to sound too naive or stupid. It's a game. If you do not play by the rules, some other girl will come along and give him what he wants." Nga said, "In Vietnam, it's a man's world. We spoil them and give them everything. We fall in love, they cheat, and we hold it all inside." I was silent for several minutes, trying to take in everything that they were saying, when Chi turned to me and said,

> When you live in Vietnam for a long time, you too will learn that things here are never what they seem. You have to learn that Vietnamese women will always look good on the outside. We take care of our bodies with makeup,

clothes, and plastic surgery. It is all on the outside. But on the inside, we are going crazy. We look modern, but we are still living in Vietnam, so we cannot act like Viet Kieu or Western women, because men come to Vietnam to be around *Vietnamese* women. They are looking for the *old* Vietnam.

This conversation captured the tension that women experienced at a critical moment in Vietnam's transition. To make money, sex workers had to embody the new and modern, but at the same time, they realized that they had to play into Viet Kieu men's nostalgic desire to be around "traditional" Vietnamese women. To explain what they meant by *traditional*, Thuy-Tien told me, "A lot of men come in here and complain about Western women. They tell us that Western women forgot where they came from, and that they do not know their place in the house. Viet Kieu women hate us because we give men what they will not give them." Nga jumped in and said, "We are young and better looking too. Why do you think so many Viet Kieu men steal money from their wives back at home and give it to us?" I asked, "Why?" She said, "Because we make men feel like they are at home in Vietnam. . . . We root them here and help them feel connected to Vietnam." I asked, "How?" She said, "You have to learn how to flirt in Vietnamese. Viet Kieu men love that. It is deeper, more endearing; it is more passionate, bitter, and spicy [*dang cai*]."

I asked several Viet Kieu men what they thought about the type of flirting that took place inside bars like Lavender. Tony, a twenty-seven-year-old man, said to me, "It is cute. It is so cute. It kind of makes your heart melt a little bit, you know [*laughing as he places his hand over his heart*]. It is just one of those things that hits the spot." I probed a bit more and asked him what he meant, and he said, "It is just deeper, you know, or more meaningful. It's the language of the *motherland*. I know that the girls don't mean it, and they probably don't talk to their real boyfriends like this anymore. But it's a way of just showing care." I pushed a little harder and asked, "Care?" He said, "You know, that's the problem with Western women like you. You don't understand that there is a difference between showing care and being submissive. The women in here, they are not weak women; they will fight with you. But they know how to get their way while still making men feel like men."

As Tony described it, flirting allowed women to embody nation-as-home for a group of diasporic men looking to feel rooted in the motherland. Women's performances of femininity played into men's nostalgic sense of an old Vietnam, allowing men to hold on to vestiges of the past and import them into Vietnam's modernizing present. Male clients wanted to be around women whose bodies looked modern but who could engage in flirtatious deferential performances of femininity, thereby allowing them to assert their dominance in a modern patriarchal order.

Sex workers altered their bodies and presentations of self both to preserve a past where women deferred to men and to reveal Vietnam's future as a country on the move. Their ability to perform a nostalgic femininity allowed men to feel as though the global center was shifting away from the West and toward Asia, a place where modernization did not necessarily accompany shifting ideals related to gender equality. That men were invested in gendered *difference* was key to an effective masquerade that allowed workers to capitalize on men's nostalgic remittances.

THIRD WORLD DEPENDENCY IN SECRETS AND NAUGHTY GIRLS

Men come in here for Asian women who are, without exception, dark, sleek, well groomed, and dressed in a way that is sexy but not trashy. The girls from the village look clean and innocent. They are comfortable with the fact that they are not men. They don't have to establish their masculinity, or act like femaleness is a diseased condition. This place is an escape from American women. Asian gals will eat [American women] alive.

—Edward, fifty-nine-year-old man from the United States

Although the socioeconomic class of the clientele differed between Secrets and Naughty Girls, sex workers in both bars shared similar embodiments that dramatically distinguished them from women who catered to Viet Kieu men or local elite businessmen. These women altered their bodies to cater to their clients' implicit and sometimes explicit racial desires, resonant with what several other scholars have found among sex tourists in the Caribbean.[16] Unlike the workers in Khong Sao Bar and Lavender, the women who catered to Westerners were careful *not* to present themselves as pan-Asian modern subjects. Instead, they capitalized on their embodiment of Third World dependency.

Workers in Secrets and Naughty Girls made no effort to lighten their skin. In fact, the owners of both bars capitalized on women's darker complexions. When I asked the women why they preferred having darker complexions, Lilly, the owner of Secrets, told me, "Men like brown skin, Kim. They like it. I like it, too. Look better." Lilly indeed was darker than all the other women in the bar. She prided herself on her skin color, stating (in English), "Every afternoon around 2 P.M., I put on my bathing suit and I go lay on the hammock I tied up [on the roof], to make my skin more brown. People laugh. They say, 'Why you look so dark, Lilly?' But I say, 'Because I like it.'" Lilly and Tina, the owners of the expat and tourist bars, respectively, had by far the darkest complexions of all the women I studied.

While Lilly and Tina both embraced the tan aesthetic that they built their businesses on, several of the other women working in the bar had more ambivalent feelings about dark skin and used bronzers as part of a costume to play a role. Xuong, a twenty-six-year-old woman working in Naughty Girls, said to me, "The men here like darker skin and women who just came up from the village. The girls who just come up from the villages always get the most clients because they look the most innocent and fresh. Men like women with dark skin. They will always touch you and say, 'Wow, your skin is so dark and soft. . . .' But I like to have light skin, because when I go home to the village, I want to look like a city girl, not a poor village girl." Altering their skin color was the most notable strategy these women adopted to racialize their bodies in a way that would exaggerate their appearance as poor women in a Third World country. Dark skin provided a narrative of poor, rural labor that could hide women's experiences of factory work and service work in HCMC. For many of the workers, the dark complexion was a lotion that they could apply to their skin for work and wash off when going about their lives outside of sex work.

Women who catered to Westerners also applied their makeup differently than sex workers in other niches. Sex workers at Secrets and Naughty Girls were much more ostentatious with their eye makeup, working to produce a smoky-eye effect. This smoky eye highlighted their darker features, making them look more exotic and sexually appealing.

The women who worked for Western expatriates and backpackers did not make as much money as the women who catered to elite Vietnamese businessmen and Viet Kieus. Therefore, compared to women in the high-end niche markets, fewer women who catered to Westerners purchased plastic surgery. Those who did, opted for surgical procedures that differed from the types high-end women chose. Sex workers who catered to Western men generally chose to have breast implants or liposuction rather than nose jobs. Among the forty women I studied in the two bars catering to Westerners, roughly one-third had breast implants, while less than 20 percent had had nose jobs.

In my conversations with women who had had plastic surgery, I asked how they prioritized their procedures. Thao, a twenty-three-year-old worker, said to me, "I have a friend who got breast implants, and she knew a doctor who could give me surgery for cheap. I sold my motorbike to get the surgery because I know that men like bigger boobs. I thought that if I could get more clients, then I could make the money back to buy a newer motorbike. . . . They don't notice nose jobs. It does not make them [aroused]." For Thao, getting breasts implants was a strategic investment in her body capital to attract more clients. Breast implants, she believed, made her body not only aesthetically appealing but also sexually desirable. These technological changes had less to do with signifying Thao's upward mobility, modernization, or progress than with trying to appeal to her clients' sexualized desires.

One day, as I was chatting with Mai-Lan and Yen-Nhi in Secrets, I asked the women why they chose to have breast implants when nose jobs were cheaper. Yen-Nhi replied, "Some women get nose jobs because it makes their face look better . . . [or] to change their luck in life. But men always like boobs. . . . They like to run their fingers down our chest." I then asked, "Do you ever want to get a nose job, double eyelid surgery, or breast implants to look more Western?" Mai-Lan replied, "Western men come to Vietnam because they think Vietnamese women are beautiful, not because they want women who look Western. The girls who always get picked first in these bars are the ones who just came up from the village or who just started working." Yen-Nhi said, "None of those women had plastic surgery. Men want a Vietnamese girl. That is what they like." This conversation highlighted the racialized and sexualized desires of clients in Secrets. Both women believed that men would reward them if they could successfully pull off a dark aesthetic that conveyed rural authenticity.[17]

Mai-Lan and Yen-Nhi's perceptions of their clients' racialized desires were substantiated during my conversations with several expatriate Westerners. One evening, Alex, a thirty-nine-year-old ceramic exporter from France, said to me, "There are a few of us who have been in Vietnam for a couple of years now, and we all know the tricks these girls have up their sleeve. Stay away from city girls who know how to hustle. If you are an expat in Vietnam and you know better, then you go for the village girls, because they are the real deal. . . . They are the real Vietnam. . . . They are not greedy or chasing after this urban lifestyle of consuming new things." Expats like Alex wanted to be with recent migrants to the city because they felt that rural women provided them with an authentic experience of Vietnam. As the quote suggests, rather than acknowledging that the upwardly mobile urbanite is also authentically Vietnamese, Alex preferred women who represented his vision of a Vietnam where the majority of people were trapped in Third World poverty.

Although most sex workers in Secrets and Naughty Girls migrated to the city to experience upward mobility, they were strategic about when and how they displayed their access to foreign capital. All the women in both bars had two cell phones: the cheapest Nokia, worth twenty U.S. dollars, and another, more expensive phone. Several women had iPhones, which typically sold in the Vietnamese market for between two hundred and a thousand U.S. dollars, depending on the grade of the phone. They also purchased new dresses and urban clothing that they rarely wore to work. Women who worked in Secrets were required to wear uniforms, which were often sexier versions of the traditional Vietnamese *ao dai* (dress). This uniform allowed women to embody an ethnically authentic Vietnam. Naughty Girls did not require a uniform, but the women almost always wore jean shorts, tank tops, and plastic high heels to highlight their sexual appeal. Many of these women owned nicer clothing, but they chose to wear outfits that would convey to their clients both overt sexuality and their status as victims of Third World poverty. While their embodiments were similar, sex workers in Secrets and Naughty Girls engaged in different performances of femininity for expatriates living in Vietnam and budget travelers touring Vietnam.

Localizing Expats and Performing Third World Dependency

One key difference between Secrets and Naughty Girls was that the sex workers in Secrets played a critical role as cultural brokers for Western businessmen, while workers in Naughty Girls served primarily as tour guides for men looking for an "authentic" experience of Third World, rural Vietnam. In their attempts to succeed in Vietnam, Western businessmen often tried to gain local knowledge by learning the language and culture and by forming relationships with local women who made them feel desired. Through various efforts, the men in this niche constructed a distinctly racialized masculinity through their use of language with women in the bar.

When I first started working in the bar, I was surprised to find that my ability to speak English was useless because many of the clients preferred to speak Vietnamese. By speaking and flirting in Vietnamese, they had access to Vietnamese honorifics for asserting themselves as higher than women, referring to themselves as *anh* (higher) and to the women as *em* (lower) instead of using the English terms *you* and *me*, which do not denote status. They often flirted in Vietnamese, saying things to the women like: "Em khoe khong?" (How are you?) or "Hom nay em mac ao dep qua. Sexy lam!" (You are wearing a pretty dress. Very sexy!) The act of speaking Vietnamese allowed them to draw on local language tools to reinforce a subordinated Vietnamese femininity and prove their worth in the local economy by displaying knowledge of Vietnamese. Sex workers capitalized on these honorifics by carefully employing them in every encounter, allowing men to feel superior. Although the clients in Secrets knew I was an American, several men refused to speak English with me. The women in the bar commented that forcing me to speak Vietnamese enabled clients to put me in my place—that is, to reinforce a gender hierarchy. Thus, white businessmen drew on the Vietnamese language to assert a racialized masculinity as neocolonials and worldly cosmopolitans. Moreover, in venues like these, women served as cultural brokers for men. As Alex, the client from France, introduced earlier, explained to me, "We call them long-haired dictionaries. . . . All expats need one in order to localize."

In addition, the use of Vietnamese allowed Western men to adopt the local style of flirtation through indirect communication. These expats could then take pleasure in acting and consuming the "native" culture. The predictability of the scripts within the bar helped men feel connected to Vietnam as a place where they were beginning to plant new roots. As Timothy, a forty-seven-year-old expat who had been in and out of Vietnam during the preceding three years or more, explained, "My work requires me to travel a lot. I spend most of my time in Vietnam, but I am always in and out of the country. Sometimes you just want to go to that place[,] . . . that place where everyone knows your name[,] . . . where things are just predictable. . . . It helps to ease a lot of my [anxieties], because everyone who lives and works here knows how unpredictable everything else can be." Lilly, the owner of the bar, understood this full well and made it a point to teach the workers the importance of remembering the clients' names. She explained to me (in English), "This not a tourist bar, where men come for one drink and not come back. I want them to feel comfortable and come back. If we remember customer name, they feel closer to us."

In addition to helping expatriate men localize, sex workers in both Naughty Girls and Secrets engaged in performances of virtuous Third

World poverty. Through the English lessons that I provided at Naughty Girls three afternoons a week, I learned of women's strategies to perform Third World dependency. Many of the women were excited about the opportunity to work with someone who would help them translate the stories they used to elicit cash gifts from clients without judging them for duping the men. During the lessons, I helped women translate a series of stock emails, text messages, and phrases that they could use with their clients. I translated phrases into broken English like, "My motorbike broke down I have to walk to work. Can you help me buy new motorbike?" and "My father very sick and no one in my family help so I have to work. I am from An Giang village. You go to village before?"

During these lessons, I asked many of the women why they lied to their clients or why they were careful not to display too much wealth. Diem-Hang explicitly stated, "The men like to meet poor village girls. If you show them that you have nice clothes or new phones, they will start to lecture you about how you should save your money so that you can quit working. If you do not show them what you have, they will feel sorry for you, think that you are poor, and give you money." Even though the women were much more financially secure than family members who worked in the rice fields, in manufacturing industries, or even as service workers in HCMC, they could not display their new wealth to their clients. Many of the clients thought sex work was acceptable only if the women were flat broke and had no other options. To them, this was not a respectable profession if the women could afford to do something else. This was very different from the appreciation Vietnamese men have for the sex workers in Khong Sao Bar. In the high-end niche market, clients recognized that the women were skilled and therefore deserving of some degree of respect for their work attracting foreign capital into the country. In the niche market catering to Westerners, however, women proved their respectability by portraying Vietnam as an impoverished Third World nation, inferior to the wealthy West, and by presenting themselves as innocent victims of that poverty.

To portray an authentically Third World Vietnam, women did more than simply alter their bodies by choosing cheap or traditional clothing and darkening their skin and eyelids. They also used trips to villages in the Mekong Delta to provide clients with a visceral experience of Third World poverty and appeal to their generosity as relatively wealthy Westerners. On these trips, women would introduce men to their "families" to tie their own self-presentation to the poverty the men witnessed.

Often, however, these families were fake. Thuy-Linh explained, "I am going to Kien Giang tomorrow with one of the guys here because he wants to see my village. But most of my family lives in Saigon now. . . . I am taking him to stay with Vi's family so that he will think I am really poor and maybe give me money to rebuild the house or help my 'family' out." When the women in the bar first told me about their fake village families and the trips that they organized to take with their clients, I was struck by their awareness of their clients' desire to see Vietnam as a developing Third World country rather than as an emerging hotbed of global investment. These men wanted to visit villages where they could walk through rice fields, ride bicycles, and bargain in street markets. More often than not, sex workers were happy to play along with their clients' desires, because doing so enabled them to ask for larger sums of money. Like the women in Katherine Frank's study on strippers in the United States, the women in Naughty Girls and Secrets played on their clients' sympathy for the material inequalities and constraints that might shape a woman's decision to engage in sex work.[18]

Upon their return from these trips to the Mekong Delta, many of the clients explained that they were moved to altruism by the impoverished conditions they had seen. For example, after spending three days in a village with Nhi's family, John, a man in his late fifties or early sixties, commented, "There are so many things that we in the West take for granted. Roofs over our heads, hot water, shoes. . . . When I was with Nhi, I had to shower with buckets of cold water. It was so disgusting because I was brushing my teeth and I didn't realize that the bucket had a bunch of maggots in there. I felt these tiny worms swimming around in my mouth that I had to spit it out." It is important to note that the women did not buy into the story of Vietnam's inferiority; instead, they capitalized on their clients' desire, in this case by deliberately placing buckets with maggots in the outdoor shower. Such visceral experiences of poverty allowed workers to ask their clients for a large sum of money. Indeed, John sympathized with Nhi's poverty so much that he gave her family U.S.$500 to install a new shower.

Regardless of whether they were real or staged, these visits to the village allowed workers to capitalize on Vietnam's shifting position in the global economy. Men provided women with both large and small amounts of money, or what I call benevolent remittances, to help them find a morally respectable trade, escape poverty, and transition their standard of living from basic to comfortable. Consequently, even though sex work allowed some women to purchase nicer clothing and expensive cellular phones, they had to hide their wealth and perform poverty because those items symbolized access to global capital, mobility, status, and most important, dignity in their work.

The complexity of Vietnam's contemporary political economy maps onto sex workers' competing technologies of embodiment and performances of femininity. The sex industry shapes and is shaped by broader economic forces, such as rapid local development, the global growth of "frontier markets" seeking to be the next major economic players, and the emergence of a homegrown superelite that remains plugged into the international political economy. In Vietnam, the changing source of FDI capital, from the West to Asian markets, translates into a new group of Vietnamese sex workers, who satisfy the needs of their Asian clientele to help augment the increasing status of the region.

The growth of competing embodied ideals fueled new configurations of modernity, wherein sex workers in Vietnam did not embrace Western standards of beauty. Instead, they worked to emulate women in more developed Asian countries, emphasizing Vietnam's regional position in relation to Hong Kong, Korea, and Japan. In Khong Sao Bar and Lavender, sex workers and clients worked together to signify a new embodied ideal of pan-Asian modernity and nostalgic cosmopolitanism that hinged on regional and non-Western standards of beauty. Indeed, wealthy local Vietnamese men who entertained their Asian business partners used women's bodies to illustrate their nation's modernization.

Sex workers who catered to Western men consciously embodied Third World dependency, playing on their clients' racialized desires and imaginations of Vietnam as a poverty-stricken country. These women were conscious of globalized racial discourses and strategically consumed and reproduced representations of Vietnamese women as the needy, exotic other. Although most Western men acknowledged Vietnam's rapid economic development, many sought what they called the "authentic" Vietnam, which was untouched by processes of globalization. They imagined the "real" Vietnam as poor, rural villages situated among verdant rice paddies and sought out memorable experiences of Third World poverty.

Sex workers' competing technologies of embodiment come to represent the changing dynamics of race/nation and the increasing recognition of previously marginalized countries in the global arena as a result of globalization. Sex workers' bodies in Khong Sao Bar and Lavender were molded by technologies that reflected Vietnam's striving to emerge as another "rising tiger." However, not all women could secure a foothold in the rapidly developing sectors of the economy, and some women turned to other niche markets and other technologies of embodiment in order to appeal to Western men's desires for Third World dependency. Regardless, women across all niches of sex work altered their bodies to fit clients' particular racialized and classed desires, and their divergent technologies of embodiment reflected tensions within Vietnam's gendered landscape. These competing technologies of embodiment and competing performances of femininity allowed workers in the different niche markets to capitalize on their clients' different ties to global capital.

Workers in Khong Sao Bar who helped project confidence in the Vietnamese market through South-to-South FDI projects were able to capitalize on Asian-based capital investments. Workers in all other bars sought overseas remittances—a different kind of market money that took on different meanings for workers drawing on Viet Kieu men's nostalgia or Western men's benevolence. Importantly, even as some sex workers relied on performances of dependency to tap into remittances from Western men, Vietnam's dependency on Western capital was fading. Therefore, in the historical moment of my research, Vietnam was in the process of rejecting a past of colonial dependency and embracing a vision of the future in which East Asia is the new financial center of global capitalism. In light of these changes in the global imaginary, women across all niches of sex work altered their bodies to fit the varied desires of men with access to foreign capital because, after all, that's what sells.

7

Sex Workers' Economic Trajectories

One evening, Nga, a twenty-year-old hostess, brought her nineteen-year-old friend Yen-Nhi to Khong Sao Bar to help Yen-Nhi find work. Hanh, the head mommy, carefully looked Yen-Nhi over before asking, "Where do you live?" Yen-Nhi replied, "I just came up from Chau Doc [a village four hours from Ho Chi Minh City] a few days ago. I am staying at Nga's house to see if I can find work in the city. If it works out [*nieu hop*], then I will stay. If not, I will return to the village." Hanh replied, "You can try it for a few days and see if this bar is the right fit for you. Some people are lucky in here, and some people are a better match in a different bar." Yen-Nhi shyly bowed her head and thanked Hanh. Then Nga grabbed Yen-Nhi's arm and led her to the back room to get dressed. An hour later, the three of us were riding in the backseat of a black Mercedes S-Class sedan on our way to a private party. When we arrived, Yen-Nhi fumbled with the door handle as she struggled to open it, commenting under her breath that this was her first time riding in a private car.

For many of the women in this study, sex work was an opportunity to move into new social spaces. It was not uncommon to see women like Yen-Nhi go from the back of a motorbike to a Mercedes in the same day. Yet most of what we know about sex workers revolves around their day-to-day interactions with clients; few ethnographers tell a story of how women's lives are transformed through sex work or how their trajectories of mobility may vary according to the particular niche market they occupy in a segmented industry.

In times of rapid economic change, individuals and groups may experience accelerated opportunities for mobility, moving upward or downward in status or class position in what sociologist Pierre Bourdieu calls "the trajectory effect, which allows for individual and collective class mobility."[1] Sex workers across the four bars experienced two different trajectories of social mobility in the context of Vietnam's rapidly changing economy: rapidly oscillating upward and downward mobility; and steady upward mobility.

Sex workers who catered to wealthy local Vietnamese men and Viet Kieu men experienced volatile economic mobility. Like Yen-Nhi, these women often went from poor rural areas to spaces that housed some of HCMC's most exclusive elites indulging in conspicuous consumption. Their trajectories contrasted with the slow and steady upward mobility characteristic of sex workers serving Western clients, who imposed paternalistic Western values concerning money, which involved saving money and delaying gratification.

Related to the issue of mobility is the theme of convertibility: workers converted the money they earned in the city to social status and respectability in their home villages.[2] During return trips to their villages, sex workers in all niches of HCMC's sex industry destigmatized sex work through outward modes of consumption and gift giving. They capitalized on new market conditions by creatively converting their access to global and local currencies into social status, and they drew heavily on their access to cash and gifts to alter family members', friends', and villagers' perceptions of sex work. In the face of rapid economic restructuring, cities like HCMC become critical sites where the First World and Third World collide, and where women in multiple niche markets straddle the boundary between First World wealth and Third World poverty.

NEW TRAJECTORIES OF UPWARD MOBILITY IN HCMC'S GLOBAL SEX INDUSTRY

From a Motorbike to a Mercedes and Back: Rapid Upward and Downward Mobility

Workers in Khong Sao Bar and Lavender often straddled First World luxury and Third World poverty as they developed new strategies for mobility. The large amount of money flowing through the high-end niches created a situation in which women quickly gained access to large sums of cash. These sums were known locally as hot money (*tien nong*), the kind of money made in the illicit economy that flows out or gets spent as quickly as it comes in. Workers who generated money through sex work could not predict how much money they would generate or how quickly that money might come in. Often the money would flow out through unexpected expenses related to a sudden illness or death or a family member's sudden loss of income.[3]

Of the fifty women I studied in the two high-end niche markets, none had more than a high school education and most came from poor rural and urban families. Of the twenty-five women working in Khong Sao Bar, seventeen came straight from a nearby village into sex work, while only eight came from poor urban families. Those who came to the city directly from the village went straight into sex work with the help of their social networks and the mommies who had come to their villages to seek out beautiful women. As Hanh explained to me, "It is better for me to bring in young, very pretty girls from the village, because they have the look that my clients like. They look more innocent and pure. The men are rich and powerful, and sometimes they need to have a place where they can go to relax and have fun without people knowing who they are. Village girls do not know anything about the men, except that they are rich, and the men like to keep it like that."

The clients' desire for anonymity and privacy led the bar to hire workers from poor rural backgrounds strictly on the basis of their looks. Many of the women entered the bar through an introduction by a friend or through direct contact in the village with one of the mommies. During my months working as a hostess in each of the bars, I watched three workers enter the bar and transform in a matter of weeks. As the new women worked to adapt to the bar, I was able to collect stories about the other women's trajectories of mobility as they reflected on their own transformations. For example, Nhi, a twenty-four-year-old hostess who returned to Khong Sao Bar after being away for several months, described her experiences with rapid upward and downward mobility, saying,

> Seven months ago, when I first came to work in the city, I was a different person. I was young and shy, but I knew that I was beautiful because men used to beg me to come in to their tables. So I was stuck-up [*chanh*]. I would run around from table to table. I remember holding the first one million dong [fifty U.S. dollars] in my hands thinking that I had never held this much money in my hands before. I made that in the first hour of work on just tips.

The clients loved me. I got an iPhone, money for new clothes, and someone paid for me to get my nose fixed. I went from riding around on a motorbike to riding in nice cars. They spoiled me.

Then, I fell in love with this [local Vietnamese] man, and I thought he loved me. He [set me up] in one of his condos and told me that he wanted me to quit. He told me that he would give me two thousand U.S. dollars a month and a free house if I quit working. Everyone told me not to listen to him, but I was stuck-up and I thought I was better than even the mommies. After two months he found a new girl to play with, and he got bored with me. She took over the apartment and I had to move out. I had nothing; my hands were empty [*hai ban tay trang*]. I got on a motorbike taxi for the first time in three months, and I just cried because I felt like a princess who lost her riches. So here I am, back for a job. No one says anything to me, because they all know; but I feel ashamed. It is a lot harder to get back in on tables again. I have to work to build up my network of clients again.

Tears dripped down Nhi's face as she spoke of her humiliation. Though the other women tried to console her and help her get in on tables by introducing her to new clients, I watched as she fumbled to make the most of what she had. When I asked her why she decided to come back to sex work, she said to me, "I got used to the high life and to always having money in my pockets. If I quit, I will have to go back to the village, get married, and settle down. I want to try one more time and, this time, be smarter with the money I make."

Nhi's trajectory is a characteristic story of rapid upward and downward mobility after stepping into sex work in Khong Sao Bar. As young women from the village entered the hostess bar, their tastes began to change and so did their consumption patterns. As I discussed in chapter 6, women who catered to wealthy local Vietnamese men acquired a taste for global luxury items, tailored clothing, and plastic surgery. These new consumption patterns were possible only because women had access to so much more expendable income than they had had before entering sex work. Hanh, the head mommy, tried her best to teach them how to manage their money, save, and invest in small businesses back in their hometowns to protect them from hard falls like Nhi's. Vy, a twenty-three-year-old worker, said to me,

I wish that I were as lucky as Hanh. She makes a lot of money and has different businesses. I try to save money, but it is hard because now I am taking care of too many people. I am paying for my older brother's college and my older sister to go to beauty school. I send money to my parents. When I get depressed about money, I spend it on clothes because I need something to relieve the pressure that I have. I know that I am getting too old to work here, and I will have nothing to show for it if my siblings do not take care of me later. Life is strange; when you have money you have a lot of it, but when you are poor, you are so poor you cannot even eat.

The precariousness of Vy and Nhi's economic status was common in the niche market that catered to local Vietnamese and other Asian businessmen. Women entered the bar and maintained their status because of their novelty value; over the years, they had to invest in plastic surgery to give their clients something new to look at. However, this lifestyle was never easy to maintain, because the more money they made, the more pressure they felt to invest in their bodily capital to stay in the game. And ultimately, most hostesses experience downward mobility as they age out of the sex industry, unless they carefully plan their exit by saving enough money to invest in another business.

One evening, I went with a group of sex workers from Khong Sao Bar to have dinner with a group of clients in an upscale Vietnamese restaurant. The clients shut down the restaurant for the night so they could enjoy both exclusive service and privacy in the restaurant. While the newer workers at the table fumbled with the silverware and the food, the more experienced sex workers comfortably ordered the restaurant workers around. After dinner, we all made our way back to the bar, where the workers spent the rest of the evening drinking, dancing, and singing karaoke. At the end of the night, some of the more experienced workers instructed the newer women on the importance of learning how to comfortably navigate high-end spaces of fine dining. Ngoc-Anh, a twenty-three-year-old worker, explained to Thao, an eighteen-year-old worker, "Restaurants like that are uncomfortable when you first go to them, but over time you will learn how to ask for things just like the rest of us. . . . You will learn to enjoy good food and nice restaurants because the experience is different from [what happens] inside the bars."

Thao's discomfort during her first night in a restaurant highlights the displacement that new workers experienced every day as they learned to navigate new spaces of luxury, where the rules, norms, and rituals of interaction varied greatly from those in their home villages. Most of the new workers were careful to quietly observe more experienced women and men before stepping out on their own into those social spaces.

Like the women in Khong Sao Bar, workers who catered to Viet Kieu men in Lavender experienced rapid upward and downward mobility, although in a different way. Nearly all the women who worked in Lavender came from poor urban backgrounds or had migrated to the city and spent at least two years in the service sector or manufacturing occupations before entering sex work. Most of them told me that sex work was the only work they thought could bring them real economic mobility. Kieu said to me,

> My first job in Saigon was when I was sixteen. I worked in the kitchen of a restaurant cooking. Then, a year later, I worked as a receptionist at a hotel [making U.S.$150 per month]. But over the years, the price of food and gas has gone up. Everything is so expensive, and I was barely surviving, always borrowing money from friends. I kept seeing these girls come into the hotel with Viet Kieu men. At first I looked down on them, but later I saw them walking in with nicer things, [and] I got jealous. So I started working. When I realized that I could make more money having sex with one man than I could make in a whole month at the hotel, I decided that I had to close my eyes and jump [into the sex industry]. I was scared, but I knew that it was the only way I could turn my life around.

The conditions of Kieu's life before she undertook sex work propelled her into life as a bartender in a bar that catered to Viet Kieu men. Through the network of sex workers who floated in and out of the hotel at night, she learned which bars Viet Kieu men spent time in, and she went in one to ask for a job. The mommy told her that she could try it for a week to see if it was the right fit. When I asked her to describe her life since beginning work in the bar, she said to me,

> Sometimes I wish that I never stepped into this bar. My life goes up and down, up and down. I just crave stability. Some months, I make a lot of money; and some months, I am broke. It is all up to fate [*Cai gi cung cua troi cho thoi*]. With Viet Kieu men, sometimes you are lucky and you meet someone who treats you well; and then some months, you can't make any money. This one guy bought me a new motorbike and gave me a lot of money, but then when he went back to the U.S., I never heard from him again. I had to go back to the bar and start over. . . . It is hard because every time I go back to the bar, I feel nervous because I do not know who I will meet or who will fall for me. . . . One minute I am staying in a nice hotel, another minute I am in a dirty hotel. It is day by day [*Ngay nao hay ngay do*].

Because of the instability of their income, women who catered to Viet Kieu men often moved between First World luxury and Third World poverty. When they were lucky enough to have a client, they could indulge in luxurious hotels, fancy motorbikes, nice dinners, and shopping sprees. Although all these women aspired to be like the mommies who had found ways to generate a stable income through multiple investments, very few had saved any money. Of the fifty women who catered to wealthy local Vietnamese men, Asian businessmen, and Viet Kieu men, only four had saved enough money to open a small business.

The other women tried, but in times of hardship they had to go through their savings to support themselves and their families. I witnessed several women enter and exit the bar during the short two-to-three-month periods in which I was employed in each of these bars. Workers who returned to the bar after a period of not working had to get to know a whole new set of coworkers and clients.

The novelty of the clients created a structure in which workers experienced periods of great economic success and periods of failure. Having experienced rapid upward and downward economic and social mobility, moving from poor rural and urban spaces to high-end spaces where they lived in luxury apartments and acquired distinctive tastes for luxury goods, these women had to learn to feel comfortable in both spaces and social circles. Some sex workers had been in the industry long enough that they learned to anticipate the trials and triumphs. Their movement between elite and common social spaces felt most poignant to me when the women sat out on the streets eating late-night bowls of *pho* and *hu tieu* (noodles) for fifty cents after dancing in a club where the clients had spent an exorbitant amount of money on alcohol and food for the night.

From the Factory to the Bar: Slow Trajectories of Steady Upward Mobility

Sex workers who catered to Western men in Secrets and Naughty Girls experienced gradual upward mobility. They did not rise and fall as rapidly as the women who worked in Khong Sao Bar and Lavender. Roughly two-thirds of the women in both Secrets and Naughty Girls had had jobs in the manufacturing or service sectors before entering sex work. The other third of the women had not worked at all. Those women began working in the bar after seeing a friend or family member's success in this line of employment.

It was common for workers to experience rapid upward mobility during the first month of work in a bar. However, soon after their initiation they began to anticipate a steadier flow of money. For example, in a conversation with three women working in Secrets, I asked why they chose to enter the bar scene. Tam, a twenty-four-year-old sex worker who first moved to HCMC at the age of thirteen to work as a private maid, said,

> I worked as a maid for three years, and then, after the kids [in the house she worked for] grew up, they did not need me anymore, so they helped me find

work in a factory. . . . I worked in a clothing factory every day for almost twelve hours a day. It was tiring, and I did not make any money. When I worked as a maid, I did not have to pay rent, and I could send 1.5 million dong [seventy-five U.S. dollars] home each month to my parents. In the factory, I made 1.6 million dong [eighty U.S. dollars] a month, but I also had to pay for rent and buy food. I could not send as much home. I would go home crying every night because I was getting paid so little. In Vietnam, most people who are poor just accept that they are poor; but when I came to Saigon, I had dreams of making more money and living a more comfortable life. I decided to take a risk and work in a bar. I make the same money sleeping with two men that I did in a whole month in the factory, and I do not have to work long hours sitting in one place.

Like most of the women I studied in the expat and backpacker bars, Tam decided to enter into sex work not only because she thought she could make more money but also because sex work offered better working conditions. In my conversations with women who went from factories to sex work, nearly all of them spoke of themselves as strong, independent, and willing to take risks. Van, for example, said to me,

People look at the work that I do and think I am stupid because I am selling my body. They think I am uneducated or I am addicted to drugs. But the stupid people are the people who work in the factories every single day making barely enough to survive. They do not even think they are making someone else rich. They will never turn their lives around. . . . The smart ones are the ones who are bold enough to step out of the factory and onto the streets. Those are the ones who are sharp. At least in this job, I can have some hope that my life will change. Some hope, to me, is better than no hope.

In that same conversation, Chau, a twenty-one-year-old woman from the village of Chau Doc, added,

In [sex work], it is all about luck. If you get lucky and meet the right person, then your life can change. The gods give some people the chance to change their lives. I have a friend who married a white guy, and she just stays at home with the kids. She does not have to work. Her life is easy [*Cuoc doi suong lam*]. Not everyone will be lucky enough to have that life, but here the girls who are willing to roll out on the street and take risks have a chance to transform their lives, [whereas] in the factory there is no chance.

The women who left manufacturing and service-sector occupations for sex work experienced upward mobility only if they could procure clients for sex in the bars. As many of them stated, sex work provided them with the space to "hope" and "dream" about a better life. Those who were able to make it out of the factory and into sex work experienced rapid upward mobility during the first month, and after that they earned a steady income that came directly from providing sexual services. While many of these workers certainly earned more money, their patterns of social mobility did not resemble those of women who catered to local Vietnamese men and Viet Kieu men. As I discussed in chapter 6, workers who catered to Western men did not have to alter their bodies or consumption patterns to embody their wealth, and instead they worked to look like Third World subjects. Thao, a twenty-six-year-old worker, explained to me, "I do not buy fancy clothes to wear at work. The men who come here need to think that sex workers are poor so that they will help us. If they think we have money, why would they give money to us?"

Because they dressed to display a sexualized form of poverty while at work, the sex workers in these niche markets did not spend nearly as much money on new designer handbags, tailor-made dresses, or plastic surgery as women in the higher-paying sectors. Sex workers who catered to white men indeed experienced dramatic changes in their lifestyles in terms of their changing tastes in consumption, modes of transportation, or living arrangements. But they did not move in and out of high-end spaces as often as women who catered to men in higher-tiered bars. In times when their money from clients did not flow as generously, they did not have to make significant changes to their lifestyles.

Male clients played a crucial role in easing these women into slow but steady upward mobility. Clients tried to teach workers how to manage their money by commenting on appropriate spending and explaining strategies to create savings. One night in Secrets, I listened as Kevin, a forty-seven-year-old man from Virginia, lectured Thoa, a twenty-five-year-old woman, in broken Vietnamese: "I do not understand people in Vietnam sometimes. How much was this cell phone? You buy expensive phone but you no save money for emergency. Why you need fancy phone? I buy cheap phone [*pointing to his basic Nokia phone*], same, same." He then turned to me and said in English, "Everyone in this country is poor, but they all have a cell phone because they do not know how to save their money." He continued: "They just live for the day and spend, spend, spend." While local Vietnamese and Viet Kieu men engaged in various forms of conspicuous consumption and encouraged workers to do the same to embody pan-Asian modernity, Western men like Kevin were often critical of women's consumption patterns. These men critiqued the effects of globalization, noting that it had created an ethos that prompted people in developing countries like Vietnam to purchase luxuries before necessities.

By 2010, many of the expatriate men who returned to Vietnam frequently on business were well aware of the ways in which women performed Third World dependency. And while they still gave the women money, they monitored their expenditures. David, a thirty-eight-year-old man from France, explained to me why he carefully monitored the construction on his girlfriend's family home in the village: "Any smart donor knows that you cannot just give money freely. You need to see a plan and be part of the whole process. I want to be part of every step, so I will pay as construction is taking place. Otherwise, she [his girlfriend] will run off and do God knows what with the money."

Expatriate clients went to great lengths to manage the money they spent on their girlfriends. One client said to me, "The market is different in the East than in the West. There is no set price for anything; you have to bargain for everything. So, sometimes, women will tell you that it costs four thousand U.S. dollars to expand the house, when it only costs two thousand. They eat up the other two thousand. So I make sure to ask around about the cost before giving them any money. The worst money spent is wasted money." The methods men used to ensure that the money they provided was used for basic necessities rather than conspicuous consumption led workers to experience slow and gradual pathways to upward mobility. Sex workers often had to prove to their clients that the large sums of money they asked for to remodel a village home or care for an ailing parent were actually spent on those needs. As a result, women earmarked their money for different purposes.[4] Sex workers often considered the money they earned from brief and casual encounters as their own, and they would use this money to pay for their living expenses and luxury goods and to help their parents. However, they often had to report to their clients about how they used the large sums of money they received, so they set that money aside for specific purposes.

When women asked their clients-turned-boyfriends for financial assistance to start a business, they also had to accept the men's input and advice on budgeting and investing properly. These lectures were filled with messages of delayed gratification. I sat with women on several nights as they sketched their budgets on bar receipts or napkins. They thought about opening small cafes, after-hours food stalls, spas, beauty salons, restaurants, clothing shops, and bars. While nearly all the women had dreams of opening their own businesses, very few acquired the capital necessary to get their businesses going. During the time I spent in Secrets, Thao was the only woman able to do so: she gathered from a boyfriend the U.S.$10,000 she needed in order to become an active partner, and take an equity stake, in one-third of a small bar. Her boyfriend, Steven, a fifty-eight-year-old expatriate from Australia, told me,

> I am always wary of partnerships in countries like Vietnam, because someone can take your money and run [away] with it. But I see this as an investment so that she can learn the business rather than jumping the gun and doing something on her own. I did not want her to be a sole owner, because I worried that she would not know how to manage a large amount of money. So far, the business has been under, but I am hoping it will pick up in the next few months. . . . At least she is working toward something long-term instead of trying to get it from sex.

Steven regarded the money he spent helping his girlfriend buy into a bar as honest money with long-term benefits. However, he also worried that if Thao succeeded financially, she would become too independent and leave him. Two months after Thao's bar opened, when I came by with Lilly to show support for her business, Steven said to me, "I do not want her to make too much money." When I asked why, he said, "Because she will become like Lilly over here. . . . She will have so much money and won't need me." Steven provided his girlfriend with a way of generating income that allowed her to think about a long-term future where she would not need sex with clients to earn money. However, by limiting her to merely partnership in the bar, rather than sole ownership, Steven also regulated the amount of money Thao would earn. As a result, she experienced a steady trajectory of upward mobility rather than the rapid trajectory that might have been possible had she been sole owner of a bar. The carefully monitored exchanges of money and intimacy in this kind of relationship effectively transformed sex workers into docile subjects who aligned with the Western value of frugality.

Although clients tried to manage sex workers' money, the workers still found ways to maintain cash stashes for special uses or emergencies. Rather than creating fictive crises, they offered to run errands for men like helping them purchase airfare, hotel rooms, or bus tickets through a travel agent, so that they could add to the cost and have some money to spare. The amount of money that women generated in this way was generally not enough to create a large spike in their income. While most women occasionally bought expensive cellular phones, jewelry, or new clothing, their tastes stayed relatively constant compared to those of women in the higher-tiered niches. Male clients often lectured workers on how to "save their money" with the hope of teaching them the value of hard work and delayed gratification. In this era of upward mobility through entrepreneurship, these women served as small "development" projects for men looking to invest in the workers' futures. Rather than freely giving women money, the men acted as microlenders, financing small businesses. As a result of these factors, most women who worked in bars catering to Western men did not experience the rapid, volatile mobility of the other niches but instead had slower, steadier trajectories toward upward mobility.

CONVERTIBILITY: FROM THE CITY TO THE VILLAGE

At the end of my time in each bar, I accompanied a group of workers on a trip to their hometown to meet their parents and siblings and see what their lives had been like when they were growing up. These four trips, with women from the four different bars, were also going-away presents and gestures of farewell from them to me, marking the end of my time of getting to know the women and becoming friends with them. At first, I did not think of these trips as fieldwork; I saw them as vacations away from the city, during which I could get away from my work, ride my bike through rice paddies, and stay up late in the company of friends without having to perform any emotional labor. However, after all four trips to the different villages, I began to notice that issues of convertibility were salient for women across all niches.

Scholars have long documented the multiple ways in which global men convert their First World citizenship and Western dollars into social status across transnational social fields.[5] Global men who come to Vietnam alter their consumption patterns for a short while to earn the social respect and dignity that they struggle to obtain in their home countries. During my trips to the villages, I noticed that sex workers engaged in similar forms of conversion as they moved between rural and urban spaces. Scholars have not yet theorized this practice of domestic convertibility across urban spaces and rural villages. By working in the sex industry, some women had access to global capital that flowed through the hands of overseas men, and others to global capital that passed through the hands of wealthy local men. Regardless of the ways in which women accessed global capital, and regardless of their patterns of consumption while living in HCMC, all the workers in my study converted their urban dollars into social status in the villages.

This became clear to me while preparing for a trip to the village of Tay Ninh near the Cambodian border. Lilly, the owner of Secrets, told the women from her village that she was going to hire a private van, and anyone who wanted to accompany her was welcome. Seven of the women from the bar asked to come along, and she gladly accepted them all. A few days before leaving, the women dragged me out at 7 A.M. to go shopping so they could purchase an array of gifts for their family members. I watched as they carefully negotiated for electronic items, including a television, a refrigerator, a karaoke machine, a rice cooker, and several small kitchen appliances. We also shopped for clothes for the young children back in the village, makeup for the adult women, and liquor for the men. I was amazed at how full the van was after we packed in all these items. During the eight-hour van ride, Tam, a twenty-three-year-old woman, received a call in which her sister told her that their mother had invited several people in the neighborhood over for dinner to celebrate Tam's homecoming. Disappointingly, several people had declined the invitation, saying that her mother was a disgrace for allowing her daughter to sell her body. One neighbor even said, "It is bad karma to be around dirty money." Tam began sobbing, and everyone in the van tried to console her. Then Lilly turned to everyone and said, "Who cares about those people and what they think? They do not know anything. They are the same stupid people whose lives will never change, because they are not savvy enough to get out there and try something different. You just have to work hard and be successful. Let them talk, who cares? Because money talks. When we get to the village with all these gifts, people will shut up. People are scared of money; and when you have it, they will defer to you. Watch and learn."

The other women chimed in, reminding Tam that women who worked in the sex industry built the largest and most modern homes in the villages. People never look at those houses with shame, because, as Lilly said, money talks. The notion that "money talks" struck me as I realized that workers spent a great deal of their earnings, and some even went into debt, to bring modern commodities to their villages. However, the act of gift giving was not merely about providing their family members with basic necessities. Workers also gave gifts to manage the stigma attached to their work. In effect, like the Viet Kieu men I discussed in chapter 3, they converted their access to global capital to achieve a sense of dignity and status in their villages.

As the van pulled into in the village at 11 P.M., I woke up and looked outside the window to see dozens of people awaiting the women's arrival. They helped unload the van, and we went inside to eat chicken and rice porridge. I watched as family members gushed over the new electronics while neighbors looked on shyly but with envy. Three of the returning women were cousins and the other four were friends from the same area, so all their families congregated in the same house for the evening. Two men set up a karaoke system, and people began to sing so loudly that their voices echoed down the street. The young children ran in and out, modeling their new clothes. Lilly brought out three bottles of Johnnie Walker Black Label and sat drinking with the men. Typically in the village, the women cooked and ate in the kitchen area while the men sat out front, eating and drinking with each other. However, on this night, the visiting sex workers were all invited to sit, eat, and drink with the men. Lilly, Ai, Diep, Binh, and I sat with the men while Tam, Chau, and Tuyen moved back and forth between the kitchen, where their family members were preparing food, and the front table, where the men sat, sang, drank, and ate together.

After awhile, Chu Manh, the father of one of the girls, began tearing up and drunkenly said to me, "This household would be nothing without the women and their sacrifices." We all grew silent as Lilly tried to turn the seriousness of the conversation into a joke by saying, "Why? Because you would starve to death?" We all laughed, and then Chu Manh said what I heard many times on my visits to other villages as well: "People used to think that girls were worthless because after they grew up, they would marry into someone else's family. Today girls are gold, because they sacrifice everything to take care of their families." Lilly again joked, saying, "Hold your tongue until after we are married." We laughed and continued drinking until everyone grew tired and went to bed.

The next morning at eight, Tam woke me up and asked if I would like to go with them to the market, because that was where the whole village gathered in the morning. I watched as the women put on their newest clothing, items that they had purchased in the city but saved for a special occasion. Then we climbed on motorbikes to head into the market. The women walked among the stalls with pride, purchasing food, snacks, and goodies without even bargaining for the right price. Lilly commented out loud, "Everything is so cheap here compared to Saigon," as she pulled a wad of cash from her pocket for everyone to see. People stared at us as we walked through the market; some of them snickered behind our backs, while others nicely asked how long we would be in town. I turned to Lilly and asked her, "Do you ever worry that someone will rob you when they see how much money you carry around?" She said, "Some of these people made Tam cry yesterday in the van. Money talks. You'll see; they will not say anything." I smiled at her, and she went on: "I have been doing this since I was thirteen. I have been through a lot, and I have to protect the girls who work for me." As we walked around, Lilly was obviously the center of attention. Several people complimented her beauty, while others brought their daughters to ask if she would be willing to hire them to work in her "restaurant." Her acts of kindness to other sex workers in public spaces both demonstrated to the people in the village that Lilly was a good person and provided her with a defense against the stigma of her work.

Later that evening, the women hosted a large party, inviting people from all around to come join in the festivities. They prepared duck, chicken, fish, and an assortment of wrapped foods steamed in banana leaves. The women came out in their nicest dresses and invited a local photographer to take their pictures. Again we sang karaoke, drank, and ate until about 2 A.M. When the sun rose, I went for a morning bike ride with Lilly, and we talked about how she used to feel bad about her mother's reputation for being a prostitute during the Vietnam War. She said,

> No one would marry my mother, because they all knew she was a prostitute for the Americans. People were afraid of being associated with anything American when the communists took over. So my mother married a Cambodian man, and my sister and I came out with dark skin. People used to make fun of how dark and skinny I was. . . . I was embarrassed to wear skirts because I hated how small my legs were. . . . [But] my dark skin has made me successful. I started out as a sex worker, and now I own four businesses. No one can talk down to me or my family. . . . I want the girls who work for me to feel good about what they are doing, because we all drag our legs out to work, hoping that we might get lucky.

I asked Lilly, "What about the ones who are unlucky? What about the ones who do not make a lot of money spreading their legs or finding a boyfriend to build them a mansion?" She said, "They come back to the village, get married, and settle down, or they stay in the city and work doing something else." I said to her, "It must be hard to come back if you have not made it." She said, "That is the risk you take. Either you are lucky or you are unlucky. That is for the gods to decide."

Workers across all niches of the sex industry turned to their villages as places where they could find a sense of dignity and respect, not through their occupation, but through the global capital they could spend and display. Most were not as fortunate as Lilly, but they contributed a significant amount of money to their families by supporting their parents and paying for their siblings' education. Workers built status and respect through the public displays of wealth on their bodies and in the gifts they brought home, which also enabled them to build social debt. They were, in effect, converting their urban status to honor and respect in their rural villages despite their stigmatized occupation.

Like the workers in Secrets and Naughty Girls, the workers in Khong Sao Bar and Lavender also invited me to accompany them on their trips to their villages. One evening, I sat down with Chu Xanh and Hanh to tell them that I would like to end my time working in Khong Sao Bar. I had gathered enough data and wanted to spend time working in a lower-tiered bar. Chu Xanh instructed me to take a week off to allow my body to rest from the months of daily alcohol consumption. He suggested that I get away from the city and accompany Yen-Nhi, the girl whose introduction to the bar opened this chapter, on a trip to her village to visit her ailing father. He explained to me,

> Yen-Nhi's father is dying; that's why she is working here. You would never know that by looking at her face, but Hanh and I knew it from the first day she came to work here. I sent one of my *linh* [underlings; *linh* translates into "soldiers" in English] to visit her father with a doctor to get an update on his status. His liver has failed and he is dying. There is nothing we can do about it, so I flew in a doctor from Singapore to come visit with him and give him enough medicine so that he can at least die the least painful death possible.

Chu Xanh informed me that he felt an obligation to take care of some of the workers' family members because the women were making huge sacrifices not merely for their own families but also for the nation. He went on: "These poor girls leave everything behind to come to the city to take care of their families, [but] they are the ones who really move money into this country in a way that no one sees. We have to do the right thing and take care of their families."

As we prepared for our departure to the village, I watched as Hanh and the two junior mommies sent the male workers in the bar out to purchase alcohol, food, and an assortment of herbal medications and teas for Yen-Nhi to bring home to her family as a token of respect. Two days later, the doctor from Singapore flew in, and Chu Xanh instructed one of his underlings to hire a private van and accompany us on the trip. The next day the doctor, Yen-Nhi, Vy-Van, Sang (the driver), Hai (Chu Xanh's underling), and I got into the van and made the four-hour journey to Can Tho. When the van pulled up to the house, Bac Tan, Yen-Nhi's father, was seated right outside the house in a wheelchair dressed in a suit. It was clear that he had been sitting there in anticipation of our arrival for some time, because his clothes were dripping in sweat from the heat. His face lit up as he embraced his daughter with tears in his eyes. We all bowed to greet him and offered our gifts. Bac

Dinh, Yen-Nhi's mother, invited us into the living room, where she poured us some tea before heading back to the kitchen to put the final touches on the food she had prepared. Yen-Nhi and I both joined her the kitchen while the doctor examined Bac Tan with the help of Hai.

In the kitchen, Yen-Nhi's mother told us that her husband recently had been drinking a lot to both numb the pain and speed up the process of his death. She said that he did not want to die a slow death. Then she told Yen-Nhi that she could not stand the thought of living alone in the village and began pressuring her to come home, get married, and settle down with someone from the village area. She jokingly brought up the names of a couple of eligible bachelors who had recently returned from Malaysia and Japan after spending several years away as construction workers. In fact, she announced, some of the single men from the village would be joining us for a dinner party at the house the following night. Yen-Nhi shifted uncomfortably and, without responding to her mother's announcement, began to take the food out to the living room.

We sat in a circle on straw mats placed on the floor, where we ate a simple Vietnamese meal—a sweet-and-sour fish soup, fried fish, caramelized braised pork and eggs, and sautéed vegetables. We all made small talk about life in Saigon, my life and family in the United States, and local gossip among neighbors in the village. As the meal wound down, Hai told Bac Tan that Chu Xanh would like to talk with him over the phone. Hai picked up the phone and called Chu Xanh and then placed him on speakerphone so that Bac Tan could hear him. Chu Xanh asked Bac Tan how he was faring. He then went on to assure Bac Tan that he would cover all costs of the Singaporean doctor and not to hesitate to ask for more medication if he needed it. Then, as he wrapped up the phone call, Chu Xanh said, "I want you to know that we are taking care of your daughter in Saigon. We will always take care of her and make sure that she is safe." He then instructed Hai to pull out a gift that Chu Xanh wanted to give to Bac Tan. Hai brought out a brand new iPhone and powered it on. Then he instructed Hai to try FaceTime (a video calling feature) so that Bac Tan could see Chu Xanh. Over the FaceTime chat, Chu Xanh said, "Hai will show you and Bac Dinh how to use this phone so that you can see your daughter every day." All of us watched as Bac Tan and Bac Dinh marveled over the phone and its video calling capabilities.

As the day wound down, Yen-Nhi took me on a motorbike tour of her village, and we spent some time alone driving down dirt roads. We stopped at a nearby river and sat on a wooden deck to watch a group of kids play in the water. As we sat there I said, "This is great; you can video call your dad every day." She then began to reflect on her life:

> My father used to drink so much. One time I got so upset with him that I told him I would let him die alone if he died from drinking too much. He got so mad that he didn't talk to me for a week. But I said that because I loved him so much. When we were kids, we were so poor, and my dad would pretend that he wasn't hungry so that my siblings could eat more food. We never said anything, because we were all so scared of him; but we knew that he was hungry because he worked all day without eating much. . . . The only thing that keeps me working in the bars is that, in my heart, I know my dad will die a less painful death. Chu Xanh has brought doctors from other countries to see my dad several times. People in the village, they see that, and they respect me for it. I have sent home enough money for my mom to keep so that, when the time comes, she will be able to pay for him to have a proper funeral.

Yen-Nhi 's decision to stay in the city and work while her ailing father spent his last days in the village with her mother, her siblings, and other relatives nearby was motivated by her desire to safeguard her father's respectability. She wanted for her father to die a respectable death, even if that meant the money she earned came from work in some of the least respectable places in the city. In doing so, she effectively transformed what once was a highly stigmatized profession into one that was at least palatable to some members of her family and village. During our visit, Chu Manh, one of her uncles, echoed the words of Tam's father, stating, "Girls are the new gold" in Vietnam's globalizing economy. Indeed, Yen-Nhi turned dust into "gold" as she capitalized on new opportunities in urban areas to remit money home, not only to help her ailing father die a less painful death, but also to enable him to leave this world with a sense of dignity and respect.

Women experienced different trajectories of mobility based on their particular niche of sex work. Workers in higher-tiered bars like Khong Sao Bar and Lavender occupied a precarious position as they straddled First World luxury and Third World poverty. Relations with wealthy local Vietnamese men and Viet Kieu men often led women to experience rapid oscillations between upward and downward economic mobility. Sex workers who catered to Western men, however, operated with a different ethic in relation to money. Western clients controlled the workers by emphasizing the necessity for hard work and the importance of saving. Workers who catered to Western expatriates and backpackers experienced upward mobility that was rapid at first, but which then reached a slow but steady pace of growth because the women were not immersed in a world that promoted conspicuous consumption of luxury items.

Across all niche markets, sex workers engaged in processes of convertibility in both rural and urban social fields. The women I met turned to the village as a place where they could acquire a sense of honor and respect through public displays of their money and in the process of gift giving. As sex workers returned home, they realized their desires to achieve economic upward mobility in an industry straddling two imaginaries of Vietnam—as a nation on the move and as a country untouched by globalization. Return visits to their villages served as visceral reminders of the precariousness of their social mobility, both in the city and in their hometowns, as they sacrificed sacred time with their families to gamble on a future with long-term economic stability.

Conclusion

Faltering Ascent

In the summer of 2013, I returned to Vietnam to find a much less vibrant economy. Only three years after my departure, foreign investors seeking returns found their money locked up in delayed projects. While some foreigners and local businessmen made out very well, others lost a great deal of money in a faltering economy. Although foreign direct investments remained stable, averaging roughly U.S.$11 billion in disbursed capital for 2011 to 2013, the country was not brokering nearly as many capital deals, nor was it growing at the rapid rate it had experienced in the years following the 2008 global financial crisis.[1] The real estate bubble had burst, and many of the Vietnamese elites in my study found their capital tied up in assets they could not sell. New political tensions, coupled with the stagnating economy, had reverberating effects on the different niche markets of the sex industry where I conducted my research.

REBIRTH AND TRANSFORMATIONS

By 2013, Khong Sao Bar had shut down. Hanh, the head mommy, said to me, "There is a Vietnamese proverb that I learned to live by: *Sinh—lao— benh—tu.* It means that a person experiences four periods in life—birth, old age, sickness, and death, before a rebirth." She continued: "That is the cycle of this business. We are reborn into a new life through the bars and all the money that comes in it; we age and get sick [from drinking], and then our time ends and we have to let other people take over." When I asked her if she knew any of the new madams or had any insight into what their client bases looked like, she laughed and responded, "Those are people's secrets . . . their livelihoods. Why would they tell me?"

I asked her, "What does your rebirth look like?" With a half smile, she said, "I was getting too old to be a madam. I wanted to get out, but I couldn't because they needed me and I was afraid of damaging those relationships. [But] when they slowed down and quit playing, I knew this was my chance to get out."

Hanh's description of her own rebirth in many ways symbolized the transformation of the broader political economy. The secrets she carried about her clients' business dealings were no longer relevant, since many of the clients began to pull themselves out of the market to engage in less risky investments abroad. As the country's economic growth slowed, so too did the lives of the key players responsible for generating that growth. Hanh settled into her role as the owner of a late-night restaurant, where she employed many of the women who used to work in Khong Sao Bar.

Across town, Lavender had shut down because it could not keep up with the competition. Several new bars had opened with skydecks and spectacular views of the city, and those bars quickly became the new hot spots frequented by Viet Kieus. When I asked Tho and Huyen, the two mommies who ran Lavender, why the bar had shut down, they told me that Anh Nguyen was pushed out because he could not keep up with the constant pressure to reinvent the space to make it the most desirable bar in town, the one where men wanted to "be seen." After the bar closed, Tho and Huyen took their money and invested it in a small clothing shop that sold replica designer handbags and clothing imported from Hong Kong. Both women were single at the time and had settled into a much slower pace of life.

Secrets and Naughty Girls were both still open, and half the women I used to work with at those two bars were still there. However, Lilly and Tina both complained about how slow business was. They were not turning as high a profit as they used to. Lilly had decided to have a child and raise him on her own after getting pregnant by a French expatriate who regularly traveled back and forth between Vietnam and France. She often brought her son to the bar to spend time with him while at work, and he became a part of the fold, doted on by clients and sex workers alike. Similarly, Tina had settled into a relationship with a Swedish man. She came to the bar less frequently now, trusting her relationships with some of the older sex workers, who managed the bar in her absence.

Across all four niche markets, the men and women I reconnected with lamented the slower pace of growth in Vietnam, the stalled construction projects scattered throughout the city, and the decreased spending on leisure activities. Lilly told me she was bracing herself during this phase of the economy, hoping it would soon pass and HCMC would pick itself up again. The sex industry lost its former vibrancy as the mommies used relationships and legitimate businesses to prepare for a new political and economic order.

POLITICAL TENSIONS AND ECONOMIC TRANSFORMATIONS

Just as the sex workers adjusted to the slowing economy, so too did many of the former clients. The men once lauded as some of Saigon's biggest playboys settled into mundane lives that did not involve as much late-night drinking and entertaining. Clients who used to patronize Khong Sao Bar eased out of their positions of political and economic power as the local commercial- and investment-banking sectors became vulnerable in the wake of a local banking crisis. Commercial banks grappling with bad debts from nonperforming real estate loans were in desperate need of liquid capital. To encourage capital flow, banks were offering a 15 percent return on all deposits.[2]

In one of the largest public scandals, the government arrested banking magnate Nguyen Duc Kien, the founder of several banks, including Asia Commercial Bank (Vietnam's fourth-largest lender), on charges that he conducted business illegally and mismanaged bank funds.[3] Rumors swirled among local elites, claiming that this arrest and others like it were related to an ongoing power struggle and rivalry between Prime Minister Nguyen Tan Dung and President Truong Tan Sang.

The prime minister controlled much of the economy and was in charge of developing and monitoring the financial sector. During Vietnam's period of rapid economic growth between 2006 and 2010, Nguyen Tan Dung was able to consolidate a great deal of power under his leadership. He had the authority to appoint the heads of state-owned banks, which controlled over 75 percent of deposits and credits in Vietnam.[4] President Truong Tan Sang, on the other hand, occupied a position of political power that was largely ceremonial, symbolic, and toothless. However, by 2013, the rivalry began to manifest itself prominently in the public eye as the president began to criticize the prime minister for mismanaging the economy, blaming him for the country's double-digit inflation and stagnating export markets. The faltering economic situation provided the president with an opportunity to test the prime minister's power. He did so by leading an investigation that would result in arrests of several banking magnates with close ties to the prime minister, on charges of corruption and mismanagement of bank funds. The arrest of banker Nguyen Duc Kien reverberated throughout the country as several other bank leaders, such as Dang Van Thanh, the CEO of Sacombank, quickly resigned their positions.

In an interview with the Asia-Pacific division of the *Financial Times,* Karolyn Seet, a banking analyst at the credit rating agency Moody's, stated, "The [arrest of major bank leaders] magnifies the general lack of transparency, weak corporate governance, fraud, corruption, and illegal trading" in Vietnam's investment industry.[5] In reference to the cross-ownership of the country's banks, Jonathan Pincus, an HCMC-based economist at the Harvard Kennedy School's Vietnam program similarly commented, "It's like a spaghetti bowl. It's very difficult to untangle the relationships because a lot of the relationships are not transparent. It presents a very difficult governance problem for the financial system."[6]

The arrests of prominent bankers illustrated Vietnam's faltering economic ascent. Westerners like Pincus and Seet blamed the stumbling economy on the Vietnamese style of broking capital deals through intimate and informal access to the economy, while wealthy local elites saw these informal business dealings as a necessary way to move capital quickly. The pressure for transparency, however, provided the president with an opportunity to take down many of the prime minister's underlings, who controlled much of the financial sector of the economy.

In follow-up conversations with some of the former clients of Khong Sao Bar, they told me that the heightened rivalry between the prime minister and the president had made them feel much more risk averse. Many were afraid that the president would target them next and would expose their informal business practices. This fear materialized for four wealthy local Vietnamese men, who were arrested with high-class sex workers in a hotel room in 2012. This incident became one of the largest public scandals in the Vietnamese news media, because it involved a famous beauty pageant winner named Vo Thi My Xuan. In the wake of the scandal, the authorities released the names of all female sex workers involved but only the initials of the male clients. The women were publicly humiliated. Public debate ensued around whether local authorities should release the names of the clients, but their names never made it into the newspapers.

While no one in my study debated whether leisure and entertainment were necessary to building social trust and informal relationships between businessmen and potential investors in Vietnam, the political tensions coupled with the public arrest of these sex workers led many of the clients who once frequented Khong Sao Bar to feel it was too risky to engage in these informal business practices. For example, Chu Xanh said to me, "We can't do things the way we used to anymore. It's too risky now. They will do anything to charge us for corruption, even if that means catching us naked in hotel rooms with sex workers." For Chu Xanh and his men, rather than continue to conduct business in hostess bars, they decided it was time to fly under the radar to avoid becoming the president's next target.

The decision to remove themselves from the center of financial transactions meant that for many of the political and economic elites, it was time to hand over the reigns to their appointed successors. Risk-averse elites who felt they had accumulated sufficient wealth groomed new players whom they could trust not to expose their previous deal-brokering business practices. These new players entered a very different kind of market, where they would have to innovate new business practices as they grappled with the shifting political economy. Although I never met any of the new key players, I was told that they often had to entertain foreign guests in much more private and secluded spaces. Rather than going out to hostess bars, the clients entertained their business partners in their private homes, where they held private parties with madams and sex workers who arrived in secret. The work that had taken place in spaces like Khong Sao Bar had essentially moved into local elite businessmen's private living quarters. Sex work continued to be a major conduit for global capital, but the form it took had to shift once again with changes in the political economy.

As Julie Chu writes, "The fortunes increasingly conjured by capitalism's vanguards through high finance—venture capital, stocks, bonds, and futures—[a]re themselves celebrations of speculation as a technology for value production."[7] This research captures a particular moment in Vietnam's local economy when there was a great deal of economic volatility, and when investment banking in the real estate market was experiencing rapid growth. Vietnam's booming markets were driven by highly speculative investments that depended heavily on local elites' ability to create value through the *perception* that Vietnam was a nation worth investing in. This was especially crucial to the country's ability to participate in new inter-Asian circuits of global capital, which profoundly transformed the local economy. At the time of my research, business dealings with foreign investors in speculative markets relied heavily on the embodied labor of women like Hanh and the sex workers she employed and trained in Khong Sao Bar. Her story and many others like it often get lost in studies of the movement of global capital that do not attend to the ways in which gendered relations are tied into the celebration of value production.

As new players enter HCMC's economy, a new set of sex workers and madams reign in the sex industry. The high-profile arrests of sex workers and their clients should not be taken to mean that the country has eliminated the informal economy crucial to brokering business deals. Instead, new players must find new spaces of leisure and entertainment and invent new strategies to build informal relationships of trust in order to attract foreign investments and yield high returns.

COCONSTITUTION OF GENDER AND GLOBAL CAPITAL

By looking closely at the coconstitutive connections between sex work and the political economy, *Dealing in Desire* reveals several consequences of the contemporary global economic situation. First, two developments in global finance—the 2008 financial crisis centered in the United States and Western Europe, and the expansion of East Asian economies—created new opportunities to rethink how race-, nation-, and class-based relations interact to produce competing local masculinities and femininities. Vietnam's increased economic openness in the context of the 2008 global economic recession elevated the position of the class of men who enjoyed access to foreign capital coming from East and Southeast Asia.

Second, globalization fractured the Vietnamese market, opening up opportunities to cater to new financial capital from different parts of the world. Just as Vietnam's new market economy created diversification in various legitimate sectors, the local sex industry also became segmented following Doi Moi. In HCMC, capital flows from Western travelers, Western businessmen, Viet Kieus visiting their homeland, and local elites split the sex industry into different niche markets. As a result, we can no longer think of the sex industry in developing economies as places where white European and American men command the highest-paying sectors. Non-Western global elites are emerging around the world, and they enter into the sex industry with aspirations to challenge the hegemony of Western masculinity. In HCMC's sex industry in particular, Vietnam's growing relationship with other Asian countries shifted the orientation of local imaginaries of the global center, away from the West and toward East and Southeast Asia.

Third, a strategic analysis of multiple performances of masculinities and femininities provides insight to the ways that different groups of male clients and female sex workers simultaneously affirmed and contested Western superiority. Together, the four niche markets of HCMC's sex industry show that, as Asia, rather than the West, became the source of foreign capital flowing into Vietnam, men and women on the ground constructed new symbolic positions. In lower-paying niche markets that catered to Western businessmen and Western budget travelers, sex bars provided men with the space to negotiate their own personal perceptions of Western decline as they projected their status anxieties onto women's bodies, affirming Western superiority. In contrast, more expensive bars catering to Viet Kieu and local elite Vietnamese businessmen provided men with a stage on which to contest Western superiority. Local elites and Viet Kieus capitalized on a particular moment of economic flux by engaging in acts of conspicuous consumption that displayed their financial dominance, in their desire to imagine a new global order that asserted the ascendancy of Vietnam and East and Southeast Asia. By looking at parallel markets where men negotiated new capital configurations, I illustrate the fact that global hierarchies are not static but are instead produced and challenged through coconstitutive relationships between global capital and different kinds of gendered bodies.

Finally, future work theorizing masculine deal-brokering must consider the place of sex work in the global economy. We must reconsider ideas of Western dominance through an empirical approach that has material implications as we think about capitalism and new differences in wealth across nations. In Vietnam's quest to assert itself as a modern nation in the new global economy, transnational capital flows are linked with intimate life in a circle of performative displays of consumerist distinction, hypermasculinity, and stylized femininity.

NEW DEALINGS IN DESIRE

In a particular moment different configurations of gender and global capital coexisted in the same locale. As William Sewell writes, "Dominant and oppositional groups interact constantly. . . . Even when they attempt to overcome or undermine each other, they are mutually shaped by their dialectical dance. . . . Moreover, dissenting or oppositional groups work to create and sustain cultural coherence among their own adherents, and they do so by many of the same strategies—hierarchization, encapsulation, exclusion, and the like—that authorities use."[8] By paying attention to how these oppositional groups work to undermine each other, we can begin to see how they in fact cohere.

Vietnam's long history of engagement with the West and the rapid changes in the contemporary economy indicate that ascension is neither a clear nor a straightforward path. Local elites, Viet Kieus, Western businessmen, and Western budget tourists inhabited four separate niche markets, each characterized by its own system of gendered, racialized, and classed relations and its own distinct social and moral order. In short, local elites worked to consolidate new elite practices in their desire to assert the ascendancy of Vietnam, while Westerners simultaneously worked to recuperate Western forms of patriarchy abroad. Although the four niche markets rarely came into contact with one another, the very existence of these separate niche markets enabled the clients and workers in them to construct competing masculinities and technologies of embodiment that simultaneously projected pan-Asian modernity, nostalgic cosmopolitanism, and Third World dependency.

Whether Western nations are declining and whether Asia's economic rise will hold out in the long run are points open to debate. But the truth of Asian ascendancy or Western decline is not central to the argument of this book; instead, this book shows the importance of how people reimagine the global order through their desires to assert a superior masculinity and reconfigure hierarchies of race and nation. Sex, after all, as Dennis Altman argues, "is a central part of the political economy of all large cities, especially those which are growing fast and therefore home to many who are uprooted, transient, desperate—or newly rich in times of political or social upheaval."[9] As new players enter the field and begin to speculate on who among them will rise to power, clients and sex workers across all sectors know that they will need to either exit these intimate economies or establish new dealings in desire.

The Empirical Puzzle and the Embodied Cost of Ethnography

In this appendix, I reflect on what it meant to do ethnography in the field of sex work in HCMC. The first part of this appendix describes the evolution of my research questions and methodological choices. I begin with my first trip to Vietnam in 2005 and the interactions that sparked my initial research interests. I then outline my preliminary phase of research, which took place in 2006–2007, before describing how my research questions shifted after I returned to Vietnam for fifteen months in 2009–2010, when I conducted the bulk of the ethnographic fieldwork for this book. I discuss how the process of ethnographic inquiry allowed serendipity to take my project down unanticipated paths that pushed me to rethink and revise my core research questions. The second half of the appendix provides a space for me to reflect on my social position, the process of gaining access and building rapport, negotiating male desire in the field, and my performances of subservience. I focus on what I call *embodied costs*— the immaterial losses that ethnographers experience as they engage in the kind of fieldwork that involves laborious embodied transformations—as well as the benefits of conducting a deeply embedded ethnography in illicit spaces and with hard-to-reach populations.

THE FIRST JOURNEY TO VIETNAM: JUNE TO AUGUST 2005

The summer before I started a PhD program in sociology at Stanford University in 2005, I decided to visit the country my parents had fled as boat refugees in 1979. My first journey to Vietnam began as a vacation. Starting my trip in Hanoi, I spent two months indulging in street foods, hiking the beautiful northern mountains of Sapa and Dalat, and soaking in the saltwater of the central coast beaches of Da Nang and Mui Ne before making my way down to Ho Chi Minh City, formerly known as Saigon.

Once I landed in HCMC, I fell in love with the bustling energy of the city. I loved the vision of hundreds of scooters flashing down streets in organized chaos; the sound of people bartering in markets; and the aroma of a wide array of food carts that filled the streets. I wanted to be more than merely a spectator—I wanted to be a part of the city. In my search for a place to rent, I met Eric and Ryan, two Western men, one from the United States and the other from Australia, who lived in a four-bedroom house with a spare room to rent in District 1, the heart of HCMC. Both men were in their early thirties and had moved to Vietnam to teach English. After I moved into the house, I discovered that Ryan had a local girlfriend living with him named Hong, who spent her evenings as a sex worker. Hong worked in bars late at night and came home in the early hours of the mornings to spend her time off with Ryan. They seemed like a cool and eclectic trio, so when they invited me to go out with them, I said yes. For several days we ate and drank at one of the bars where Hong worked, often returning home just as the sun began rise.

While I lived with Eric and Ryan, I regularly patronized a juice-and-baguette stand for breakfast. One morning, the owner of the breakfast stand scoffed at me, called me a whore, and told me that proper girls should not live with two white guys. Unbeknownst to me, I had become an item of gossip among the neighbors, who assumed that I, like Hong, was a sex worker. Shocked by her callous and inaccurate judgment of me, I retreated to the house and thought about Hong.

Physically, we shared many of the same features: jet-black hair, a petite frame, and almond-shaped eyes. Where we differed was in our history. Our differences began with a decision in 1979 that unfolded into who we would become more than twenty years later. My parents fled Vietnam as boat refugees after the fall of Saigon, while hers remained in the country. Had my parents chosen *not* to flee Vietnam, how different would Hong and I really be? While Hong did everything she could to make me feel welcome in the bar where she worked, there was a clear difference in our social strata, a difference that sparked my curiosity to learn more about the women of Saigon's nightlife and discover why their lives were deemed less proper and respectable by middle-class Vietnamese urban residents.

As a Vietnamese American woman born in the United States who knew very little about the country my parents fled, I found myself in the awkward position of being an outsider in a country I had strong cultural ties to and not knowing what to make of it.[1] After my departure from Vietnam on that first trip, I moved to Palo Alto, California, where I spent the year of the master's program in sociology at Stanford University in the library, reading everything I could get my hands on about the global sex industry. What I found were mountains of texts debating whether women were "trafficked victims," either kidnapped or otherwise forced into the sex trade, or "free agents" who willingly engaged in sex work. These texts focused primarily on female sex workers who catered to Western men on sex or dating tours in Latin America, the Caribbean, and various parts of Asia.

At Stanford I wrote my first research proposal, and in the summer of 2006 I returned to Vietnam to conduct some preliminary research. I was interested in studying other women like Hong, and I wanted to compare them with the "trafficked" women I had read about. At that time, I was trying to uncover the different pathways into sex work that involved varying degrees of coercion and freedom.

ETHNOGRAPHY: JUNE 2006 TO AUGUST 2007

With the approval of Stanford University's human subjects review committee in 2006 and a similar review committee at the University of California, where I continued my PhD in 2007, I carried out seven months of ethnographic field research in HCMC in three intervals between June 2006 and August 2007. The Stanford and UC Berkeley review committees required that I obtain verbal consent from participants to protect both workers' and clients' identities.

I began by scouring the city with local motorbike taxi drivers, who helped me map out the geographical landscape of sex work in the city. Many of them had personal ties to sex workers after regularly driving them home at the end of the night. None of the women I met had been trafficked or forced into the sex trade. Therefore, during this preliminary phase, I revised my research question and instead focused on comparing clients and sex workers across three segmented niche markets that catered to poor local Vietnamese men, Western tourists, and overseas Viet Kieus. I strategically decided to include male clients because the vast majority of the literature on sex work focused overwhelmingly on female sex workers. Moreover, studies of male clients focused primarily on Western men from developed nations traveling to less-developed nations on sex or romance tours.[2] Social scientists knew very little about non-Western men's participation in sexual commerce. For these reasons, scholars had only a partial understanding of the connection between the global sex industry and globalization. I wanted to fill that gap.

My goal was to interview both clients and sex workers across three distinct niche markets and to compare the relationships of intimacy across the different markets. The three niche markets catering to poor local Vietnamese men, Western budget travelers, and Viet Kieus were largely open to the public and therefore easier to observe. Once I had an idea of the sexual landscape, I began conducting participant observation in local bars, cafes, sex workers' homes, malls, restaurants, and on the streets.

As I ventured into the different sites, I was able to convince some of the women to sit down and talk with me in a formal tape-recorded interview. This methodology, however, soon proved to generate very thin data. After the first thirteen interviews, I began to reach a point of saturation where the same narratives of poverty kept coming up over and over again. It made me feel as though the data I had generated was barely scratching the surface. This became even clearer after I asked to follow the women in their daily lives. Women who catered to Viet Kieus, for example, often claimed that they had entered into sex work because of poverty, but as I followed them to their homes and into shopping centers, I quickly learned that they came from families that were fairly wealthy by local standards and even in comparison to many people I knew in the United States.[3] In addition, while many sex workers understandably refused to sit down for a formal tape-recorded interview, they were frequently receptive to letting me follow them more informally as they went about their daily lives. Therefore, I decided to drop interviewing as the primary method of research and instead opted to conduct ethnographic field research.

In this first phase of my research, I conducted the kind of participant observation that allowed me to be more of an *observer* and less of a participant. As an observer, I spent time in the bars as a paying customer who ordered drinks. I identified myself as a researcher and, with the bar owners' and workers' consent, was able to take careful notes on the *interactions* that developed between clients and sex workers. This allowed for a kind of in-depth analysis that would otherwise be lost in interviews that were often one-sided.

Before asking any women to participate in my project, I first spent time in local bars and on the streets to meet and develop rapport with various sex workers, clients, and bar owners. I then conducted intensive participant observation and informal interviews with the individual sex workers who agreed to take part in my study. Being an overseas Vietnamese woman helped me gain access to female sex workers, because many of them saw me as nonthreatening compared to local Vietnamese men and women, who many workers thought of as either undercover police or local journalists. All the women knew that I was a researcher from the United States who would eventually write about their lives with their names changed. They knew about my research, but did not seem to find it important; they cared more about my family history and my life overseas—information that would help them situate me in their mental universe.

All the clients, too, knew that I was a researcher from the United States. Overseas white backpackers and Viet Kieu clients in my study were much more open with me than local Vietnamese men were. White backpackers and Viet Kieu men could converse with me in English and talk about their lives overseas and the dynamics of their relationships in HCMC. For example, one client said, "It's so nice to talk to someone who speaks English fluently and who isn't going to judge me. I've been dying to talk to someone about this, but I can't talk to anyone back at home, because, you know, they have all these stereotypes about Asia. And people here [in Vietnam] all speak broken English, so it's hard to talk deeply about these things."

While in the field, I also spent time in Internet cafes helping sex workers read emails and conduct instant-message conversations with their overseas "boyfriends." I helped these women find remittance centers and went with them to pick up remittances from their overseas partners. Between my research periods in HCMC, I also conducted extensive chat-room conversations and online correspondence with informants via e-mail. Through this online and off-line fieldwork, I learned that sex workers and their clients often told lies to each other about various aspects of their relationships—lies that I kept confidential for both parties.

In the initial seven months of fieldwork, I spent three days a week conducting field research and three days writing field notes. On a typical research day, I spent the mornings in barbershops that doubled as brothels, where women catered to poor and working-class locals; I spent afternoons having lunch or coffee and shopping with clients and sex workers; and I spent my evenings in bars where women would meet Western backpackers and Viet Kieu men. I spoke mostly in Vietnamese with clients and sex workers in the niche market that catered to low-income locals, and in a mixture of English and Vietnamese in the other niche markets. I wrote all my field notes in English but highlighted key phrases in Vietnamese. I used pseudonyms in my field notes to ensure confidentiality in the event that local authorities asked to look through my computer. Although I never knew of anyone who had a computer searched by the police, these rumors circulated among researchers working in Vietnam and were enough to make me take extra precautions to safeguard my data. During this preliminary phase of research, I conducted informal interviews with a total of 56 sex workers and 27 clients: 12 workers and 4 clients in the low-income, local niche market, 31 workers and 15 clients in the Western backpacker niche market, and 11 workers and 7 clients in the Viet Kieu niche market.

PARTICIPANT OBSERVATION: JUNE 2009 AND AUGUST 2010

In June 2009, I returned to Vietnam to conduct another fifteen months of ethnography. Following Michael Burawoy's approach of reflexive ethnography,[4] I began by revisiting the spaces that catered to Viet Kieus, Western tourists, and poor local Vietnamese men to examine how the sex industry had changed three years after Vietnam's integration into the World Trade Organization.

As I reentered the field, I quickly learned that much had changed in HCMC's sex industry. The global financial crisis of 2008 had led to an influx of Western businessmen who had lost their jobs in the United States and Europe and sought new opportunities in Vietnam's booming market economy. In addition, the rapid increase in foreign direct investments from other parts of Asia meant that wealthy local Vietnamese men who were channeling FDI into the nation experienced a similar increase in status and power. These macropolitical and macroeconomic transformations proved difficult to ignore, since both clients and sex workers talked about them in my interviews. In this second phase, I incorporated two new groups of clients: wealthy Vietnamese men and Western expatriates.

As a result of these economic transformations, I found myself revising my research questions. Through my talks with sex workers and clients, I formulated the new questions that ultimately animated the heart of this book: (a) how had Vietnam's economic volatility destabilized the terms on which diverse men understood their masculinity that hinged on local women's various performances of femininity, and (b) how did these transformations provide male clients with the tools to claim or reclaim masculine hegemony?

In order to streamline my field research, I decided to focus on the niche markets where male clients were connected to global capital flows—in this case FDI and overseas remittance money. Therefore, I dropped the niche market that catered to poor local Vietnamese men situated on the outskirts of HCMC because that niche market operated at "Saigon's edge," or what Erik Harms refers to as the periphery or nonurban margins of HCMC, largely disconnected from networks of male clients linked to foreign money.[5]

My decision to focus on both male clients and female sex workers led me to conduct the kind of grounded ethnography that involved both "studying up" and "studying down." Most urban sociologists and anthropologists either "study down" by centering their projects on marginalized people living in poverty, involved in gang activity, or subjected to exploitative working conditions, or they "study up" by focusing on privileged people who belong to a powerful world of high finance.[6] It was only by including male clients in this study that I came to see the importance of studying up. The men opened my eyes to the broader links between sex work and global capital flows. This project examines both the privileged male clients directly connected to FDI and overseas remittances and the local Vietnamese sex workers who generally operate at the margins of the formal economy. That is, by studying up and studying down, I shifted my research from a simple study of stratified markets to one that would highlight the productive frictions produced between privileged men and marginal women whose relationships led to new and divergent constructions of masculinity and embodied femininities. These divergent constructions led me to think about new ways in which gendered relations are coconstituted within global and local economic processes.

Obtaining Permission to Conduct Research via Local Institutions

In order to conduct this research in HCMC, I had to seek permission from a local university or research institute in order to obtain the necessary visas and permissions. In the wake of President George W. Bush's 2006 visit to Vietnam, the Vietnamese government initiated an effort to shut down all the local bars and clubs, making any study related to the topic of "sex trafficking" or "sex work" a sensitive topic that would garner closer scrutiny of the researchers. At the time, President Bush was an avid antitrafficking advocate who had recently signed the Trafficking Victims Protection Reauthorization Act (H.R. 972), in 2005, directing the U.S. Agency for International Development, the U.S. State Department, and the U.S. Department of Defense to incorporate antitrafficking and protection measures for vulnerable populations around the world.

In this context, as someone who would eventually spend time in the illicit spaces of the sex industry, I worried about being arrested and charged with aiding and abetting "sex trafficking" if I were caught up in a police sweep. At that time, local police often conflated sex workers with trafficked victims in their efforts to increase the numbers in their reports of "saved women." Therefore, I decided it would be best to have the formal sponsorship of two different visa-granting institutions for international research. After submitting my research proposals and jumping through the necessary bureaucratic hoops, I eventually obtained permission to conduct research in the local bars and clubs from both the University of Social Sciences at Vietnam National University and the Southern Institute of Sustainable Development in HCMC.

While many local researchers in Vietnam had conducted research on street-level sex work between poor local Vietnamese men and local Vietnamese sex workers, virtually no one had gained access to spaces that catered to Westerners, Viet Kieus, or wealthy local Vietnamese clients. Thus, the university officials and researchers who oversaw my research project at Vietnam National University and the Southern Institute of Sustainable Development could not advise me on how to conduct my research or gain access to these bars. Rather, they provided me with the freedom to conduct research on my own with minimal surveillance. Although I reported monthly to both the university and the institute, organized workshops on ethnographic research methods, and presented preliminary findings at the end of my research stay, I had a great deal of freedom in the research process. I was not required to hire a local research assistant or to be accompanied by an official as I conducted my fieldwork, because the university and institute felt that such requirements would infringe on my ability to access these research sites.

To ensure my safety, a professor at the University of Social Sciences in HCMC introduced me to a local police officer, who provided me with documentation that legitimated me as a researcher in the event that I was arrested during a police sweep. This document provided me with peace of mind as I navigated the different field sites. In the end, however, the connections that I made in the bars proved to be more critical to my safety than my connection to the research institutions or with this local police officer.

Access and Rapport in the Bars

With approval from the two research institutions in Vietnam and the Committee for the Protection of Human Subjects at UC Berkeley, I decided to work as a hostess during this phase of my research to gather data more as a *participant* than as a stand-alone observer. Working in the bars provided me with deeper insights into the backstage relationships among owners, mommies, police, the mafia, clients, and sex workers in multiple bars.[7] Gaining access to each of the bars was an arduous process because I had to learn to manage myriad relationships. The bar structures and clientele were all quite different, which meant that I had to try on different hats, alter my embodiment in different ways, and manage a new set of relationships in each space.

I first obtained access by asking to work in a bar that catered to Viet Kieu men. The owner of Lavender, Anh Nguyen, was a Viet Kieu sympathetic to the project because I was a Viet Kieu woman who had traveled to Vietnam alone, without any family or social contacts to lean on. He took me under his wing as a younger sister and introduced me to alcohol distributors connected to a network of bar owners in HCMC. Through the connections with the alcohol distributors, I met Lilly, the owner of Secrets, and Tina, the owner of Naughty Girls. Both women invited me to come work in their bars because of my language ability in English and Vietnamese and my willingness to work for free. Through my personal circle, a local Vietnamese man offered to help me gain access to the most exclusive club in town, a bar that catered to a clientele of elite Vietnamese businessmen, in exchange for translation services for his company. Those translation services later developed as he trusted me to help him broker several business deals. Khong Sao Bar was much more discreet than the other bars I worked in and would allow me to build relationships with high-level officials and businessmen.

I built social debt with the clients who frequented Khong Sao Bar by working as a free consultant translating company pamphlets, copyediting emails, reviewing the language in different companies' business plans, and sitting in on business meetings for a variety of clients. My role was to verify the political capital of some of the men in a country rife with corruption, where a lot of people pretended to have the political connections needed for licensing and permits. Importantly, I allowed them to use my name because their business partners could trace me back to a legitimate institution (UC Berkeley) and file a formal complaint if the men's political ties proved to be false. I also served as a translator without accepting any kind of monetary payment or commission for the deals that I helped to broker. This role enabled me to spend time with the businessmen outside the bars, visiting construction sites, spending time on golf courses, dining with them, and helping entertain foreign clients by introducing them to my coworkers in the bars. This networking allowed me to get a sense of the scope of the diverse projects of each company and to understand how local Vietnamese men conduct business compared to other Asian men and Western businessmen.

Rather than seeking monetary payment, I sought in-kind payment for my services. For example, one night after having successfully closed my third deal on a land development project, one of my informants, Chu Xanh (a wealthy local Vietnamese businessman), handed me a black plastic bag and told me it was a gift for all my hard work. Because it would have been rude to open the gift in front of them in this cultural context, I waited to open the bag in the privacy of my own home. Thinking that the bag contained some kind of foreign dessert from a recent trip they took to South Korea, I wrapped it on the handle of my motorbike and rode home with it. When I got home, I was shocked to find nearly $10,000 dollars in cash in the bag. Panicked, I immediately asked to meet the men for a late-night dinner and coffee. There, I returned the bag of cash and told them that I could not accept it. They tried to tell me that it was standard practice to pay brokers a commission.

Because I was unwilling to accept their money, they asked how they could repay my services. I took this opportunity to ask the men to help introduce me to the bar owners and mommies in Khong Sao Bar, where I would like to conduct research. I told them that my dissertation advisor would not grant my PhD if I came home without data for my dissertation. In effect, I had built up some social debt that I wanted to cash in on for access to a research site. This was effective, because the madams and bar owners felt a similar kind of social debt to the clients who frequented the bars. The businessmen drew on this debt to ask the mommies and bar owners to allow me to work in Khong Sao Bar and to help me successfully fit into the space. The mommies and bar owners welcomed me and taught me how to navigate interactions with clients and other sex workers in the bar. They did this in part to pay back their social debts, but also because they were curiously interested in seeing how long a Viet Kieu women could last while performing acts of submission in this bar.

Working with a network of powerful men often made me wary of my safety because I was privy to some of the clients' private business dealings. I felt like I had to be hypervigilant as I worked to manage my relationships with powerful, elite local male clients who had the money and connections to take me down or push me out of Vietnam. I grew anxious and paranoid as I managed this complex array of relationships. The clients made it clear that I needed to tread carefully and manage all my relationships with caution. One client said to me, "If something happens to you and it gets all over the news, none of us will be there to catch you, because there would be too much at stake for us. We can take you only so far. You have to be the one to take your research and your work the rest of the way." Another client reminded me, "Know who you are and where you are. In this country, if you piss off the wrong person, someone can 'accidentally' knock you over on your motorbike and you can disappear just like that." For the first four weeks, I came home from work nervous, exhausted, and drained.

I relied heavily on key informants like Chu Xanh and Chu Thach to coach me on how to manage my relationships with wealthy businessmen, so that those men would not fear I might compromise their anonymity. Following their advice, I took what Gary Alan Fine calls "Deep Cover," never announcing my role as a researcher among the men that I did not interview for this study in Khong Sao Bar.[8] Around the men whom I would interview and the sex workers, madams, and bar owners, I maintained a "Shallow Cover,"[9] where I explicitly announced my role as a researcher without getting into the specifics of my research questions. My informants warned me that being too open about my research project would compromise the anonymity of the research subjects who would eventually agree to participate in my project. For example, Chu Xanh explained to me, "Saigon is very small. If everyone in town knows you as the girl who studies the sex industry, then any one of my guys who are out with you in public would be associated with the sex industry." In order to maintain my research subjects' anonymity, only twenty-five of the men in this niche market knew of my status as a researcher. There were many times when, as a bar hostess, I sat at tables with men who did not know that I was a researcher. To fulfill a promise I made to one of the mommies and to the bar owners, and to stay in line with the ethics of informed consent, I did not include those men in any of my field notes. Because Lavender, Secrets, and Naughty Girls operated in publicly visible sites, I could maintain a much more "Explicit Cover,"[10] letting everyone in those bars know I was a researcher. There, no one seemed to express any kind of concern that I would comprise their anonymity.

I spent two and a half months to three months in each of three bars: Khong Sao Bar, Lavender, and Secrets. While I could never pass as a local Vietnamese woman, in Khong Sao Bar and Lavender I learned how to adjust my gait, serve, take orders, smile when people criticized my weight, and remain silent when men touched me inappropriately. I was also ten years older than most of the sex workers and overweight according to local standards, which made me nonthreatening to the women and enabled my rapport with them. My personal feelings of shame and vulnerability in the field enabled me to empathize and connect with so many of my research subjects. I will never forget the night that I stayed up really late with two of the workers in Khong Sao Bar, after everyone had gone home, as they tried to teach me how to sing several key songs in Vietnamese, and while I taught them how to pronounce various words for the English songs that they were practicing. That night, we lamented both the fact that we spent so much of our time working and reworking our bodies in order to get picked in the lineup and the emotional exhaustion that we felt as a result of having to be constantly attuned to the clients' needs and desires. Our shared shame and struggle provided that late-night bonding moment in Khong Sao Bar, as well as many others like it in the other bars where I conducted research.

In each of those bars, I worked as a participant observer from noon until 2 A.M. seven days a week. I chose not to live with any of the other sex workers, so that I could spend the mornings writing my field notes away from the bar. I diligently wrote field notes and transcribed the interviews from notes on my phone every morning. However, after nine months of the continuous alcohol consumption that was required in Khong Sao Bar, Lavender, and Secrets, I decided to scale back. Therefore, I conducted ethnography in Naughty Girls less as a participant and more as an observer. I made myself useful in this bar by serving as an English instructor during the day and a patron of the bar at night. In this niche market, I conducted fieldwork three to four nights per week. I spent my afternoons from noon to 4 P.M. in the bar teaching the women English. Then, in the evenings, I spent time in the bar getting to know some of the clients.

In all four bars, I spent the first two weeks learning the women's names, figuring out the appropriate style of dress and makeup, learning how to mix drinks, and building rapport with all the people in the bar. I realized that, after about two weeks of being in each bar, I needed to ask directed and pointed questions in my conversations with the clients and sex workers to get at some of the themes that I was interested in uncovering. Therefore, I prepared and memorized two interview guides, one for clients and one for sex workers, which allowed me to conduct two to three interviews per night. Each interview lasted anywhere from two to seven hours.

I began the interviews with basic background questions about where the individuals were from, their occupations, their experience before they began bar work or before their arrival in Vietnam, and their recent activity, such as traveling or working in Vietnam. I then began to ask intimate questions about their private lives, which included marriage and family life, extramarital affairs, and details about their relationships, including their emotional experiences, expectations, and anxieties related to topics such as love, care, and deception. While none of the sex workers I studied knew very much about the other niches of the sex industry, male clients had a lot to say about other niche markets in relation to symbolic boundaries drawn along racial, national, and class hierarchies. I inquired about men's feelings and experiences related to moving through varied spaces in Vietnam and in transnational circuits. I interviewed the men in a variety of settings—bars, coffee shops, their offices, and on car rides to development project sites.

Between June 2009 and May 2010, I got to know hundreds of sex workers and clients across five niches of HCMC's sex industry. I decided to narrow my project to 40–50 clients and sex workers in each niche market. In the second phase of research, between 2009 and 2010, I interviewed a total of 193 individuals: 90 clients, 90 sex workers, 8 mommies, and 5 bar owners who consented to being a part of my study.

Male Desire and Performing Subservience

Because I was a highly educated Vietnamese American woman working on a degree from a prestigious university, many of the men and women initially wrote me off as a feminist who, they assumed, would not be sympathetic to the gendered relations that took place in the bar. However, ethnography often requires some form of deep acting to overcome subjects' initial resistance. My acts of public subordination toward the men and secondary role in support of the women were crucial in opening doors to workers' and clients' most intimate feelings and secrets. As one Viet Kieu put it, "[Since] you are willing to get down and do the dirty work, you blend in, and people see you as local. They will open up." With the sex workers, my willingness to drink the alcohol they drank and subject myself to some of the clients' unsolicited touches without acting like I was "too good for that" led the workers to eventually warm up to me. Indeed, it was the shared sense of responsibility for performative acts of submission that helped me build a relationship with many of the sex workers I met.

Even though I could never pass as a local, my willingness to be vulnerable made many men sympathize with my project. As a *participant*-observer, I was drawn into a set of objectifying and sexualizing rituals in which male clients' powerful gaze constructed various notions of female desirability.[11] In becoming part of these very gendered processes, I felt exposed every time a group of men came into the bar and I had to stand in the lineup while the clients looked at women's bodies and explicitly judged them. Attractive women "got in on tables" and less attractive women had to depend on friends or a set of regular customers. In the lineup at Khong Sao Bar, some of the clients had no problem calling me fat, old, and unattractive.

At that time, I was twenty-six years old and a size extralarge by local standards. It was clear that I was a bit too old for the high-end bars, and I always felt like I was on the cusp of getting kicked out because I was not someone whom clients came into the bar to see. These daily comments about my body made me feel an incredible pressure to manage my weight and give my body a serious makeover to conform to the desirable aesthetics in each bar. My personal life was consumed with fieldwork. Anytime I was not in the bars, I was either writing field notes or at the gym frantically trying to lose weight. Yet at the same time, as many of the clients got to know me and watched as I worked diligently to conform to the gendered relations in each space, they expressed a great deal of sympathy for my research project. Some of those men went to great lengths to protect me from having to subject myself to constant scrutiny. For example, one client brought his four-year-old son into the bar several times, and it was my role to feed him, play with him, and even take him toy shopping in a cab while the men drank and talked business. This allowed me to escape into a motherlike role, which men in the bars often relegated to the realm of sexually unapproachable.

My subject position also varied from bar to bar. I realized that it was easier for me to be submissive to wealthy local Vietnamese and Viet Kieu men in Khong Sao Bar and Lavender because I was raised in a family where hierarchal structures were embedded in language and interaction. I could easily draw on my family history to put myself below the men both physically and through language. However, it was much more challenging for me to act submissive to white men in Secrets and Naughty Girls. I was far better educated than many of them and found it politically difficult to engage in acts of submission to them.

think some of the men could tell I looked down on them by the way that treated them, sometimes refusing to get their drinks or shooting them dirty looks when they were overly aggressive with my body. What I found most fascinating was how they tried to put me in my place by speaking to me in Vietnamese, thus forcing me to use honorifics denoting "higher" and "lower." They referred to themselves as *anh* (male higher) and to me as *em* (female lower). Many of them were condescending, and some even asked me to come work for them, knowing my level of education and English-speaking abilities. One client jokingly offered to take me in as his "sex-retary" for U.S.$300 a month. I remember feeling an overwhelming desire to punch him in the face, but instead I smiled, bowed my head, and thanked him for the job offer.

Similar to my experiences in Khong Sao Bar and Lavender, many of the men in Secrets and Naughty Girls often commented on how my "foreign" body was not as attractive or appealing in these local spaces. One client said to me, "It must be hard to be the ugly duckling in this bar. . . . I guess that's just how it works here. Local girls make women like you look fat!" Yet for all the negative comments I received, my willingness to sit through critique provided me with a window of opportunity to ask questions about their personal lives. Many of our discussions revolved around our shared feelings of Western decline and its effect on our experiences of settling into the local spaces in Vietnam. Several of the men found my engagement in deeper conversations about their lives in their respective home countries and their experiences in Vietnam to be cathartic and therapeutic.

While engaging in these acts, I started to think about the conflation of "submission" with "care." The Western-educated side of me who entered the field with feminist blinders would have described all these acts as gestures of submission—the typical Vietnamese hostess-worker being submissive to make men feel more masculine. However, many of the workers encouraged me to rethink my understanding of submission. To them, submissive gestures were acts of "care" that men paid for, and men sometimes reciprocated this care in small ways, by making sure to feed the women, by fending off clients who were too sexually aggressive, or by caring for the workers' ailing parents and providing those workers with the means to start a new business or rebuild a village home.

Drawing on three case studies of conservative field sites, feminist ethnographers Orit Avishai, Lynne Gerber, and Jennifer Randles argue that feminism can operate as a blinder that limits our ability to see and interpret empirical realities that do not conform with feminist expectations.[12] They call for researchers' personal reflexivity regarding the possibility for true egalitarian relations between the researcher and her research subjects. As a feminist and a female researcher, I often found myself grappling with such contradictions in the field. The following section describes the embodied costs of conducting the kind of ethnography that does not conform with feminist expectations.

THE EMBODIED COSTS OF ETHNOGRAPHY

Erving Goffman once noted that the goal of an ethnographer is to subject himself, his body, his positionality, and his own social situation to the set of contingencies that play upon a set of individuals, so that he can physically and eco-logically penetrate their social circle.[13] The goal of the researcher is to accept both the desirable and the undesirable aspects of her field sites by "tuning" her body in the field in such a way that it enables the researcher to feel as her par-ticipants feel. However, in doing so, ethnographers often have to draw bounda-ries in their field sites and with their research subjects. They often have to decide how much they are willing to do on a day-to-day basis or how involved they are willing to get in their research subjects' lives for the sake of gathering data.[14] These ethnographers incur embodied costs—or what we as researchers some-times lose or give up in the process. The acts of female submission I participated in were ones that do not appear in ethnographies conducted by men who study drugs, gangs, or the informal economy.

In my field sites and in the world of academia, people often joke that I chose a "fun" research topic. For example, Jason, a twenty-nine-year-old colleague from the United States, jokingly asked me, "Wow, so you get to party all night and call that fieldwork?" This kind of field research, however, was far from fun. Even the process of getting dressed for work was laborious. And in order to maintain my focus in a setting where I was required to consume alcohol, I lined my stomach with ginger and drank a variety of herbal medicines.

After doing ethnography in the field of sex work in Vietnam for fifteen months, I found that this work had begun to wear on me. Global ethnographers studying down often become what Jordanna Matlon (citing Bourdieu) refers to as "exotic objects of prestige," where the research subjects' association with the researcher brings them status.[15] However, in my experience, my education and all the achievements I had celebrated in my life did not matter to the people I studied. Instead, in my work inside the bars, what mattered was whether I could make myself physically attractive in a way that was desirable to the clients while also making myself useful to the madams and other women by drinking, con-versing with men, dancing, and singing. This ethnography involved such a deep sense of embeddedness that the daily role-playing blurred the boundaries of my real life. Late one night, I came home from work in the bar and prepared to wash the layers of makeup off my face. Standing over the bathroom sink, I real-ized I no longer recognized my own face in the mirror. I burst into tears. All my anxieties came to the fore. In the bars, I was invisible and undesirable, sur-rounded by beautiful, savvy women ten years younger than myself. I knew that I would never survive in the world of hostess bars if it were my real life.

The process of field research forced me to adapt to a completely different environment, compared with my life in the United States. Analytically, I knew that altering my body and immersing myself in a particular ethical world were critical components in gaining a deep understanding of relations in the various bars. However, I also had to learn to pull myself out of these embodied modal-ities and ethical worlds when I returned to the field. When I first returned to Berkeley, Barrie Thorne commented on the way that I now shaped my eye-brows. She reminded me that I would need to undo my embodiment as a host-ess-worker to navigate the university hallways again. I had to find new clothing and a new way of inhabiting my body that would allow me to desexualize myself around others. Now, nearly four years later, I still find myself serving everyone's dish at a dinner table and clinking my glass below theirs when cheering. These are the kinds of embodied costs that have forever changed the way that I think and maneuver in my daily life, embodied costs that have taken years to undo.

DESIRABLE RETURNS

The embodied costs did not come without rewards. Had I not gone through these embodied transformations, my analysis would not have had the same degree of richness, depth, or accuracy. I would have never been able to connect with my research subjects on the emotional level that was crucial to pulling out the stories that make up the heart of this book. My own subjectivity helped me to uncover the moral and ethical codes between and among workers and clients, the varied performances of masculinity and femininity, and the stories of mobility. Moreover, the relationships and friendships that I developed in the field were immensely fulfilling and long lasting. Some of the people I least expected help from provided me with the most access, help, and guidance. I am deeply indebted to Curly, TTV, TinTin, and Anh Cua Ti (self-given pseudonyms), who not only provided me with access to the spaces I describe in this book but also acted as key informants who taught me a great deal about how to carry myself and manage my relationships. These men drew on their social networks to help me gain access to bars where I felt safe. Without them and their connections, this project would never have been possible. I am also grateful to Lilly and Tina, who took me under their wings and helped me feel comfortable in spaces that catered to Western men. And this project would not have been the same without the ninety men and ninety women who taught me how to dress, drink, serve, and adapt to the bars.

By the end of my time in each bar, I felt a personal connection to the women and men who had shared some of their secrets and desires, which then became the bedrock for some of the longest-lasting friendships. I realize that my authorship of this book, drafted in the comfort and safety of my life as an academic in the United States, has given me the power to reframe and reconstruct the many conversations and interactions that I witnessed and in which I took part. I can only hope that in my writing I have done justice to the complex and dynamic relations that took place in these spaces, as they do elsewhere in social life.

APPENDIX NOTES

1. I did not know very much about Vietnam, because the war experience was so traumatic for my parents that they rarely talked about their home country. When I initially told my parents that I would like to return to Vietnam for a visit alone, they were concerned for my safety because they could not imagine a Vietnam that had moved on from the war.

2. See, for example, Brennan (2004); Kempadoo (2004). Moreover, these researchers have written about clients primarily in Western contexts as lonely men (Flowers [1998]) seeking love (Brennan [2004]), emotional intimacy (Sanders [2008]), or a "girlfriend experience" (Bernstein [2007]).

3. For an expanded analysis of the clients and sex workers that I met between 2006 and 2007, see Hoang (2010, 2011).

4. Burawoy (2003).

5. Harms (2011, 4).

6. For examples of studying down, see Venkatesh (2013); Wacquant (2004); Contreras (2013); Ralph (2014). For examples of studying up, see Ho (2009); Knorr Cetina (forthcoming); Mears (2011, 2013); Ong (1999); Khan (2011); Benzecry (2011).

7. Allison (1994); Parreñas (2011); Zheng (2009b).

8. Fine (1980, 1993).

9. Ibid. In her ethnography of modeling agencies, Ashley Mears (2011), too, describes her strategy of taking on a "Shallow Cover."

10. Fine (1980, 1993).

11. This is a process that C. J. Pascoe (2007, 176) describes in her study of adolescent boys.

12. Avishai et al. (2012).

13. Goffman (1989).

14. Wacquant (2004); Burawoy (1979); Salzinger (2003).

15. Matlon (2014).

Notes

INTRODUCTION

1. A "sexscape," as defined by Denise Brennan (2004), "is a new kind of global sexual landscape . . . where the practices of sex work are linked to the broader forces of the global economy" (15–16).

2. When discussing money, I refer to U.S. dollars throughout this book in order to simplify the sums for Western readers. However, the money exchanged was always in Vietnamese dong (VND).

3. Though the term *remittance* is commonly used to refer to money sent to the homeland by members of the diaspora, I believe this term is also an apt description of the money sent by Western men back to a country where they attempted to establish a new sense of "home" through their relationships with sex workers. Their lump-sum and gift remittances to sex workers are distinct from tourist dollars or contributions made by expatriates to the local economy.

4. Zelizer (1997, 5).

5. For an in-depth analysis of global capital flows across major cities, see Sassen (2000, 2001, 2007).

6. See Chu (2010); Harvey (2012); Iwabuchi (2002); Kelsky (1999); Kondo (1990); Ong (1999); Rofel (1999).

7. Iwabuchi (2002); Kelsky (1999).

8. Harvey (2012); Iwabuchi (2002); Koolhaas (2004); Ong (2011).

9. Benz and Lassignardie (2013).

10. World Bank (2012); Zoellick (2010).

11. Ong (2011).

12. Harvey (2012).

13. Carlson (forthcoming). For more on the context of American decline, see also Randles (2013).

14. GSO Vietnam (2011).

15. Ibid.

16. Ibid. The 32 percent in figure 3 represents all other countries combined. Among those countries, no single country supplied a larger percentage of FDI in Vietnam than the countries named in this figure.

17. Nam (2011).

18. As late as 1987, the national economy was dominated by agriculture, which accounted for 40 percent of the GDP. See GSO Vietnam (2009). According to a report by the General Statistics Office of Vietnam (2011) on FDI by sector, the top five investment projects for the period 2005–2010 included manufacturing, real estate, hotels and tourism, construction, and information communication.

19. Ho (2009, 32–33). See also Arrighi (1996); LiPuma and Lee (2004).

20. Ho (2009, 32).

21. For examples in China, see Osburg (2013); Otis (2012); Zheng (2007, 2009b); for examples in Japan, see Allison (1994); Parreñas (2011); for examples in South Korea, see Lie (1995).

22. For more on the trilateral partnerships between state officials, private entrepreneurs, and foreign investors, see Nguyen-Vo (2008).

23. Ibid., 13.

24. Ibid., 3–6.

25. Nam (2012).

26. For more on the inextricable relationships between the economy and intimacy, see Boris and Parreñas (2010); Zelizer (2005). For more on the variation in markets, see Almeling (2011); Otis (2012).

27. The number of studies that look at male clients is very limited. For more on male clients, see Bernstein (2007); Prasad (1999); Sanders (2008).

28. Tsing (2005).

29. Glenn (2009); España-Maram (2006); Hearn and Blagojevic (2013); Patil (2009); Yuval-Davis (2011).

30. McClintock (1995, 5), emphasis in the original.

31. Chu (2010, 5–6).

32. Tsing (2005).

33. Massey (1993).

34. Bourdieu (1984).

35. Tsing (2005).

36. Braun (2011).

37. West and Zimmerman (1987).

38. Brennan (2005); Kempadoo (2005); Limoncelli (2010); Masika (2002); Parreñas (2011); Shelley (2010).

39. Brennan (2004); Bernstein (2007); Parreñas (2011); Kotiswaran (2011).

40. Lynch (2007); Mahmood (2005).

41. For more detail on the first phase of research, see Hoang (2010, 2011).

42. See Allison (1994); Parreñas (2011); Zheng (2009a, 2009b).

43. Throughout the text, I refer to the latter category of men by the colloquial term *expats*. Not all these men resided exclusively in Vietnam. Some lived in more than one country, and some were visitors who made regular business trips to Vietnam. However, all these men sought to establish a sense of "home"

in HCMC, and it was their connection to the country—not merely to individual women—that prompted their remittances.

44. I was not paid by the bar owner in any of these bars. However, I earned money through client tips. This amount varied, depending on the bar, but ranged between U.S.$100 and $500 per month. I made much less than the other women because I did not embody any of the particular femininities that were considered desirable in the bar and because I refused to leave with clients.

45. *Backstage* and *frontstage* are terms introduced by Goffman (1959) to describe behavior in social situations that is hidden from the public eye, and that which is visible to the public, respectively.

46. Contreras (2013, 19).

47. Ibid., 26–27.

48. For more examples of the gendered dilemmas of fieldwork, see Chapkis (1997, 211–231); Bernstein (2007, 189–202).

49. Lynch (2007, 8).

CHAPTER 1. SEX WORK IN HCMC, 1867–PRESENT

1. Many local Vietnamese often refer to Ho Chi Minh City as Saigon in their colloquial references to the city.

2. Loomba (1998); Manalansan (2004).

3. Hoang (2010, 2011).

4. GSO Vietnam (2011).

5. For other studies of Asian modernity, see Arrighi (2007); Ong (1999).

6. Cooper (2001).

7. Guenel (1997, 149).

8. Ibid. I use the terms *prostitution* and *sex work* somewhat interchangeably in this chapter. In contemporary writings, the latter is favored in antiabolitionist legal discourse to recognize women's work as a form of labor in the sex industry, while the latter is used primarily to assert a victim status. However, *sex work* was not a term coined or used during the period of French colonialism or U.S. imperialism. Therefore, I use the term *prostitution* in those contexts to maintain the social and historical specificity.

9. McCune (1937).

10. Rodriguez (2008).

11. Stoler (1991, 1992).

12. This type of makeshift structure, as described by local journalist Vu Trong Phung (1937 [2011]), was made of thatch and bamboo.

13. Rodriguez (2008).

14. See Phung (1937 [2011], 45). This estimated number is very low because it does not account for the large number of women involved in clandestine prostitution rings. See Cherry (2011). Research on prostitution during the colonial period in Vietnam focuses mostly on Vietnamese and French representations of women as prostitutes but not on prostitution itself. See Bradley (2001); Marr (1980); Tai (1992). According to French historian Alain Corbin (1991), the prostitute does not write about herself. Thus, as historian Haydon Cherry points out, prostitutes, like others who composed the urban poor in Saigon, left few traces in

colonial archives. What is known about prostitution is drawn mainly from legal documents, which frame these women as objects of regulation and control. See Cherry (2011); Marcondes and Edmonds (1967). Moreover, most of the texts that examine prostitution do not describe how the market met these needs, nor do they provide a portrait of the social lives of women working in the sex trade. Instead, these texts focus on the regulation and control of women whom officials feared would spread syphilis, thereby pathologizing desires for Vietnamese women's bodies. By the late 1930s there were an estimated four hundred establishments servicing the commercial sex trade. See Malarney (2011, 22).

15. Proschan (2002).

16. Roger Charbonnier (1936, 17) provides evidence of a hierarchical structure to sex work in his discussion of the fees different clients paid. Women who catered to a "coolie" charged 1–2 hao, those who serviced a solider or laborer charged 2.5–3 hao, and those who serviced a Vietnamese noncommissioned officer or European solider charged 5 hao. The highest-paid women were those who catered to highly ranked European officers at 20–30 hao. At that time, a copy of a local Vietnamese newspaper cost 3 hao, and a high-quality satin top cost 200 hao.

17. Ibid.

18. Tracol-Huynh (2010) looked into the national archives of the Centre des Archives d'Outre-Mer in Aix-en-Provence and in the Vietnamese National Archives Centres 1 and 2. Boittin et al. (2011).

19. Virgitti and Joyeux (1938).

20. Wood (1986).

21. Vo (2011).

22. Sun (2004).

23. Enloe (1990); Sun (2004).

24. Cheng (2010); Enloe (1990); Lee (2010).

25. "Boom-Boom, Chop-Chop" (2008).

26. Ibid.

27. Sun (2004, 131).

28. Barry (1979).

29. Jamieson (1995).

30. Gay (1985).

31. Gustafsson (2011); Hayslip and Wurts (1990); Sun (2004).

32. Barry (1996); Brownmiller (1975).

33. Brownmiller (1975).

34. Hayslip and Wurts (1990).

35. Gustafsson (2011).

36. Taylor (1999).

37. Nguyen-Vo (2008).

38. Ibid., 4.

39. Ibid.

40. Small (2012); Thai (2006); Truitt (2007).

41. For overseas remittance figures in the year 1995, see Thai (2008, 23); and for the year 2005, see World Bank (2012).

42. Pfau and Thanh (2010).

43. Hoang (2011).
44. Ibid., 9–11. See also Gainsborough (2003) for more on the importance of social networks under marketization.
45. Tran (2011).
46. Nguyen-Vo (2008, 12).
47. Ibid., 3.
48. Rydstrom (2006, 289).
49. Marr (1997).
50. Ibid.
51. Koh (2001, 281).
52. Ibid.
53. Ibid.
54. U.S. Department of State (2008, 2013).
55. For more on the conflicting state agendas, see Nguyen-Vo (2008).
56. *Thanh Nien News* (2011).
57. Nyblade et al. (2008). The misidentification of female sex workers as trafficked victims also occurs in other parts of the world. See Jordan (2009); Weitzer (2007).
58. The different strata of Vietnam's sex market are defined by the clients' bar and paid-sex expenditures, the women's pay, and the relative cultural prestige assigned to that niche market.
59. For examples in China, see Farrer (2009); Osburg (2013); Otis (2012); Zheng (2007). For Japan, see Allison (1994); Kondo (1990); Parreñas (2011). For South Korea, see Lie (1995).
60. Nguyen-Vo (2008).
61. Barbour-Lacey (2014).
62. Barry (1995, 131).

CHAPTER 2. THE CONTEMPORARY SEX INDUSTRY

1. Denise Brennan (2004, 15–16) uses to term *sexscape* to refer to a new kind of global sexual landscape, in which the researcher links the practices of sex work to broader forces of a globalized economy. The defining characteristics of a sexscape are (1) international travel from the developed world to the developing world, (2) consumption of paid sex, and (3) inequality.
2. For more on thick description as a research method, see Geertz (1977).
3. In order to provide anonymity to my research subjects, I have changed the names of all bars and people in my study.
4. The clients in the bar usually tipped the mommies double what they tipped hostesses. Most of the women would engage in sex work with clients after becoming familiar with them or if clients were Asian businessmen brought in by trusted local Vietnamese men.
5. Many of the women lied about their ages and told me they were at least eighteen years old. My guess is that some of them were roughly sixteen years old, based on the range of inconsistent ages they gave to other workers and the clients in the bar. Some of the women may have been older than twenty-two, but I could never confirm their ages.

6. During my first phase of research, in 2006 and 2007, I found that the high-end women who catered to Viet Kieus typically held a degree from a college or trade school, and they came from relatively wealthy families who lived in HCMC. See Hoang (2011). However, by the second phase of my research, in 2009, I found that the women who worked in Khong Sao Bar came from poor to middle-class families.

7. Top-earning hostess-workers in the bar who were requested by multiple clients earned around one hundred U.S. dollars per night from tips. Low-earning women earned thirty to sixty U.S. dollars per night, but there were many nights when we did not get asked to sit at any tables and did not earn any money. Although tips varied, clients typically tipped each girl at their table about thirty U.S. dollars. The popular women would run from one room to the next, continually rotating among multiple clients.

8. For more on the process of matchmaking among Viet Kieu men and local Vietnamese women, see Thai (2008).

9. One was an Australian man who saved his bottle and drank it over the course of five nights, which cost about the same as ordering three to four beers over five nights. The other man who ordered bottle service was a Taiwanese man who came in regularly after work. He would arrive with some of his friends, leave for dinner, and then migrate to a bar with high-end women who offered more explicit sexual services.

CHAPTER 3. NEW HIERARCHIES OF GLOBAL MEN

1. For more on "relationships on the rule of law" in China, see Osburg (2013).

2. For more on spatial and symbolic boundaries, see Lamont (2002); Lamont and Molnar (2002).

In the last ten years, a small group of scholars has moved to deconstruct narratives of male clients as a monolithic group of men looking to exert control over women. See, for example, Monto (2000); O'Connell Davidson (2003); Prasad (1999); Sanders (2008). There is a small number of empirical works describing male clients as lonely and seeking love or emotional intimacy. See, for example, Brennan (2004); Flowers (1998); Bernstein (2007); Sanders (2008). For studies of men on romance tours, see Brennan (2004); Kempadoo (2004).

3. On intersectionality, see Braun (2011); Patil (2009); on multiple masculinities, see Connell (1995); Morrell and Swart (2005). As McClintock (1995) points out, these categories "are not distinct realms of experiences, existing in splendid isolation from each other; [rather], they come into existence in and through *relations* to each other," creating hierarchies of difference that shape the men's social status positions (5). Stressing the relational dimension of material and cultural relations of power, I examine how men's performances of masculinities hinged on their structural location in categories of race, nation, class, gender, and sexuality. See, for example, España-Maram (2006); Glenn (1999); Hearn and Blagojevic (2013); Schilt (2011); Yuval-Davis (2011).

4. Several scholars advocate using a multiple-masculinities framework in order to describe different groups of men. See, for example, Pascoe (2003);

Thangaraj (2012); Woodward (1996). Morrell and Swart (2005), for example, advocate a multiple-masculinities framework in their examination of how colonialism in South Africa and the end of apartheid resulted in a system of segregated and competing patriarchies and hierarchies.

5. Scholars studying global and postcolonial masculinities tend to focus on two major approaches to gendering these global and local transformations. In the first approach, postcolonial scholars examine how tropes of exploration, conquest, and penetration of distant feminized lands helped construct masculine discourses of a global hegemonic masculinity tied to the West. See, for example, Connell and Messerschmidt (2005); Stoler (1995). Similarly, contemporary global masculinities scholars illustrate how large-scale structures like nation-states, multinational corporations, and global markets are gendered as a result of the men in charge of directing capital flows. See Acker (2004); Tienari et al. (2005). The capital flows emphasized in the literature on corporate masculinities construct an explicit dichotomy between Western distributors of capital in "core" countries and local receivers in the "periphery." See Hearn and Blagojevic (2013). Postcolonial frames further racialize and gender non-Western countries, particularly Asian countries, as inferior and feminine. See Iwabuchi (2002); Said (1979). The ideal prototypes of hegemonic masculinity that emerge in these studies are Western businessmen, bankers, officials, and intellectuals in charge of leading neoliberal policies of free market capitalism around the world. See Hooper (2000). Thus, Connell and Wood (2005) emphasize a transnational business masculinity embedded within corporate organizational hierarchies that position Western expatriates above locally born peers.

The second approach examines how marginal men react to global economic restructuring by innovating competing masculinities. See Gutmann (1996); Morrell and Swart (2005); Pringle et al. (2011). Inspired by postcolonial theory, these scholars "focu[s] on giving primacy to the agency of subaltern groups—for instance, racial, ethnic, class, and gender populations—who have been subjugated by a variety of colonial, neocolonial, and capitalist forces" (Ong 2011, 8–9). They pay close attention to the ways that subaltern resistance gives rise to different modes of colonial domination (see Spivak [1995]), highlighting frictions produced through new capital flows (see Tsing [2005]). Taking a bottom-up approach, these studies focus overwhelmingly on how men innovate competing forms of marginalized masculinities (see Connell [1995]) as they face chronic unemployment (see Izugbara [2011]; Matlon [2011]), are left behind by migrant wives (see Hoang and Yeoh [2011]), take on feminized jobs as servants (see Qayum and Ray [2010]; Ray and Qayum [2009]), and struggle with new configurations of fatherhood as a result the institutionalization of women's rights (see Wyrod [2008]).

These two parallel approaches—top-down and bottom-up—focus either on elite Western men in charge of directing global capital, or on marginal "Third World" men of color whose lives are transformed by neoliberalism, leaving unexplored the ways in which new financescapes (see Appadurai [1996]) may create room for men to reimagine competing hierarchies of nation, race, and class.

6. Braun (2011).

7. The exchange rate in 2009–2010 was one U.S. dollar for nineteen thousand Vietnamese dong.

8. The separate-spheres ideology is based on men and women performing different household roles according to their gender. For greater detail, see Zelizer (2005).

9. Cheng (2010); Bernstein and Shih (forthcoming).

10. See also Moore (2012); Kapoor (2012).

11. Brennan (2004).

12. Connell (1998).

13. Nguyen-Akbar (2014); Thai (2006).

14. During my research visits to Vietnam between 2006 and 2007, I never heard anyone use the term *Viet Cong*. Most people expressed the sentiment that it would alienate Viet Kieus, whose foreign remittances were key to the economy. However, by 2009 local Vietnamese had begun to reclaim this term to describe their economic triumphs in relation to the West.

15. Osburg (2013); Zheng (2007).

16. While this may not seem like a big tip, it is important to note that hostesses often sat in on multiple tables in what they called *chay show*—which literally means "running to perform in multiple places at once." They could earn one hundred to two hundred U.S. dollars a night simply by running from table to table.

17. This also happened in post-Soviet Russia in the 1990s—where paying more was a mark of masculine/capitalist status. Similar practices of luxury consumption were crucial to men's masculine status in contexts of global economic upheaval. See, for example, Patico (2008).

18. For other studies on "buttressing masculinity," see Parreñas (2011).

19. For more on the performance of masculinity in relation to femininity, see Connell (1995).

20. Žižek (1989, 31).

21. For more on the consumption of VIP elites in the United States and various parts of Europe, see Mears (2013).

22. Gutmann (1996).

23. In contrast to Braun's illuminating 2011 study of masculinity in large-scale development projects that privilege an international hegemonic masculinity over local masculinities, I show the reverse process, where local men work to trump an international or Western hegemonic masculinity.

CHAPTER 4. ENTREPRENEURIAL MOMMIES

1. For more works on hostess bars as spaces where men participate in male bonding rituals linked to business, see Allison (1994); Nguyen-Vo (2008); Osburg (2013); Zheng (2007).

2. Zelizer (1997).

3. For examples in Cambodia, see Nam (2011, 2012); for China, see Ai (2006); Zolkiewski and Feng (2012); Osburg (2013); Yang (2002); Zheng (2007); for Taiwan, see Shen (2003); Wong (2012); for Japan, see Allison (1994).

4. Kriz and Keating (2010).

5. I gathered this data from ethnographic field research and interviews between 2006 and 2007; see Hoang (2010; 2011).

6. Bars and clubs are lucrative businesses that can generate up to U.S.$40,000 in one evening. Therefore, there are often multiple investors in a bar who are silent partners, and one person represents the silent investors. Sometimes that person is a mommy; other times it is a bar owner who works closely with the mommy. The bar owner manages the finances and the relationships with alcohol distributors, while the mommies work on training hostess-workers and entertaining the clients.

7. Frank (2002).

8. The figures from the World Bank and General Statistics Office of Vietnam on overseas remittances, mentioned in the introduction to this book, are not broken down according to the type of remittance. Ivan Small (2012) and Hung Thai (2006) have both written extensively about remittances that overseas Vietnamese send to their families. Mytoan Nguyen-Akbar (2014) describes how overseas Vietnamese who are no longer connected to their families tend to spend their money on liquor, travel, and luxury items that they might not otherwise be able to afford in their home countries.

CHAPTER 5. AUTONOMY AND CONSENT IN SEX WORK

1. Kristof and WuDunn (2010).

2. For studies that highlight the exploitative working conditions, see Bales (2002); Farr (2005); Jeffreys (1999); Siddharth (2009).

3. Chin (2013) and Parreñas (2011). For other works on sex workers who choose to enter into the sex industry, see Brennan (2004); Brents et al. (2010); Cheng (2010); Chin (2013); Chin and Finckenauer (2012); Marcus and Snajdr (2013); Zheng (2009b).

4. There is a whole body of literature that critiques the human trafficking paradigm and the efforts to raise awareness around the issue; this literature points out that both are based on very little empirical research. See, for example, Bernstein and Shih (forthcoming); Choo (forthcoming); Haynes (2014); Jordan (2009); Mahdavi (2011); Musto (2013); Weitzer (2007).

5. For more on the distinction between force and choice in sex work, see Bernstein (1999); Chapkis (2003); Hoang and Parreñas (2014); Kempadoo (2005); Limoncelli (2010); Vance (2012).

6. For more on sexual force and coercive sex, see Farr (2005); Jeffreys (1999).

7. In a classic study of factory workers on the shop floor, Michael Burawoy (1979) theorizes worker consent by illustrating how trust and consent are central to the management of labor. Building on Burawoy's theorization of consent, I point to how, in sex work—a different organizational setting—intimacy and consent are central to establishing trust between the workers and the madams in charge of regulating the labor process.

8. Goffman (1959).

9. According to Scott (1990), "hidden transcripts" refer to the everyday forms of resistance generated through scripts that dominated persons say to

each other when they are "off stage," or when they are creating and occupying social spaces that are far beyond the gaze and control of power holders.

10. Goffman (1959).

11. For examples of fierce rivalries among sex workers in Mexico and China, see Hofmann (2011) and Zheng (2009b), respectively.

12. Zelizer (1997).

13. Parreñas (2011, 103–106).

CHAPTER 6. CONSTRUCTING DESIRABLE BODIES

1. Englund and Leach (2000); Ong (1999); Rofel (1999).

2. Otis's 2012 study of Chinese hotel service workers demonstrates that workers who cater to Westerners and wealthy locals engage in different styles of market-embodied labor practices. Similar works about South Korea (see Choo [2006]), Indonesia (see Saraswati [2010]), and the Philippines (see Cruz [2012]) highlight continuities and discontinuities both within the boundaries of nations and between nations that reflect the friction generated by the rise of Asian economies.

3. For variation in gendered ideals within nations, see also Balogun (2012); Choo (2006); Otis (2012); Saraswati (2010).

4. Mauss (1992).

5. On body work, see Gimlin (2007); on body capital, see Wacquant (1995).

6. Foucault (1988).

7. Balogun (2012).

8. Ong (2011).

9. Gal and Kligman (2000); Hanser (2008).

10. Lee (2008).

11. Glenn (2008).

12. For more on Caucasian whiteness and cosmopolitan whiteness, see Saraswati (2010).

13. A double eyelid surgery is a type of cosmetic surgery in which the doctors reshape the skin above the eyes, creating an upper-eyelid crease for eyes that do not naturally have a crease.

14. On doing gender, see West and Zimmerman (1987).

15. On nation-as-home, see Nguyen-Vo (2008); Sunindyo (1998).

16. Brennan (2004); Cabezas (2006).

17. It is important to note that women altered themselves permanently, suggesting that they viewed their work as a long-term career, not as a temporary situation.

18. Frank (2002).

CHAPTER 7. SEX WORKERS' ECONOMIC TRAJECTORIES

1. Bourdieu (1984).

2. Several scholars document themes of convertibility when referencing Viet Kieu men living in the diaspora who convert their U.S. dollars to social status in

Vietnam. For examples, see Carruthers (2002); Nguyen-Akbar (2014); Small (2012); Thai (2005); Truitt (2013).

3. For more on money in Vietnam, see Truitt (2013).

4. Zelizer (1997).

5. Carruthers (2002); Levitt (2001); Thai (2005).

CONCLUSION

1. GSO Vietnam (2013).

2. World Bank (2014).

3. Nguyen and Heath (August 21, 2012).

4. For more on the state's control of the commercial banking system in Vietnam, see Rona-Tas and Guseva (2014); Truitt (2007).

5. Bland (August 24, 2012).

6. Nguyen and Heath (August 21, 2012).

7. Chu (2010, 260).

8. Sewell (2005, 175).

9. Altman (2001, 11).

Bibliography

Acker, Joan. 2004. "Gender, Capitalism, and Globalization." *Critical Sociology* 30, no. 1: 17–42.

Ai, Jin. 2006. "Guanxi Networks in China: Its Importance and Future Trends." *China & World Economy* 14, no. 5: 105–118.

Allison, Anne. 1994. *Nightwork: Sexuality, Pleasure, and Corporate Masculinity in a Tokyo Hostess Club.* Chicago: University of Chicago.

Almeling, Rene. 2011. *Sex Cells: The Medical Market for Eggs and Sperm.* Berkeley: University of California Press.

Altman, Dennis. 2001. *Global Sex.* Chicago: University of Chicago Press.

Appadurai, Arjun. 1996. *Modernity at Large: Cultural Dimensions of Globalization.* Minneapolis: University of Minnesota Press.

Arrighi, Giovanni. 1996. *The Long Twentieth Century: Money, Power, and the Origins of Our Times.* London: Verso.

———. 2007. *Adam Smith in Beijing: Lineages of the Twenty-First Century.* London: Verso.

Avishai, Orit, Lynne Gerber, and Jennifer Randles. 2012. "The Feminist Ethnographer's Dilemma: Reconciling Progressive Research Agendas with Fieldwork Realities." *Journal of Contemporary Ethnography* 42, no. 4: 394–426.

Bales, Kevin. 2002. "Because She Looks Like a Child." In *Global Woman: Nannies, Maids, and Sex Workers in the New Economy,* edited by Barbara Ehrenreich and Arlie Hochschild, 207–229. New York: Henry Holt.

Balogun, Oluwakemi. 2012. "Cultural and Cosmopolitan: Idealized Femininity and Embodied Nationalism in Nigerian Beauty Pageants." *Gender & Society* 26, no. 3: 357–381.

Barbour-Lacey, Edward. 2014. "Vietnam Officials Struggle to Contain Burgeoning Sex Trade." AsianCorrespondent.com, March 1, http://asiancorrespondent.com/121174/vietnam-officials-struggle-to-contain-burgeoning-sex-trade.

Barry, Kathleen. 1979. *Female Sexual Slavery*. New York: New York University Press.

———. 1995. *The Prostitution of Sexuality: The Global Exploitation of Women*. New York: New York University Press.

———. 1996. Introduction to *Vietnam's Women in Transition*, edited by Kathleen Barry. New York: St. Martin's Press.

Benz, Michael, and Jean Lassignardie. 2013. *Asia-Pacific World Wealth Report*. N.p.: Merrill Lynch and Capgemini.

Benzecry, Claudio. 2011. *The Opera Fanatic: Ethnography of an Obsession*. Chicago: University of Chicago Press.

Bernstein, Elizabeth. 1999. "What's Wrong with Prostitution? What's Right with Sex Work? Comparing Markets in Female Sexual Labor." *Hastings Women's Law Journal* 10, no. 1: 91–117.

———. 2007. *Temporarily Yours: Intimacy, Authenticity, and the Commerce of Sex*. Chicago: University of Chicago Press.

Bernstein, Elizabeth, and Elena Shih. Forthcoming. "The Erotics of Authenticity: Sex Trafficking and Reality Tourism in Thailand." *Social Politics*.

Bland, Ben. 2012. "Vietnam Arrests Point to Greater Malaise." *Financial Times, Asia-Pacific*, August 24, www.ft.com/intl/cms/s/0/4f6a857e-edad-11e1-a9d7–00144feab49a.html—axzz30qSCQrq8.

Boittin, Jennifer, Christina Firpo, and Emily Church. 2011. "Hierarchies of Race and Gender in the French Colonial Empire, 1914–1946." *Historical Reflections* 37, no. 1: 60–90.

"Boom-Boom, Chop-Chop: R&R during the Vietnam War." 2008. In *Military Video*. Julian, CA: distributed by Traditional Military Videos.

Boris, Eileen, and Rhacel Parreñas. 2010. *Intimate Labors: Cultures, Technologies, and the Politics of Care*. Palo Alto, CA: Stanford University Press.

Bourdieu, Pierre. 1984. *Distinction: A Social Critique of the Judgment of Taste*. Cambridge, MA: Harvard University Press.

Bradley, Mark. 2001. "Contests of Memory: Remembering and Forgetting War in Contemporary Vietnamese Cinema." In *The Country of Memory: Remaking the Past in Late Socialist Vietnam*, edited by Hue-Tam Ho Tai, 196–226. Berkeley: University of California Press.

Braun, Yvonne. 2011. "The Reproduction on Inequality: Race, Class, Gender, and the Social Organization of Work at Sites of Large-Scale Development Projects." *Social Problems* 58, no. 2: 281–303.

Brennan, Denise. 2004. *What's Love Got to Do with it? Transnational Desires and Sex Tourism in the Dominican Republic*. Durham, NC: Duke University Press.

———. 2005. "Methodological Challenges in Research with Trafficked Persons: Tales from the Field." *International Migration* 43, no. 1–2: 35–54.

Brents, Barbara, Crystal Jackson, and Kathryn Hausbeck. 2010. *The State of Sex: Tourism, Sex and Sin in the New American Heartland*. New York: Routledge.

Brownmiller, Susan. 1975. *Against Our Will: Men, Women, and Rape*. New York: Simon and Schuster.

Burawoy, Michael. 1979. *Manufacturing Consent: Changes in the Labor Process under Monopoly Capitalism*. Chicago: University of Chicago Press.

———. 2003. "Revisits: An Outline of a Theory of Reflexive Ethnography." *American Sociological Review* 68, no. 5: 645–679.

Cabezas, Amalia. 2006. "The Eroticization of Labor in Cuba's All-Inclusive Resorts: Performing Race, Class and Gender in the New Tourist Economy." *Social Identities* 12, no. 5: 507–521.

Carlson, Jennifer. Forthcoming. *Citizen-Protectors: The Everyday Politics of Guns in an Age of Decline.* New York: Oxford University Press.

Carruthers, Ashley. 2002. "The Accumulation of National Belonging in Transnational Fields: Ways of Being at Home in Vietnam." *Identities: Global Studies in Culture and Power* 9, no. 4: 423–444.

Chapkis, Wendy. 1997. *Live Sex Acts: Women Performing Erotic Labor.* New York: Routledge.

———. 2003. "Trafficking, Migration, and the Law: Protecting Innocents, Punishing Immigrants." *Gender & Society* 17, no. 6: 923–937.

Charbonnier, Roger. 1936. *Contribution à l'étude de la prophylaxie antivénérienne à Hanoi* [Contribution to antivenereal prophylaxis in Hanoï]. Paris: Jouve.

Cheng, Sealing. 2010. *On the Move for Love: Migrant Entertainers and the U.S. Military in South Korea.* Philadelphia: University of Pennsylvania Press.

Cherry, Haydon. 2011. "Down and Out in Saigon: A Social History of the Urban Poor, 1863–1939." PhD diss., Yale University.

Chin, Christine. 2013. *Cosmopolitan Sex Workers: Women and Migration in a Global City.* New York: Oxford University Press.

Chin, Ko-Lin, and James Finckenauer. 2012. *Selling Sex Overseas: Chinese Women and the Realities of Prostitution and Global Sex Trafficking.* New York: New York University Press.

Choo, Hae Yeon. 2006. "Gendered Modernity and Ethnicized Citizenship: North Korean Settlers in Contemporary Korea." *Gender & Society* 20, no. 5: 576–604.

———. Forthcoming. *Citizenship beyond the Books: Gender, Labor, and Migrant Rights in South Korea.* Stanford, CA: Stanford University Press.

Chu, Julie. 2010. *Cosmologies of Credit: Transnational Mobility and the Politics of Destination in China.* Durham, NC: Duke University Press.

Connell, R. W. 1995. *Masculinities.* Berkeley: University of California Press.

———. 1998. "Masculinities and Globalization." *Men and Masculinities* 1, no. 1: 3–23.

Connell, R. W., and James Messerschmidt. 2005. "Hegemonic Masculinity: Rethinking the Concept." *Gender & Society* 19, no. 6: 829–859.

Connell, R. W., and Julian Wood. 2005. "Globalization and Business Masculinities." *Men and Masculinities* 7, no. 4: 347–364.

Contreras, Randol. 2013. *The Stickup Kids: Race, Drugs, Violence, and the American Dream.* Berkeley: University of California Press.

Cooper, Nicola. 2001. *France in Indochina Colonial Encounters.* Oxford: Berg.

Corbin, Alain. 1991. *Le Temps, le désir et l'horreur: Essais sur le dix-neuvième siècle* [Time, desire, and horror: Essays on the nineteenth century]. Paris: Aubier.

Cruz, Denise. 2012. *Transpacific Femininities: The Making of the Modern Filipina.* Durham, NC: Duke University Press.

Englund, Harri, and James Leach. 2000. "Ethnography and the Meta-Narratives of Modernity." *Current Anthropology* 41, no. 2: 225–248.

Enloe, Cynthia. 1990. *Bananas, Beaches, and Bases: Making Feminist Sense of International Politics.* Berkeley: University of California Press.

España-Maram, Linda. 2006. *Creating Masculinity in Los Angeles's Little Manila: Working-Class Filipinos and Popular Culture, 1920s–1950s.* New York: Columbia University Press.

Farr, Kathryn. 2005. *Sex Trafficking: The Global Market in Women and Children.* New York: Worth.

Farrer, James. 2009. "Shanghai Bars: Patchwork Globalization and Flexible Cosmopolitanism in Reform-Era Urban Leisure Spaces." *Chinese Sociology and Anthropology* 42, no. 2: 22–38.

Fine, Gary Alan. 1980. "Cracking Diamonds: The Relationship between Observer Role and Observed Content in Little League Baseball Settings." In *Fieldwork Experience: Qualitative Approaches to Social Research,* edited by William Shaffir, Robert Stebbins, and Allan Turowetz, 117–132. New York: St. Martin's Press.

———. 1993. "Ten Lies of Ethnography: Moral Dilemmas of Field Research." *Journal of Contemporary Ethnography* 22:267–294.

Flowers, Amy. 1998. *The Fantasy Factory: An Insider's View of the Phone Sex Industry.* Philadelphia: University of Pennsylvania Press.

Foucault, Michel. 1988. "Technologies of the Self." In *Technologies of the Self: A Seminar with Michel Foucault,* edited by Luther Martin, Huck Gutman, and Patrick Hutton, 16–49. Amherst: University of Massachusetts Press.

Frank, Katherine. 2002. *G-Strings and Sympathy: Strip Club Regulars and Male Desire.* Durham, NC: Duke University Press.

Gainsborough, Martin. 2003. *Changing Political Economy of Vietnam: The Case of Ho Chi Minh City (Rethinking Southeast Asia).* New York: RoutledgeCurzon.

Gal, Susan, and Gail Kligman. 2000. *The Politics of Gender after Socialism.* Princeton, NJ: Princeton University Press.

Gay, Jill. 1985. "The 'Patriotic' Prostitute." *The Progressive* 49, no. 2: 34.

Geertz, Clifford. 1977. *The Interpretation of Cultures.* New York: Basic Books.

Gimlin, Debra. 2007. "What Is 'Body Work'? A Review of the Literature." *Sociology Compass* 1, no. 1: 353–370.

Glenn, Evelyn Nakano. 1999. "The Social Construction and Institutionalization of Gender and Race: An Integrative Framework." In *Revisioning Gender,* edited by Myra Ferree, Judith Lorber, and Beth Hess, 3–43. New York: Sage.

———. 2008. "Yearning for Lightness: Transnational Circuits in the Marketing and Consumption of Skin Lighteners." *Gender & Society* 22, no. 3: 281–302.

———. 2009. "Consuming Lightness: Segmented Markets and Global Capital in the Skin-Whitening Trade." In *Shades of Difference: Why Skin Color Matters,* edited by Evelyn Nakano Glenn, 166–187. Palo Alto, CA: Stanford University Press.

Goffman, Erving. 1959. *The Presentation of Self in Everyday Life.* New York: Doubleday.

———. 1989. "On Fieldwork," translated by Lyn H. Lofland. *Journal of Contemporary Ethnography* 18, no. 2: 123–132.

GSO Vietnam. 2009. *Report on Labour Force Survey.* Edited by Ministry of Planning and Investment. Hanoi: General Statistics Office of Vietnam.

———. 2011. *Foreign Direct Investment Projects Licensed in Period 1988–2010.* Edited by Investment Department. Hanoi: General Statistics Office of Vietnam.

———. 2013. *Foreign Direct Investment Projects Licensed in Period 1988–2013.* Edited by Investment Department. Hanoi: General Statistics Office of Vietnam.

Guenel, Annick. 1997. "Sexually Transmitted Diseases in Vietnam and Cambodia since the French Colonial Period." In *Sex, Disease, and Society,* edited by Milton Lewis, Scott Bamber, and Michael Waugh, 139–153. Westport, CT: Greenwood Press.

Gustafsson, Mai Lan. 2011. "'Freedom. Money. Fun. Love': The Warlore of Vietnamese Bargirls." *Oral History Review* 38, no 2: 308–330.

Gutmann, Matthew. 1996. *The Meanings of Macho: Being a Man in Mexico.* Berkeley: University of California Press.

Hanser, Amy. 2008. *Service Encounters: Class, Gender and the Market for Social Distinction in Urban China.* Stanford, CA: Stanford University Press.

Harms, Erik. 2011. *Saigon's Edge: On the Margins of Ho Chi Minh City.* Minneapolis: University of Minnesota Press.

Harvey, David. 2012. *Rebel Cities: From the Right to the City to the Urban Revolution.* London: Verso.

Haynes, Dina. 2014. "The Celebritization of Human Trafficking." *Annals of the American Academy of Political and Social Science* 653, no. 1: 25–45.

Hayslip, Le Ly, and Jay Wurts. 1990. *When Heaven and Earth Changed Places.* New York: Penguin.

Hearn, Jeff, and Marina Blagojevic. 2013. "Introducing and Rethinking Transnational Men." In *Rethinking Transnational Men: Beyond, between, and within Nations,* edited by Jeff Hearn, Marina Blagojevic, and Katherine Harrison, 1–26. New York: Routledge.

Ho, Karen. 2009. *Liquidated: An Ethnography of Wall Street.* Durham, NC: Duke University Press.

Hoang, Kimberly Kay. 2010. "Economies of Emotion, Familiarity, Fantasy and Desire: Emotional Labor in Ho Chi Minh City's Sex Industry." *Sexualities* 13, no. 2: 255–272.

———. 2011. "'She's Not a Low-Class Dirty Girl': Sex Work in Ho Chi Minh City, Vietnam." *Journal of Contemporary Ethnography* 40, no. 4: 367–396.

Hoang, Kimberly Kay, and Rhacel Parreñas, eds. 2014. *Human Trafficking Reconsidered: Rethinking the Problem, Envisioning New Solutions.* New York: International Debate Education Association.

Hoang, Lan Anh, and Brenda Yeoh. 2011. "Breadwinning Wives and 'Left-Behind' Husbands: Men and Masculinities in the Vietnamese Transnational Family." *Gender & Society* 25, no. 6: 717–739.

Hofmann, Susanne. 2011. "Corporeal Entrepreneurialism and Neoliberal Agency in the Sex Trade at the US-Mexican Border." *Women's Studies Quarterly* 38, no. 3–4: 233–256.

Hooper, Charlotte. 2000. *Manly States: Masculinities, International Relations, and Gender Politics.* New York: Columbia University Press.

Iwabuchi, Koichi. 2002. *Recentering Globalization: Popular Culture and Japanese Transnationalism.* Durham, NC: Duke University Press.

Izugbara, Chimaraoke. 2011. "Poverty, Masculine Violence, and the Transformation of Men: Ethnographic Notes from Kenyan Slums." In *Men and Masculinities around the World: Transforming Men's Practices,* edited by Elisabetta Ruspini, Jeff Hearn, Bob Pease, and Keith Pringle, 235–246. New York: Palgrave Macmillan.

Jamieson, Neil. 1995. *Understanding Vietnam.* Berkeley: University of California Press.

Jeffreys, Sheila. 1999. "Globalizing Sexual Exploitation: Sex Tourism and the Traffic in Women." *Leisure Studies* 18, no. 3: 179–186.

Jordan, Ann. 2009. "Sex Trafficking: The Abolitionist Fallacy." Human Rights Issue, *Foreign Policy in Focus* (March 19).

Kapoor, Ilan. 2012. *Celebrity Humanitarianism: The Ideology of Global Charity.* New York: Routledge.

Kelsky, Karen. 1999. "Gender, Modernity, and Eroticized Internationalism in Japan." *Cultural Anthropology* 14, no. 2: 229–255.

Kempadoo, Kamala. 2004. *Sexing the Caribbean.* New York: Routledge.

———. 2005. *Trafficking and Prostitution Reconsidered: New Perspectives on Migration, Sex Work and Human Rights.* Boulder, CO: Paradigm.

Khan, Shamus. 2011. *Privilege: The Making of an Adolescent Elite at St. Paul's School.* Princeton, NJ: Princeton University Press.

Knorr Cetina, Karin. Forthcoming. *Maverick Markets: The Virtual Societies of Financial Markets.* Chicago: University of Chicago Press.

Koh, David. 2001. "Negotiating the Socialist State in Vietnam through Local Administrators: The Case of Karaoke Shops." *Journal of Social Issues in Southeast Asia* 16, no. 2: 279–305.

Kondo, Dorinne K. 1990. *Crafting Selves: Power, Gender, and Discourses of Identity in a Japanese Workplace.* Chicago: University of Chicago Press.

Koolhaas, Rem. 2004. "Beijing Manifesto." *Wired,* August.

Kotiswaran, Prabha. 2011. *Dangerous Sex, Invisible Labors: Sex Work and the Law in India.* Princeton, NJ: Princeton University Press.

Kristof, Nicholas, and Sheryl WuDunn. 2010. *Half the Sky: Turning Oppression into Opportunity.* New York: Random House.

Kriz, Anton, and Bryon Keating. 2010. "Business Relationships in China: Lessons about Deep Trust." *Asia Pacific Business Review* 16, no. 3: 299–318.

Lamont, Michele. 2002. *The Dignity of Working Men: Morality and the Boundaries of Race, Class, and Immigration.* Cambridge, MA: Harvard University Press.

Lamont, Michele, and Virag Molnar. 2002. "The Study of Boundaries in the Social Sciences." *Annual Review of Sociology* 28:167–195.

Lee, Jin-Kyung. 2010. *Service Economies: Militarism, Sex Work, and Migrant Labor in South Korea.* Minneapolis: University of Minnesota Press.

Lee, Sharon. 2008. "Lessons from 'Around the World with Oprah': Neoliberalism, Race, and the (Geo)politics of Beauty." *Women and Performance: A Journal of Feminist Theory* 18, no. 1: 25–41.

Levitt, Peggy. 2001. *The Transnational Villagers*. Berkeley: University of California Press.

Lie, John. 1995. "The Transformation of Sexual Work in 20th-Century Korea." *Gender & Society* 9, no. 3: 310–327.

Limoncelli, Stephanie. 2010. *The Politics of Trafficking*. Palo Alto, CA: Stanford University Press.

LiPuma, Edward, and Benjamin Lee. 2004. *Financial Derivatives and the Globalization of Risk*. Durham, NC: Duke University Press.

Loomba, Ania. 1998. *Colonialism/Postcolonialism*. London: Routledge.

Lynch, Caitrin. 2007. *Juki Girls, Good Girls*. Ithaca, NY: Cornell University Press.

Mahdavi, Pardis. 2011. *Gridlock: Labor, Migration, and Human Trafficking in Dubai*. Palo Alto, CA: Stanford University Press.

Mahmood, Saba. 2005. *Politics of Piety: The Islamic Revival and the Feminist Subject*. Princeton, NJ: Princeton University Press.

Malarney, Shaun Kingsley. 2011. Translator's note to *Luc Xi: Prostitution and Venereal Disease in Colonial Hanoi*. Honolulu: University of Hawai'i Press.

Manalansan, Martin F., IV. 2004. *Global Divas: Filipino Gay Men in the Diaspora*. Durham, NC: Duke University Press.

Marcondes, Ruth Sandoval, and Scott Edmonds. 1967. "Health Knowledge of Prostitutes in Saigon, Vietnam: A Study of Health Attitudes and Habits Relating to Venereal Diseases Taken from a Group of Prostitutes." *Revista de Saúde Pública* (University of São Paulo) 1, no. 1: 18–23.

Marcus, Anthony, and Edward Snajdr. 2013. "Anti-anti-trafficking? Toward Critical Ethnographies of Human Trafficking." *Dialectical Anthropology* 37, no. 2: 191–194.

Marr, David. 1980. *Vietnamese Tradition on Trial, 1920–1945*. Berkeley: University of California Press.

———. 1997. "Vietnamese Youth in the 1990s." *Vietnam Review* 2, no. 1: 288–354.

Masika, Rachel, ed. 2002. *Gender, Trafficking, and Slavery*. Oxford: Oxfam.

Massey, Doreen. 1993. "Power-Geometry and a Progressive Sense of Place." In *Mapping the Futures: Local Cultures, Global Change*, edited by John Bird, Barry Curtis, Tim Putnam, and Lisa Tickner, 59–69. New York: Routledge.

Matlon, Jordanna. 2011. "Il Est Garçon: Marginal Abidjanais Masculinity and the Politics of Representation." *Poetics* 39, no. 5: 380–406.

———. 2014. "'Elsewhere': An Essay on Borderland Ethnography in the Informal African City." *Ethnography*, doi: 10.1177/1466138113513527.

Mauss, Marcel. 1992. "Techniques of the Body" (1934). In *Incorporations*, edited by Jonathan Crary and Sanford Kwinter. Cambridge, MA: MIT Press.

McClintock, Anne. 1995. *Imperial Leather: Race, Gender and Sexuality in the Colonial Contest*. New York: Routledge.

McCune, Shannon. 1937. "Saigon, French Indo-China." *Journal of Geography* 36, no. 1: 24–34.

Mears, Ashley. 2011. *Pricing Beauty: The Making of a Fashion Model*. Berkeley: University of California Press.

———. 2013. "Elite Social Spaces: Visibility and Gendered Capitals among the Global VIP." Presentation at Crisis in the City, Society for the Advancement of Socio-Economics, Milan, Italy, June 20.

Monto, Martin. 2000. "Why Men Seek Out Prostitutes." In *Sex for Sale*, edited by Ronald Weitzer, 67–82. New York: Routledge.

Moore, Thomas. 2012. "Saving Friends or Strangers? Critical Humanitarianism and the Geopolitics of International Law." *Review of International Studies* 39, no. 4: 1–23.

Morrell, Robert, and Sandra Swart. 2005. "Men in the Third World: Postcolonial Perspectives on Masculinity." In *Handbook of Studies on Men and Masculinities*, edited by Michael Kimmel, R. W. Connell, and Jeff Hearn. Thousand Oaks, CA: Sage.

Musto, Jennifer. 2013. "Domestic Minor Sex Trafficking and the Detention-to-Protection Pipeline." *Dialectical Anthropology* 37, no. 2: 257–276.

Nam, Sylvia. 2011. "Phnom Penh: From the Politics of Ruin to the Possibilities of Return." *Traditional Dwellings and Settlements Review* 22, no. 1: 55–68.

———. 2012. "Speculative Urbanism: The Remaking of Phnom Penh." PhD diss., University of California, Berkeley.

Nguyen, Kieu Giang, and Nick Heath. 2012. "Vietnam's Arrest of Bank Mogul Sparks Slide in Financial Stocks." *Bloomberg Businessweek*, August 21, www.businessweek.com/printer/articles/310868?type=bloomberg.

Nguyen-Akbar, Mytoan. 2014. "The Tensions of Diasporic 'Return' Migration: How Class and Money Create Distance in Vietnamese Transnational Family." *Journal of Contemporary Ethnography* 43, no. 2: 176–201.

Nguyen-Vo, Thu-Huong. 2008. *The Ironies of Freedom: Sex, Culture, and Neoliberal Governance in Vietnam*. Seattle: University of Washington Press.

Nyblade, Laura, Thu Hong Khuat, Van Anh Nguyen, Jessica Ogden, Aparna Jain, Anne Stangl, Zayid Douglas, Tao Nguyen, and Kim Ashburn. 2008. *Communities Confront HIV Stigma in Viet Nam: Participatory Interventions Reduce HIV Stigma in Two Provinces*. Edited by International Center for Research on Women. Washington, DC: International Center for Research on Women.

O'Connell Davidson, Julia. 2003. "Sleeping with the Enemy? Some Problems with Feminist Abolitionist Calls to Penalize Those Who Buy Commercial Sex." *Social Policy and Society* 2:55–63.

Ong, Aihwa. 1999. *Flexible Citizenship: The Cultural Logics of Transnationality*. Durham, NC: Duke University Press.

———. 2011. "Introduction: Worlding Cities, or the Art of Being Global." In *Worlding Cities: Asian Experiments and the Art of Being Global*, edited by Ananya Roy and Aihwa Ong, 1–26. Oxford: Blackwell.

Osburg, John. 2013. *Anxious Wealth: Money and Morality among China's New Rich*. Stanford, CA: Stanford University Press.

Otis, Eileen. 2012. *Markets and Bodies: Women, Service Work, and the Making of Inequality in China*. Stanford, CA: Stanford University Press.

Parreñas, Rhacel. 2011. *Illicit Flirtations*. Palo Alto, CA: Stanford University Press.

Pascoe, C. J. 2003. "Multiple Masculinities?: Teenage Boys Talk about Jocks and Gender." *American Behavioral Scientist* 46, no. 10: 1423–1438.

———. 2007. *Dude, You're a Fag: Sexuality and Masculinity in High School*. Berkeley: University of California Press.

Patico, Jennifer. 2008. *Consumption and Social Change in a Post-Soviet Middle Class*. Stanford, CA: Stanford University Press.

Patil, Vrushali. 2009. "Contending Masculinities: The Gendered (Re)negotiation of Colonial Hierarchy in the United Nations Debates on Decolonization." *Theory and Society* 38, no. 2: 195–215.

Pfau, Wade, and Giang Thanh. 2010. "The Growing Role of International Remittances in the Vietnamese Economy: Evidence from the Vietnam (Household) Living Standard Surveys." In *Global Movements in the Asia Pacific*, edited by Pookong Kee and Hidetaka Yoshimatsu, 225–248. Singapore: World Scientific Publishing.

Phung, Vu Trong. 1937 [2011]. *Luc Xi: Prostitution and Venereal Disease in Colonial Hanoi*. Translated by Shaun Kingsley Malarney. Honolulu: University of Hawai'i Press.

Prasad, Monica. 1999. "The Morality of Market Exchange: Love, Money, and Contractual Justice." *Sociological Perspectives* 42, no. 2: 181–213.

Pringle, Keith, Jeff Hearn, Bob Pease, and Elisabetta Ruspini. 2011. "Introduction: Transforming Men's Practices around the World." In *Men and Masculinities around the World: Transforming Men's Practices*, edited by Elisabetta Ruspini, Jeff Hearn, Bob Pease, and Keith Pringle, 1–6. New York: Palgrave Macmillan.

Proschan, Frank. 2002. "Syphilis, Opiomania, and Pederasty: Colonial Constructions of Vietnamese (and French) Social Diseases." *Journal of the History of Sexuality* 11, no. 4: 610–636.

Qayum, Seemin, and Raka Ray. 2010. "Male Servants and the Failure of Patriarchy in Kolkata (Calcutta)." *Men and Masculinities* 13, no. 1: 111–125.

Ralph, Laurence. 2014. *Renegade Dreams: Living through Injury in Gangland Chicago*. Chicago: University of Chicago Press.

Randles, Jennifer. 2013. "Repackaging the 'Package Deal': Promoting Marriage for Low-Income Families by Targeting Paternal Identity and Reframing Marital Masculinity." *Gender & Society* 27, no. 6: 864–888.

Ray, Raka, and Seemin Qayum. 2009. *Cultures of Servitude: Modernity, Domesticity, and Class in India*. Stanford, CA: Stanford University Press.

Rodriguez, Marie-Corinne. 2008. "Insights into Prostitution in Vietnam during the Colonial Days from the Late 19th Century to the Early 1930s." Unpublished paper, University of Provence, Aix-en Provence, France.

Rofel, Lisa. 1999. *Other Modernities: Gendered Yearnings in China after Socialism*. Berkeley: University of California Press.

Rona-Tas, Akos, and Alya Guseva. 2014. *Plastic Money: Constructing Markets for Credit Cards in Eight Postcommunist Countries*. Stanford, CA: Stanford University Press.

Rydstrom, Helle. 2006. "Sexual Desires and 'Social Evils': Young Women in Rural Vietnam." *Gender, Place and Culture* 13, no. 3: 283–301.

Said, Edward. 1979. *Orientalism*. New York: Random House.

Salzinger, Leslie. 2003. *Genders in Production: Making Workers in Mexico's Global Factories*. Berkeley: University of California Press.

Sanders, Teela. 2008. *Paying for Pleasure: Men Who Buy Sex*. Portland, OR: Willan.

Saraswati, L. Ayu. 2010. "Cosmopolitan Whiteness: The Effects of and Affects of Skin-Whitening Advertisements in a Transnational Women's Magazine in Indonesia." *Meridians: Feminism, Race, Transnationalism* 10, no. 2: 15–41.

Sassen, Saskia. 2000. *Cities in a World Economy*. Thousand Oaks, CA: Pine Forge Press.

———. 2001. *The Global City: New York, London, Tokyo*. Princeton, NJ: Princeton University Press.

———. 2007. Introduction to *Deciphering the Global: Its Scales, Spaces, and Subjects*, edited by Saskia Sassen, 1–18. New York: Taylor and Francis.

Schilt, Kristen. 2011. *Just One of the Guys?: Transgender Men and the Persistence of Gender Inequality*. Chicago: University of Chicago Press.

Scott, James. 1990. *Domination and the Arts of Resistance: Hidden Transcripts*. New Haven: Yale University Press.

Sewell, William, Jr. 2005. *Logics of History: Social Theory and Social Transformation*. Chicago: University of Chicago Press.

Shelley, Louise. 2010. *Human Trafficking: A Global Perspective*. Cambridge: Cambridge University Press.

Shen, Hsiu-Hua. 2003. "Making Taiwanese Transnational Business Masculinity: Commodifying Chinese Women." Paper presented at the annual meeting of the American Sociological Association, Atlanta, Georgia, August 16.

Siddharth, Kara. 2009. *Sex Trafficking: Inside the Business of Modern Slavery*. New York: Columbia University Press.

Small, Ivan. 2012. "Currencies of Imagination: Channeling Money and Chasing Mobility in Vietnamese Remittance Economies." PhD diss., Cornell University.

Spivak, Gayatri. 1995. "Can the Subaltern Speak?" In *The Post-colonial Studies Reader*, edited by Bill Ashcroft, Gareth Griffiths, and Helen Tiffin. New York: Routledge.

Stoler, Ann. 1991. "Carnal Knowledge and Imperial Power: Gender, Race, and Morality in Colonial Asia." In *Gender at the Crossroads of Knowledge: Feminist Anthropology in the Postmodern Era*, edited by Micaela di Leonardo, 51–101. Berkeley: University of California Press.

———. 1992. "Sexual Affronts and Racial Frontiers: European Identities and the Cultural Politics of Exclusion in Colonial Southeast Asia." *Comparative Studies in Society and History* 34, no. 3: 514–551.

———. 1995. *Race and the Education of Desire*. Durham, NC: Duke University Press.

Sun, Sue. 2004. "Where the Girls Are: The Management of Venereal Disease by United States Military Forces in Vietnam." *Literature and Medicine* 23, no. 1: 66–87.

Sunindyo, Saraswati. 1998. "When the Earth Is Female and the Nation Is Mother: Gender, the Armed Forces and Nationalism in Indonesia." *Feminist Review* 58:1–21.

Tai, Hue-Tam Ho. 1992. *Radicalism and the Origins of the Vietnamese Revolution*. Cambridge, MA: Harvard University Press.

Taylor, Sandra. 1999. *Vietnamese Women at War: Fighting for Ho Chi Minh and the Revolution*. Lawrence: University Press of Kansas.

Thai, Hung. 2005. "Globalization as a Gender Strategy: Respectability, Masculinity, and Convertibility across the Vietnamese Diaspora." In *Critical Globalization Studies*, edited by William Robinson and Richard Appelbaum, 313–322. New York: Routledge.

———. 2006. "Money and Masculinity among Vietnamese Low Wage Immigrants in Transnational Families." *International Journal of Sociology of the Family* 32, no. 2: 247–271.

———. 2008. *For Better or for Worse: Vietnamese International Marriages in the New Global Economy*. New York: Rutgers University Press.

Thangaraj, Stanley. 2012. "Playing through Difference: The Black-White Logic and Interrogating South Asian American Identity." *Ethnic and Racial Studies* 35, no. 6: 988–1006.

Thanh Nien News. 2011. "Vietnam Launches Prostitution Crackdown." June 9.

Tienari, Janne, Anne-Marie Soderberg, Charlotte Holgersson, and Eero Vaara. 2005. "Gender and National Identity Constructions in the Cross-Border Merger Context." *Gender, Work and Organization* 12, no. 3: 217–241.

Tracol-Huynh, Isabelle. 2010. "Between Stigmatisation and Regulation: Prostitution in Colonial Northern Vietnam." *Culture, Health, and Sexuality* 12, no. 5: S73–S87.

Tran, Quang Minh. 2011. "Two Decades of Taiwan's FDI in Vietnam—an Analysis and Assessment." Paper presented at the seminar "Taiwan-Vietnam Economic Cooperation: Moving Towards the 2015 Vision of ASEAN Economic Integration," Hanoi, Vietnam, August 16.

Truitt, Allison. 2007. "Hot Loans and Cold Cash in Saigon." In *Money: Ethnographic Encounters*, edited by Stefan Senders and Allison Truitt, 57–68. New York: Berg.

———. 2013. *Dreaming of Money in Ho Chi Minh City*. Seattle: University of Washington Press.

Tsing, Anna. 2005. *Friction: An Ethnography of Global Connection*. Princeton, NJ: Princeton University Press.

U.S. Department of State. 2008. *William Wilberforce Trafficking Victims Protection Reauthorization Act of 2008*. Edited by Office to Monitor and Combat Trafficking in Persons. Washington, DC: U.S. Department of State.

———. 2013. *Trafficking in Persons Report*. Washington, DC: U.S. Department of State.

Vance, Carole. 2012. "Innocence and Experience: Melodramatic Narratives of Sex Trafficking and Their Consequences for Law and Policy." *History of the Present* 2, no. 2: 204–205.

Venkatesh, Sudhir. 2013. *Floating City: A Rogue Sociologist Lost and Found in New York's Underground Economy*. New York: Penguin.

Virgitti, Henri, and Bernard Joyeux. 1938. *Le Péril vénérien dans la zone suburbaine de Hanoï* [The venereal peril in the suburban zone of Hanoi]. Hanoi: Imprimerie d'Extreme-Orient.

Vo, Nghia. 2011. *Saigon: A History.* Jefferson, NC: McFarland.

Wacquant, Loic. 1995. "Pugs at Work: Bodily Capital and Bodily Labour among Professional Boxers." *Body and Society* 1:65–93.

———. 2004. *Body & Soul: Notebooks of an Apprentice Boxer.* New York: Oxford University Press.

Weitzer, Ronald. 2007. "The Social Construction of Sex Trafficking: Ideology and Institutionalization of a Moral Crusade." *Politics and Society* 35, no. 3: 447–475.

West, Candace, and Don Zimmerman. 1987. "Doing Gender." *Gender & Society* 1, no. 2: 125–151.

Wong, Jeng-Min. 2012. "The Guanxi Strategies of Taiwanese Firms in China's Economic Reforms." *Journal of Global Business Management* 8, no. 1: 111–115.

Wood, Robert. 1986. "Basic Needs and the Limits of Regime Change." In *From Marshall Aid to Debt Crisis: Foreign Aid and Development Choices in the World Economy,* edited by Robert Wood, 195–231. Berkeley: University of California Press.

Woodward, Alison. 1996. "Multinational Masculinities and European Bureaucracies." In *Men and Managers, Managers as Men,* edited by David Collinson and Jeff Hearn, 167–185. London: Sage.

World Bank. 2012. "Global Financial Development." In *Benchmarking Financial Systems around the World,* edited by Martin Čihák, Aslı Demirgüç-Kunt, Erik Feyen, and Ross Levine. Washington, DC: World Bank.

———. 2012. *Remittances Profile: Vietnam.* Washington, DC: Migration Policy Institute.

———. 2014. *Deposit Interest Rate (%): Vietnam, 2009–2013.* Washington, DC: World Bank.

Wyrod, Robert. 2008. "Between Women's Rights and Men's Authority: Masculinity and Shifting Discourses of Gender Difference in Urban Uganda." *Gender & Society* 22, no. 6: 799–823.

Yang, Mayfair Mei-hui. 2002. "The Resilience of Guanxi and Its New Deployments: A Critique of Some New Guanxi Scholarship." *China Quarterly* 170:459–476, doi: 10.1017/S000944390200027X.

Yuval-Davis, Nira. 2011. *The Politics of Belonging: Intersectional Contestations.* New York: Sage.

Zelizer, Viviana. 1997. *The Social Meaning of Money.* Princeton, NJ: Princeton University Press.

———. 2005. *The Purchase of Intimacy.* Princeton, NJ: Princeton University Press.

Zheng, Tiantian. 2007. "Cool Masculinity: Male Clients' Sex Consumption and Business Alliance in Urban China's Sex Industry." *Journal of Contemporary China* 15, no. 46: 161–182, doi: 10.1080/10670560500331815.

———. 2009a. *Ethnographies of Prostitution in Contemporary China: Gender Relations, HIV/AIDS, and Nationalism.* New York: Palgrave Macmillan.

————. 2009b. *Red Lights: The Lives of Sex Workers in Postsocialist China.* Minneapolis: University of Minnesota Press.

Žižek, Slavoj. 1989. *The Sublime Object of Ideology.* London: Verso.

Zoellick, Robert. 2010. *The End of the Third World? Modernizing Multilateralism for a Multipolar World.* Washington, DC: Woodrow Wilson Center for International Scholars.

Zolkiewski, Judy M., and Junwei Feng. 2012. "Relationship Portfolios and Guanxi in Chinese Business Strategy." *Journal of Business & Industrial Marketing* 27, no. 1:16–28.

Index

alcohol: and bottle service, 44; in business deals, 4, 41, 44–45; and conspicuous consumption, 73–74, 91; implicit rules of, 71, 137; and promotion girls, 45, 88–93, 102; and public displays of masculinity, 67–69, 73–74; revenue from, 42, 45, 100; women's consumption of, 111, 116, 133–34
Allison, Anne, 18
Almeling, Rene, 12
Altman, Dennis, 180
American imperialism, 26, 31–34, 199n8
Anh Bao, 1–2
Anh Minh, 84, 133
Anh Nguyen, 90, 92, 111, 174, 187
Anh Phat, 84
Annam, 27, 28
Asia Commercial Bank, 175
Asia-Pacific Economic Cooperation, 34
Asia-Pacific region, 8, 15
Asian ascendancy, 12–13, 51–52; male articulation of, 69, 72, 75–76. *See also* foreign direct investment: Asian based
autonomy. See consent
Avishai, Orit, 192

Bac Dinh, 170
Bac Tan, 169–170
backstage, 74, 106, 199n45; bonds of friendship, 118–20. *See also* frontstage; Goffman, Erving

bar. *See* hostess bar
beauty: pan-Asian, 131–33; Western ideals of, 130, 132–33, 135, 139. *See also* technologies of embodiment
Bernstein, Elizabeth, 194n2
body capital, 129; and plastic surgery, 134, 141–42, 147. *See also* body work; technologies of embodiment; plastic surgery
body work: and cultural ideals, 132–33; definition of, 129–30; and signaling nation's progress, 135–36, 142–43; and technologies, 129–30. *See also* body capital; plastic surgery; technologies of embodiment
boundaries: spatial and symbolic, 60, 202n2
Brennan, Denise, 197n1, 201n1
brokering capital deals, 4, 8, 11–13, 54; and relationships, 41–42, 57; and sex work, 36, 59–60, 84, 118
brokers, 12, 55, 84–85, 102, 176–78; mommies as, 78–79, 86–87; sex workers as, 148–49
Brownmiller, Susan, 30
Buddhism, 112
Burawoy, Michael, 185; and consent, 205n7
Bush, George W., 34–35, 186. *See also* United States

Cambodia, 28, 98, 115, 165
Capgemini, 6